Jasper Léonard

New York Resized

LANNOO

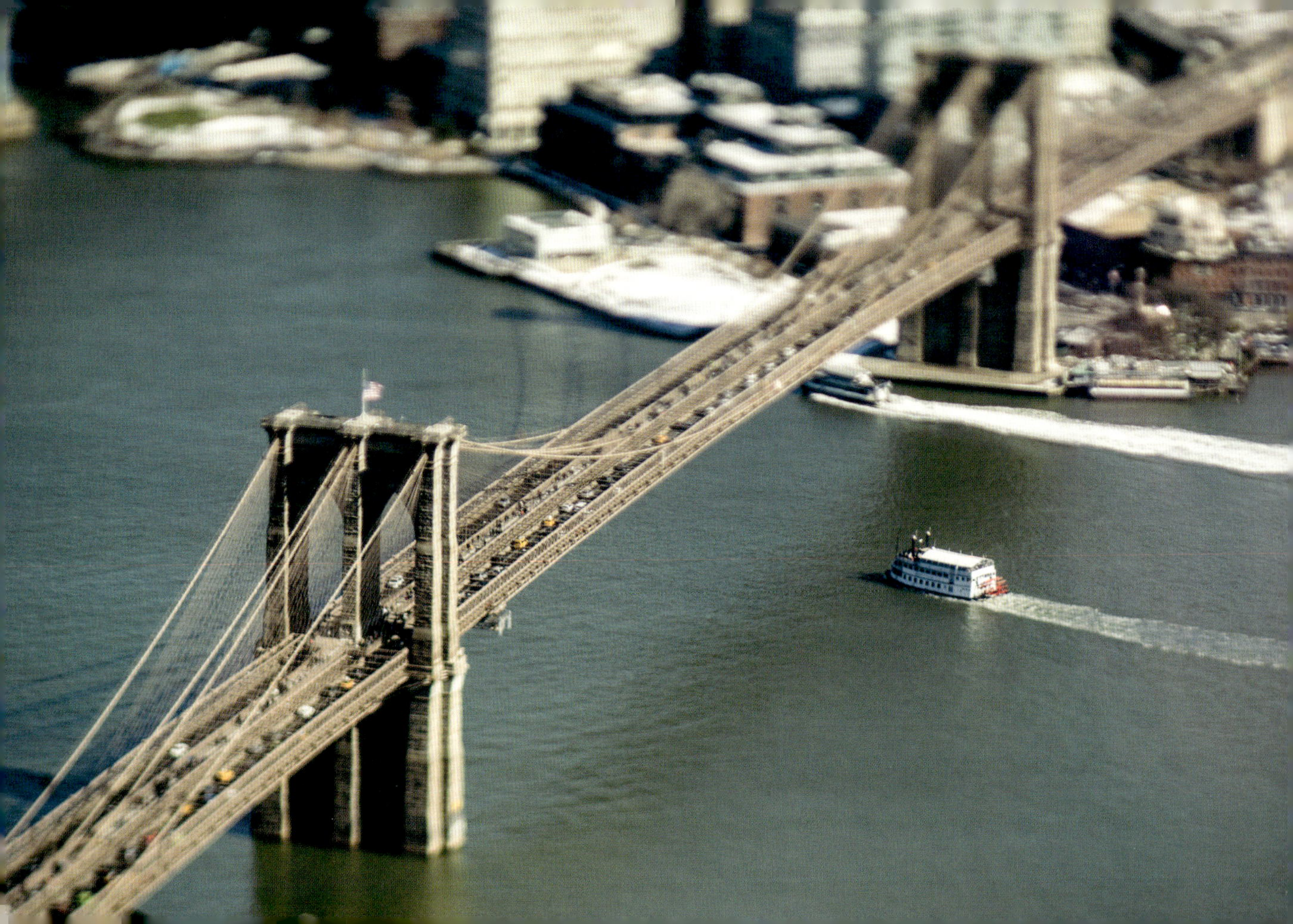

Foreword

My passion for photography developed in a very specific way: through the pleasure I experienced in tinkering impetuously with camera lenses. This cannot be called reinventing photography, but it did shape me into the photographer I am today. My photos are still indebted to these early days. My "lenses project" was also the basis for my Master's thesis in Visual Arts in 2010. One of these lenses was a 45mm Tilt-Shift in which the rubber is folded in such a way on the lens that in certain places the image loses its characteristic sharpness. With the right subject and the right perspective, the miniature effect quickly makes a realistic scene look orchestrated. Tilt-Shift sets the viewer on the wrong track, because you assume that it is a miniature photograph.

This year, I focused my lens on life in New York; often from rooftops, bridges and observatories, or from a helicopter or plane — the best places to get a bird's eye view of the city. Not a single photo was faked. The city simply ran its course and I documented it. This book not only shows New York through photographs. Throughout the book you will also find some inspirational quotes about New York that are matched with the pictures.

JASPER LÉONARD

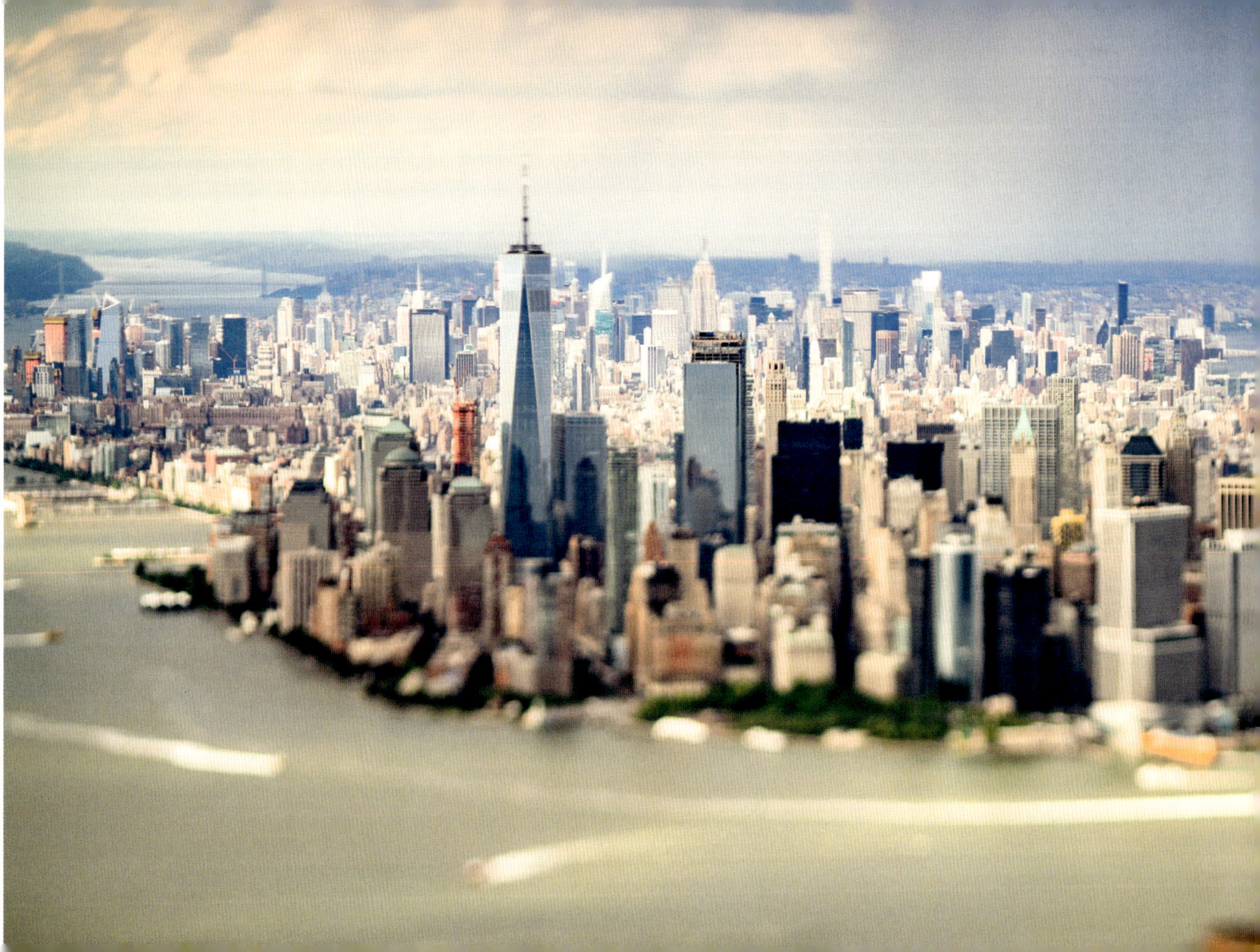

Lower Manhattan

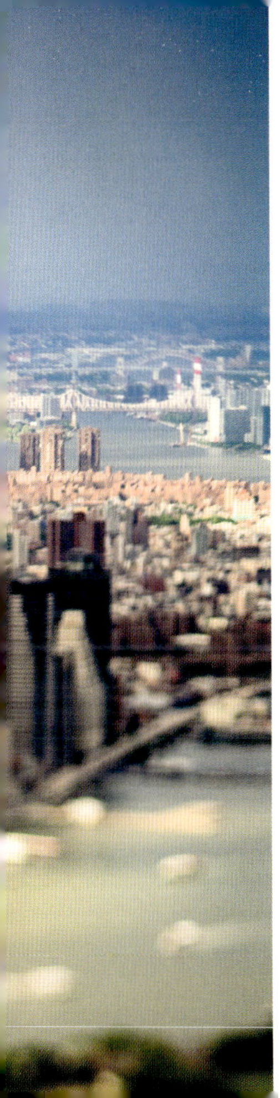

I would give the greatest sunset in the world for one sight of New York's skyline. Particularly when one can't see the details. Just the shapes. The shapes and the thought that made them. The sky over New York and the will of man made visible. What other religion do we need?

Ayn Rand

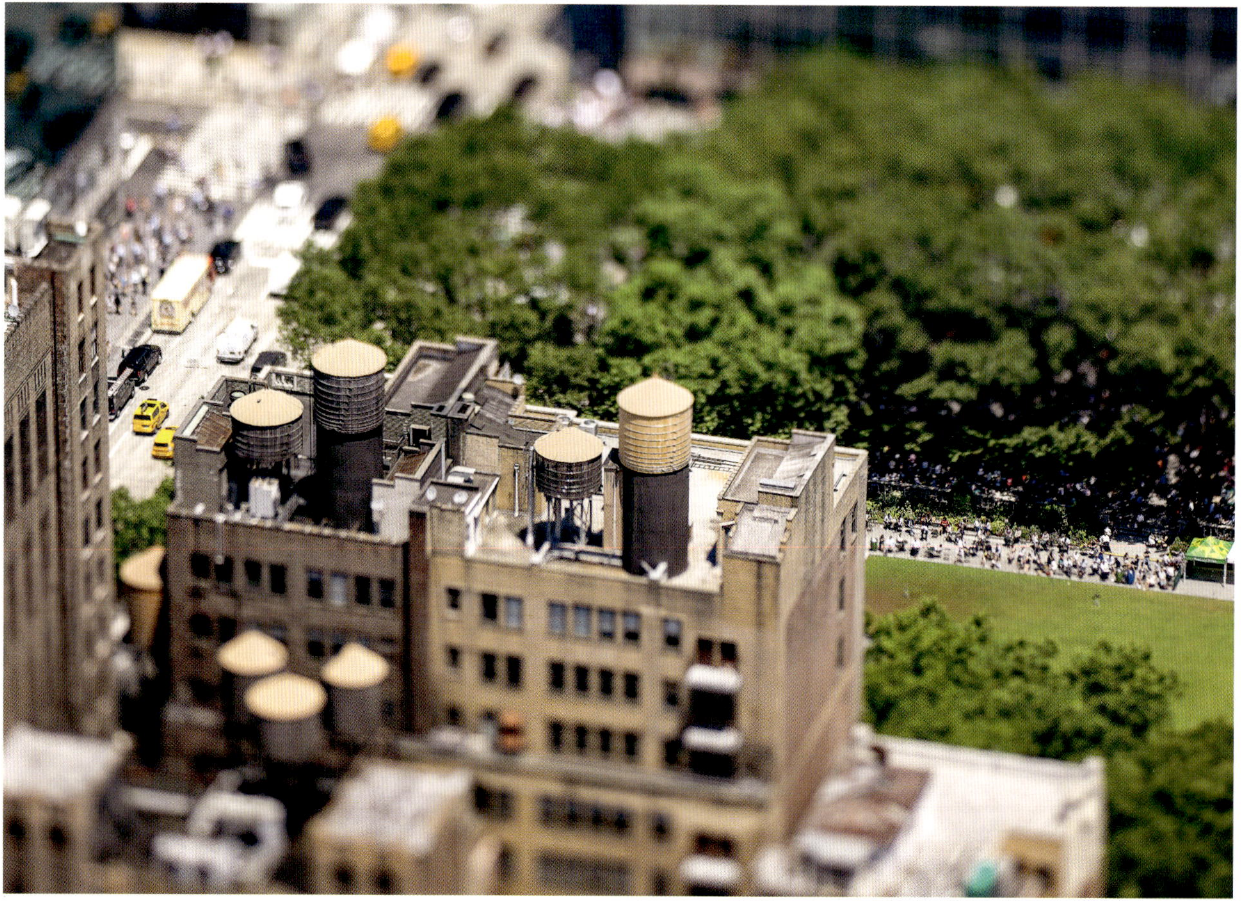

Bryant Park

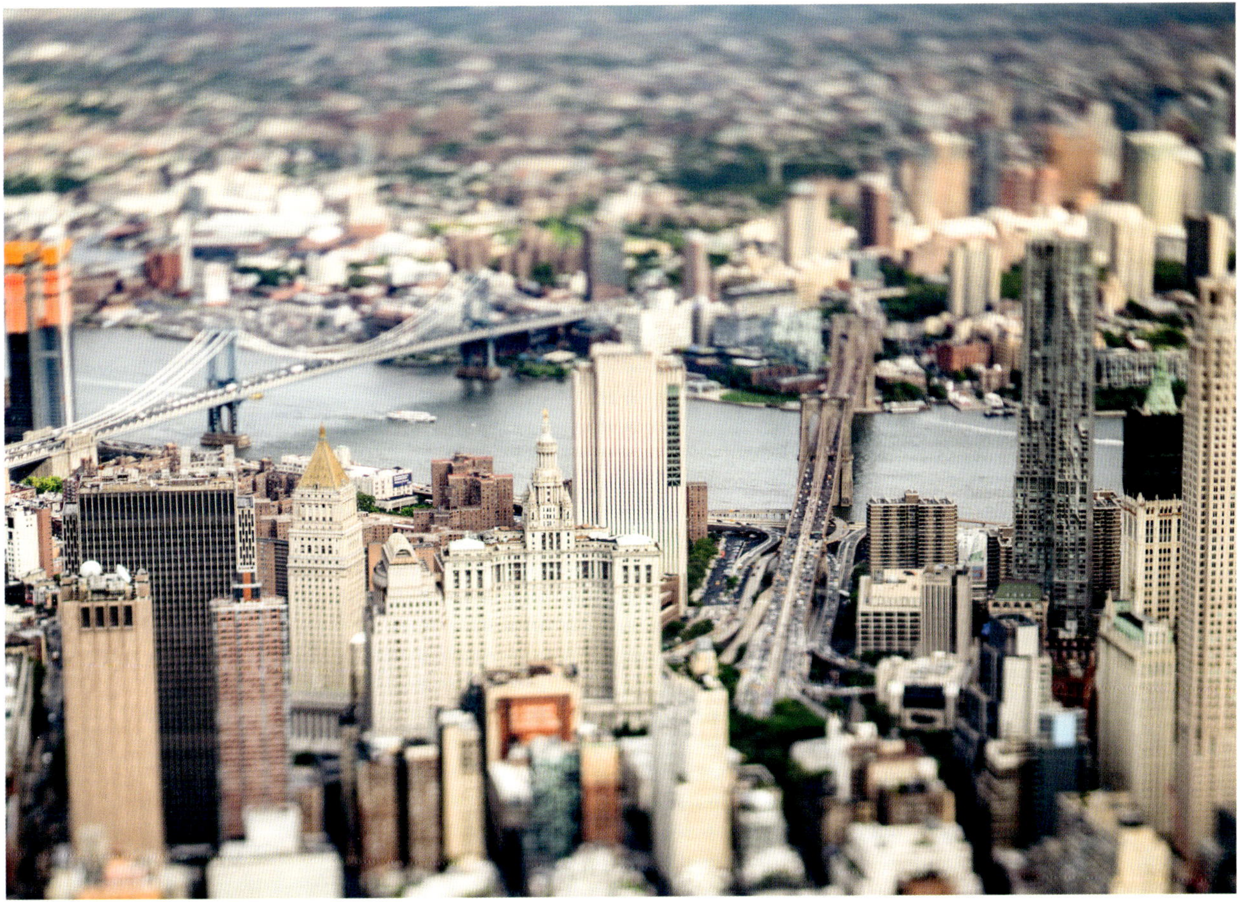

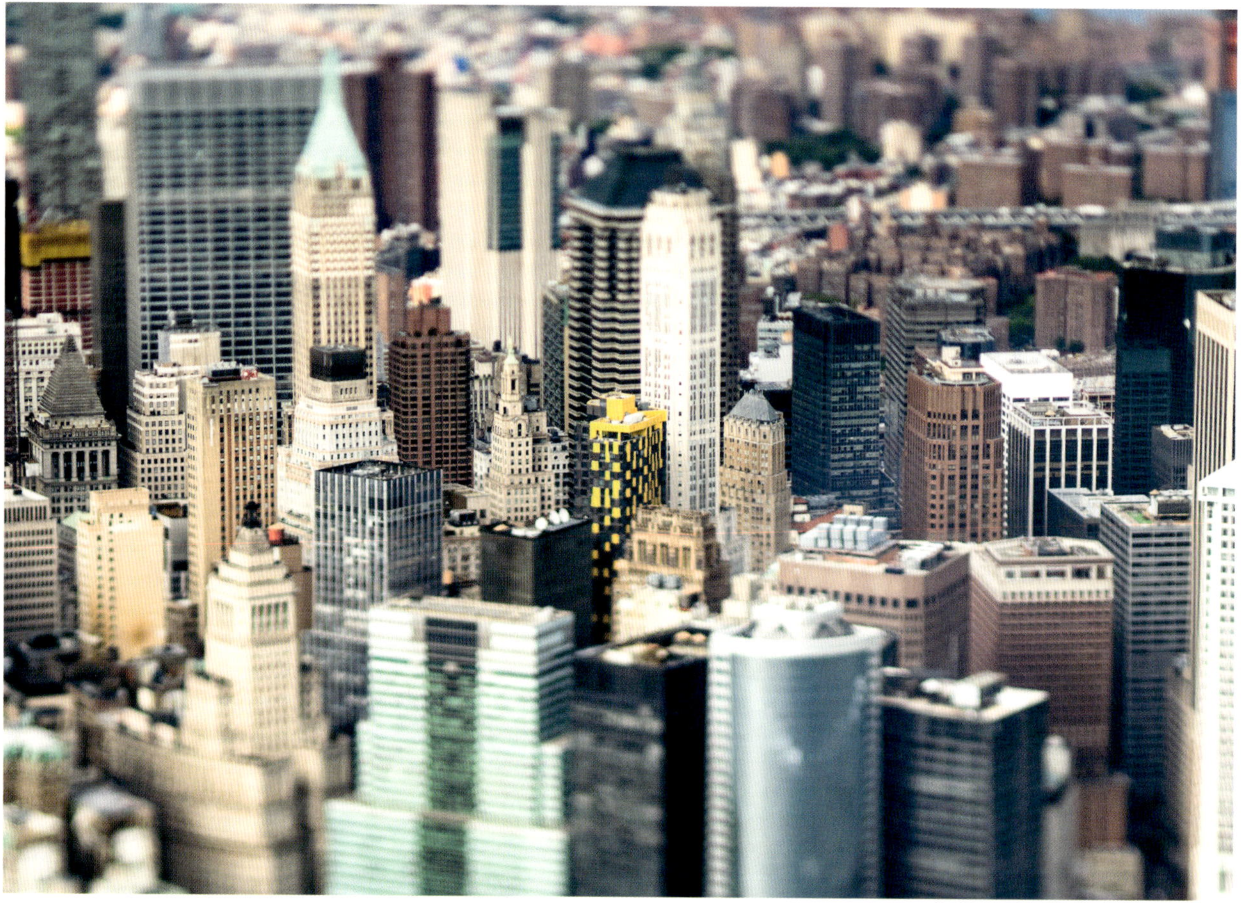

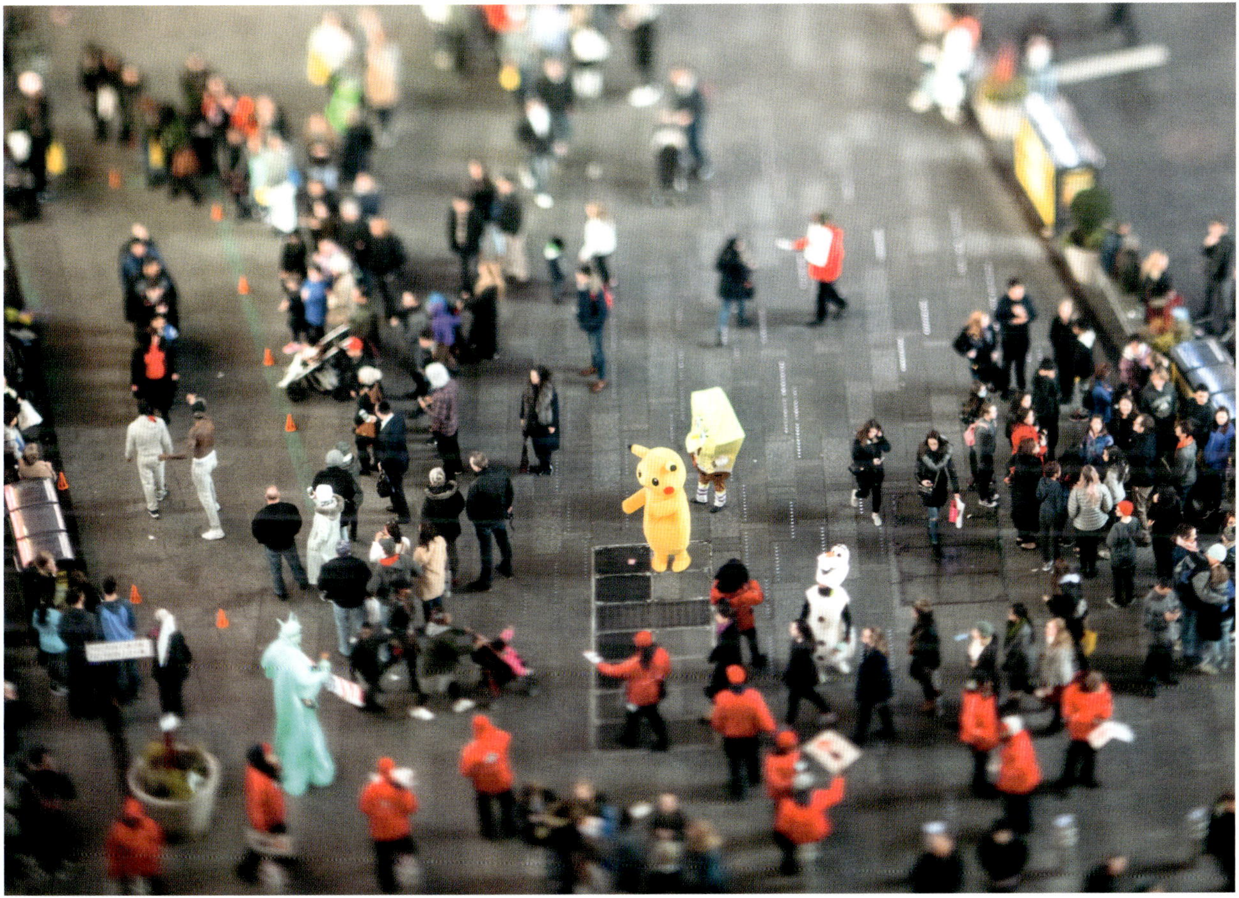

Times Square

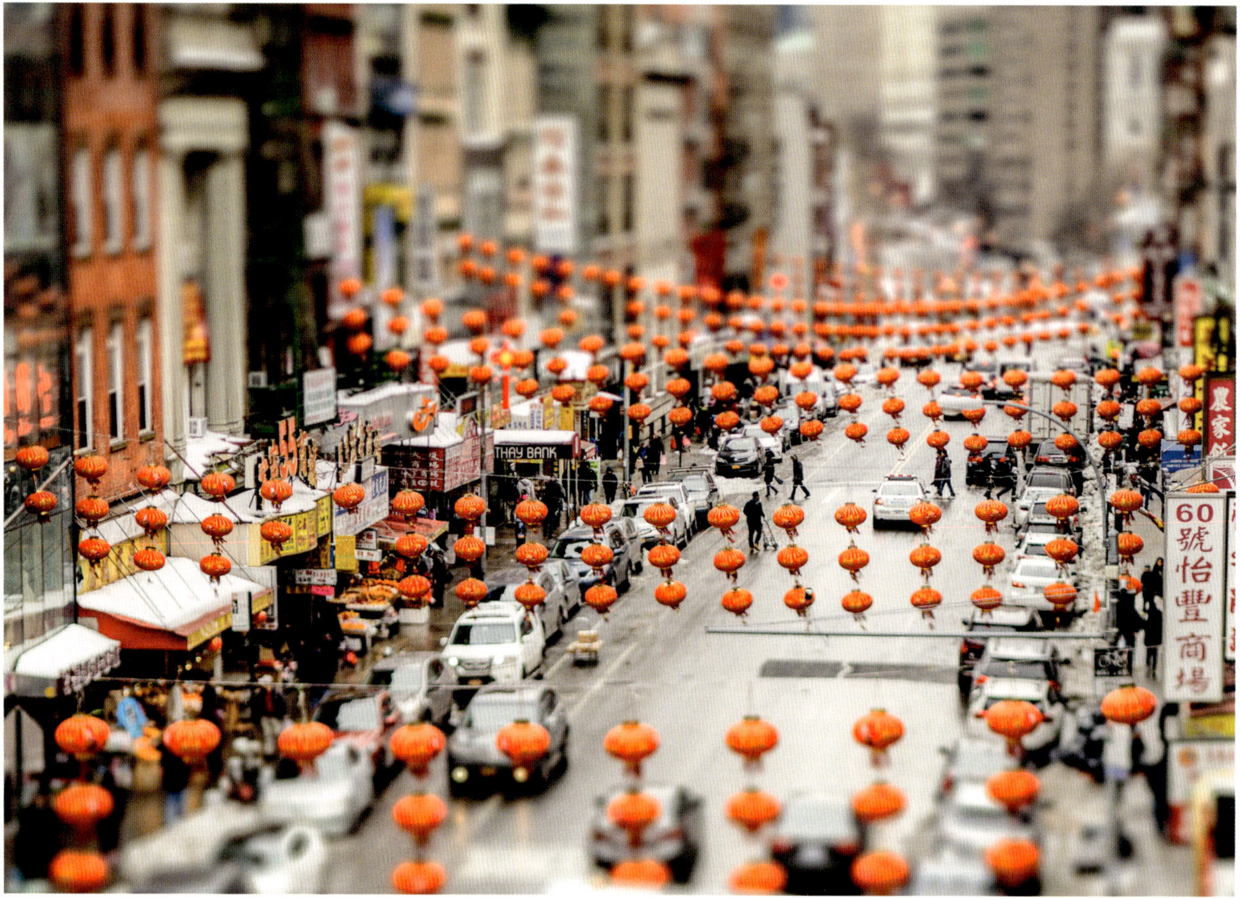
THAY BANK
60號怡豐商場

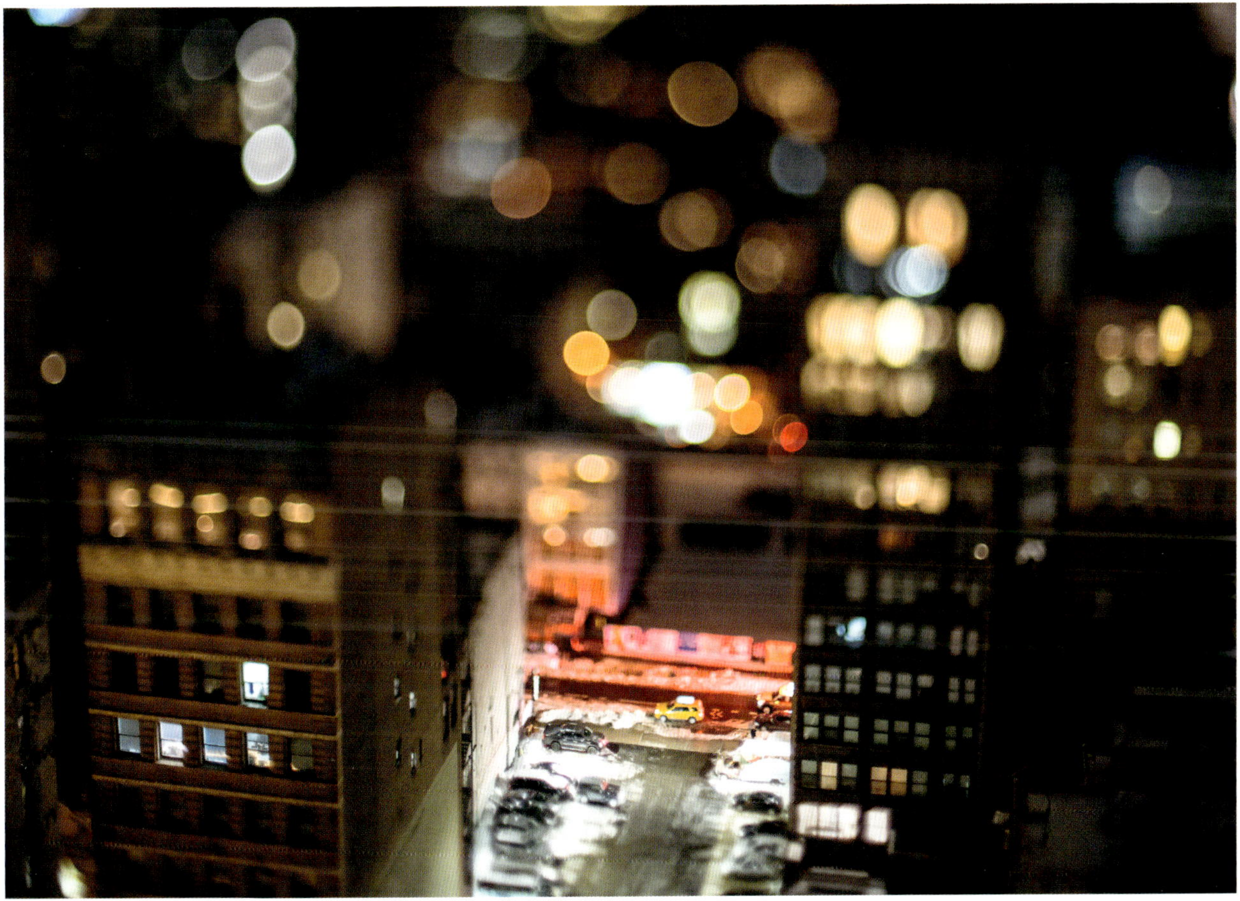

29th Street

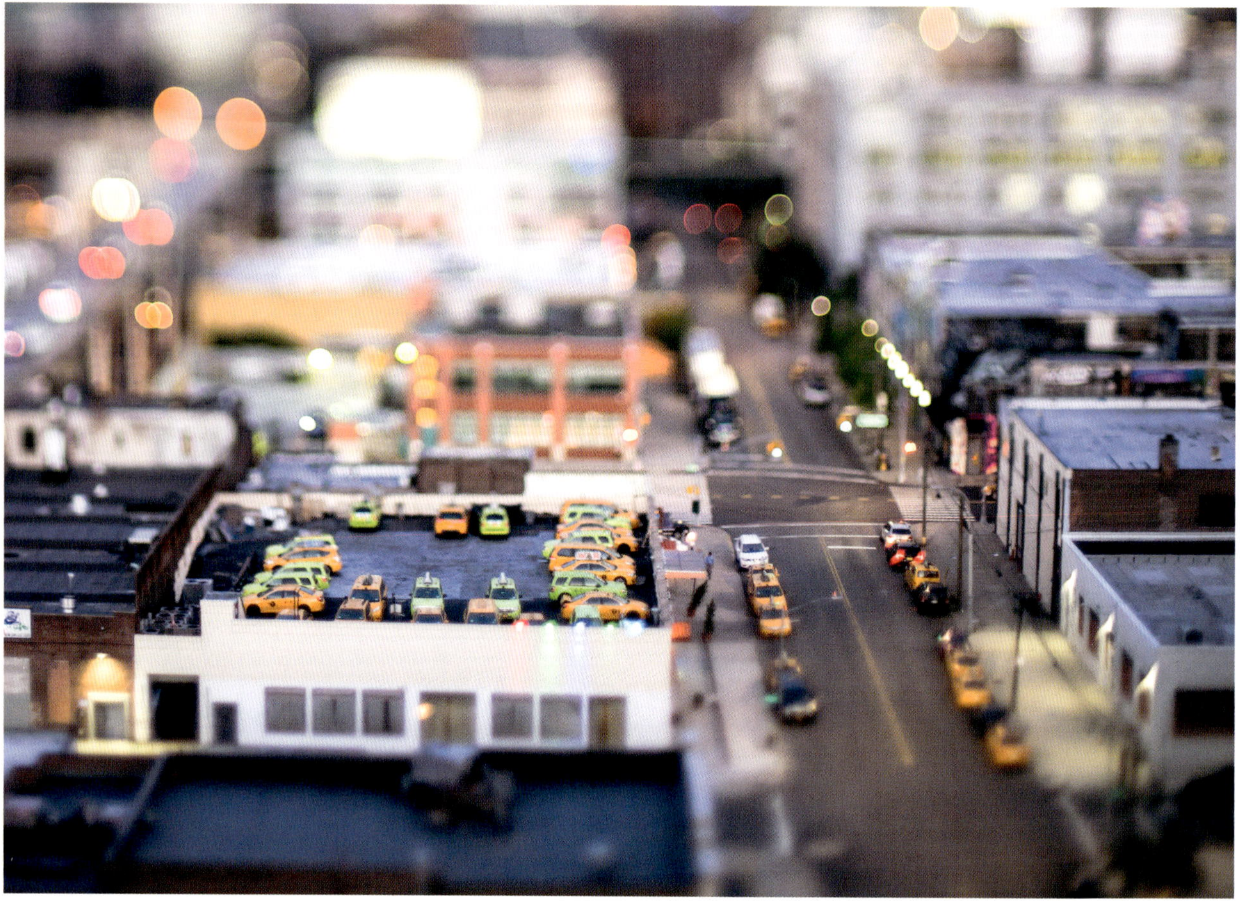

Long Island City, 43rd Ave

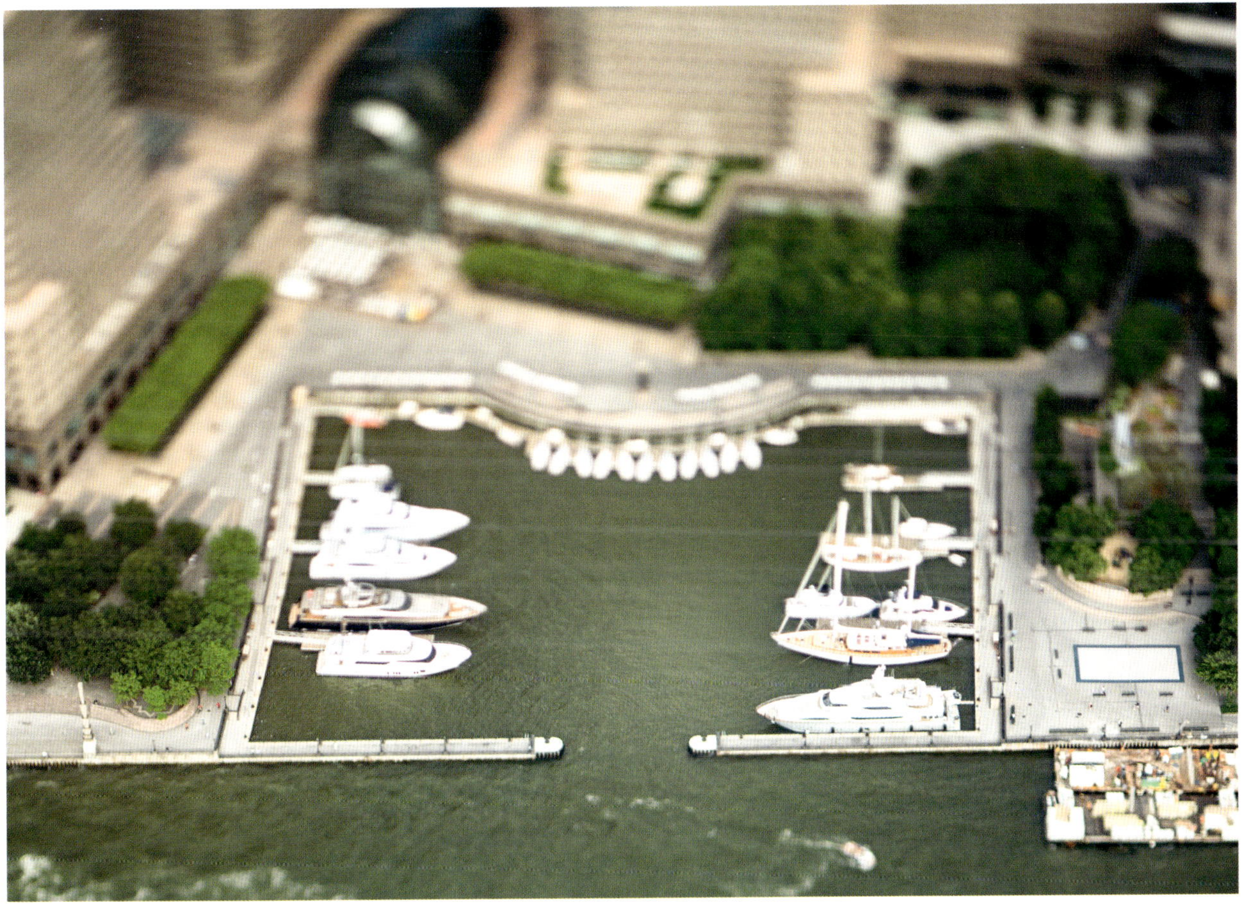

North Cove Marina

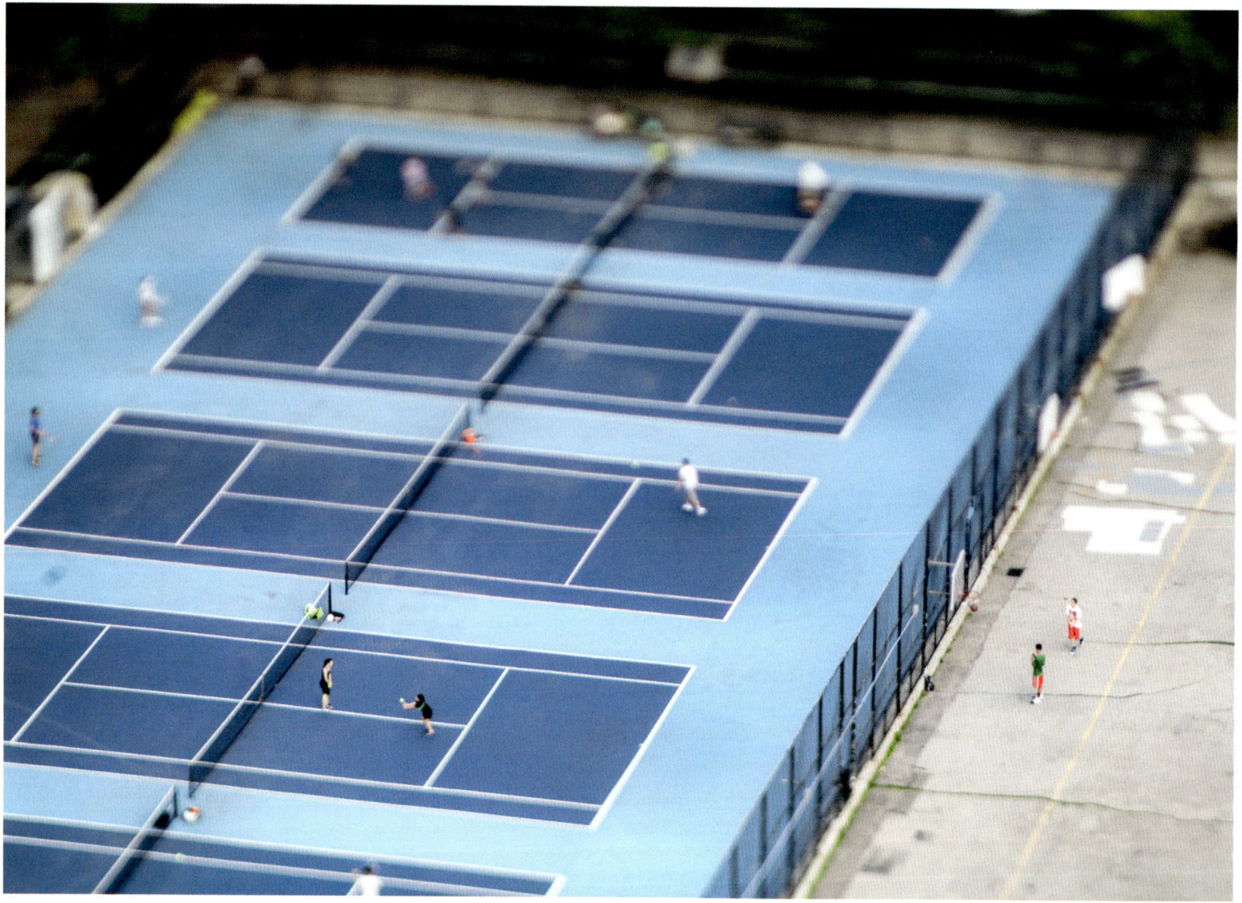

McCarren Park, Brooklyn

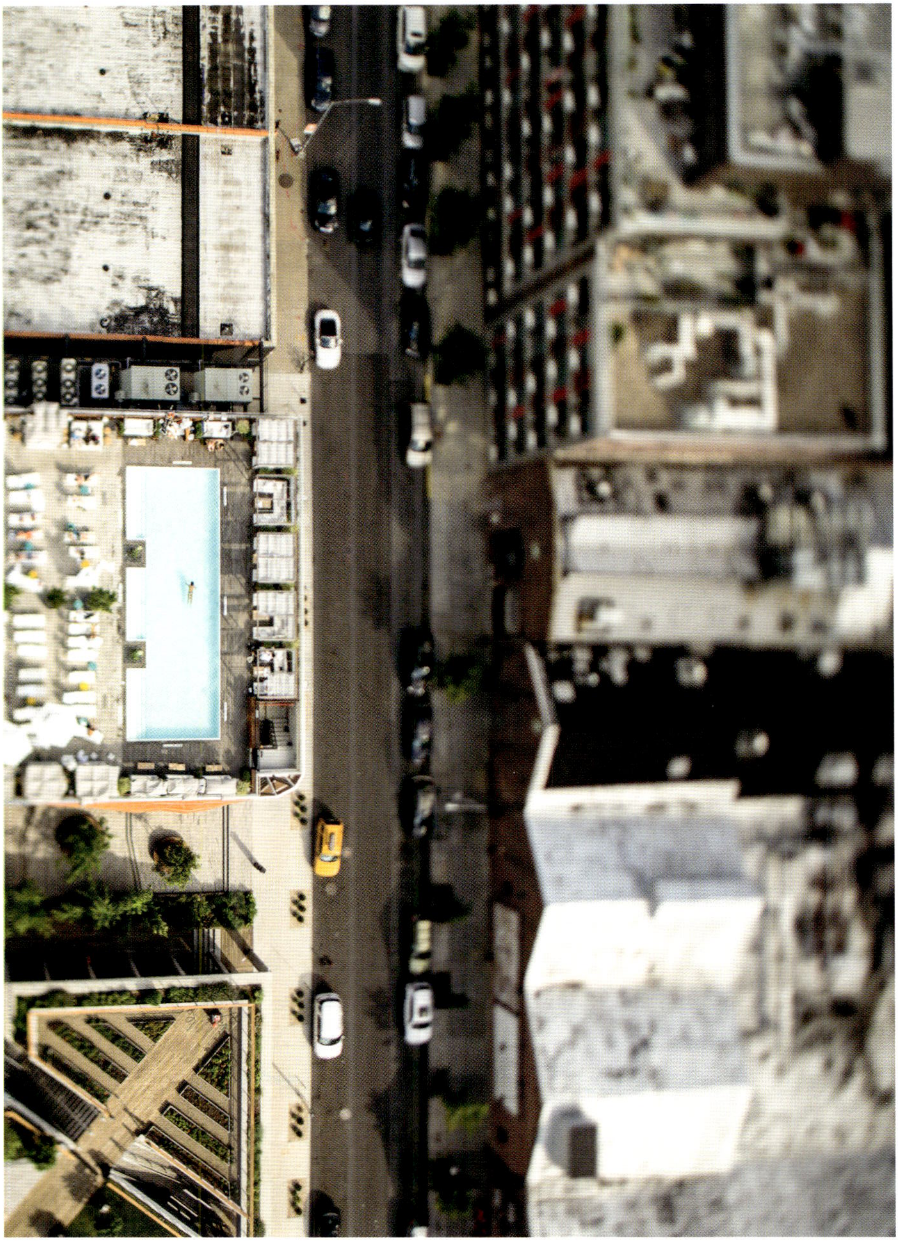

The William Vale, Brooklyn

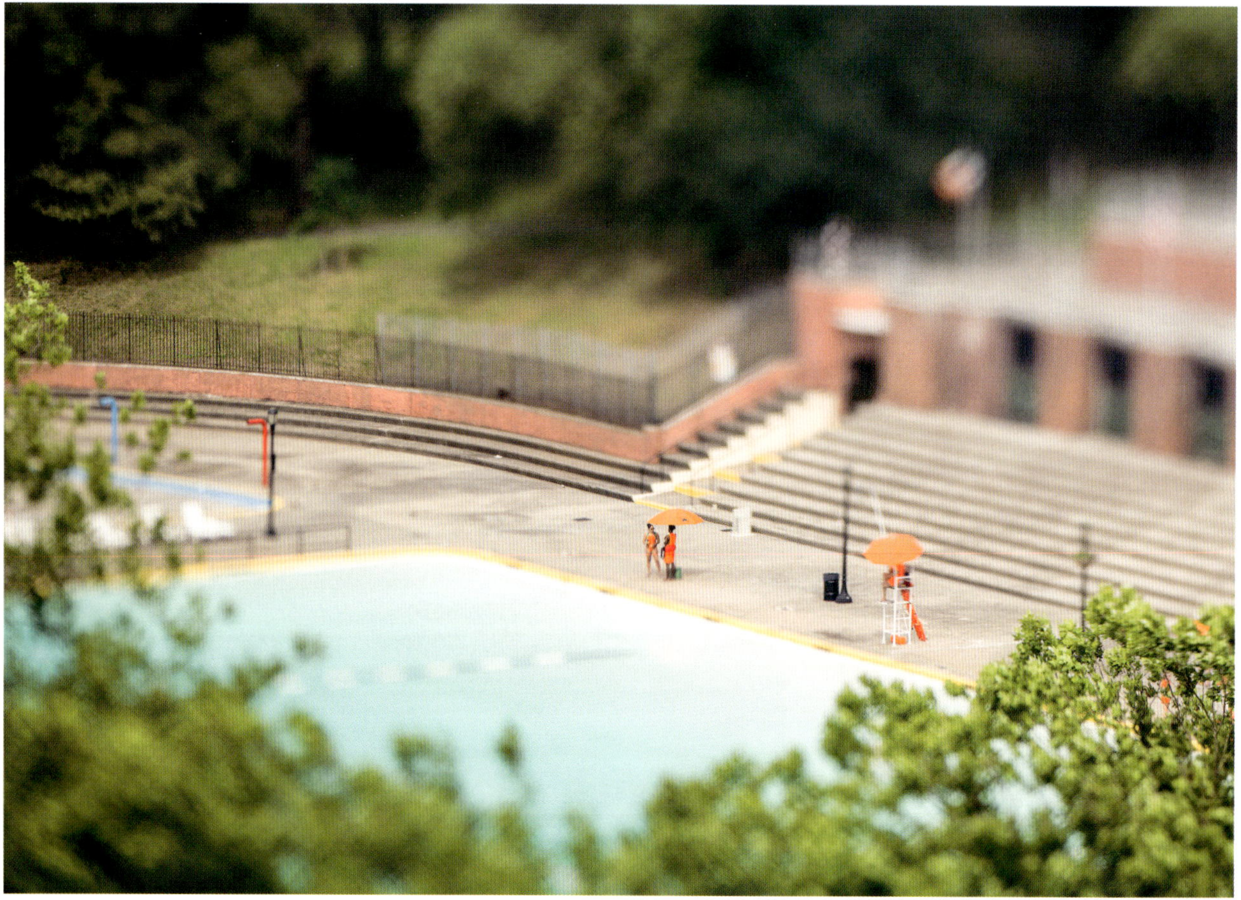

Astoria Park Pool, Queens

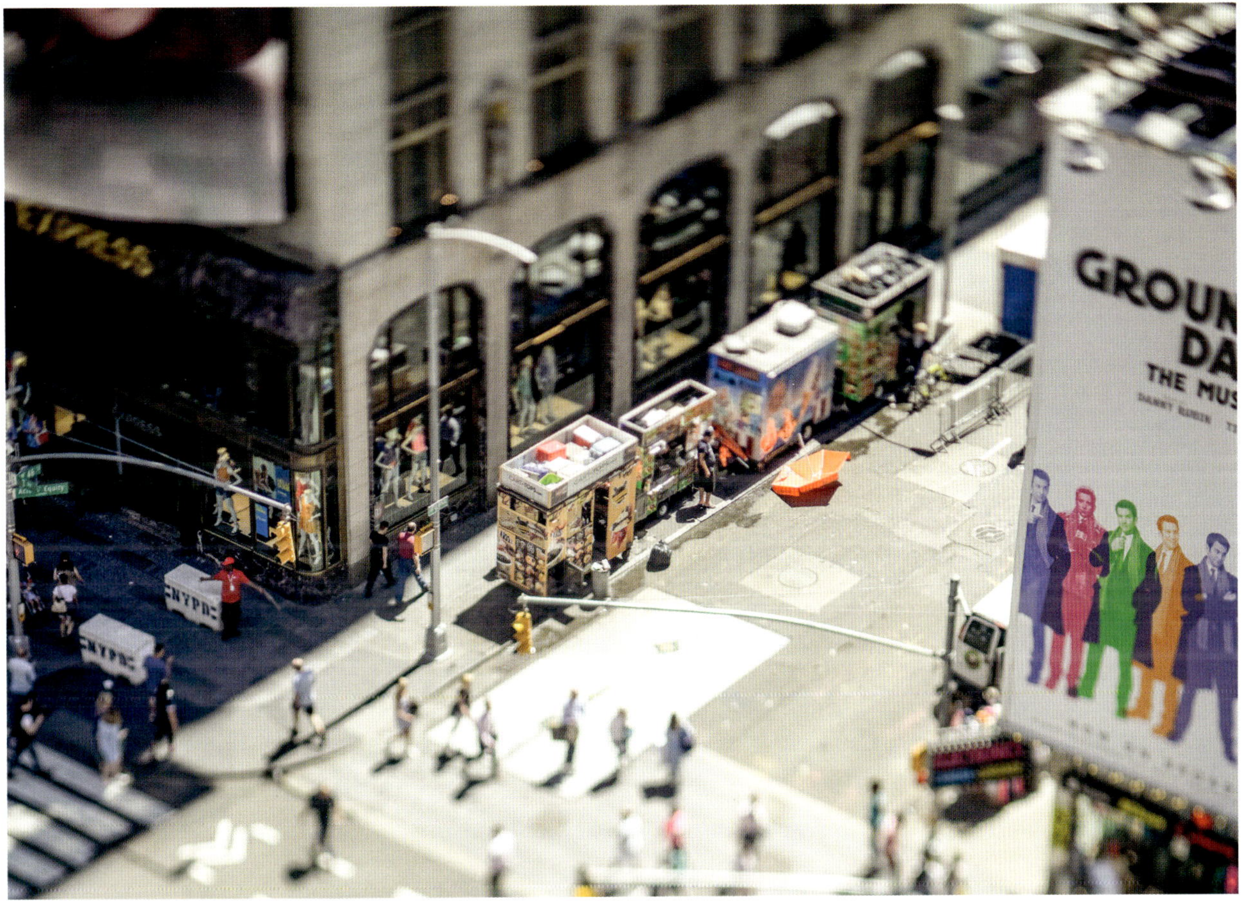

Times Square

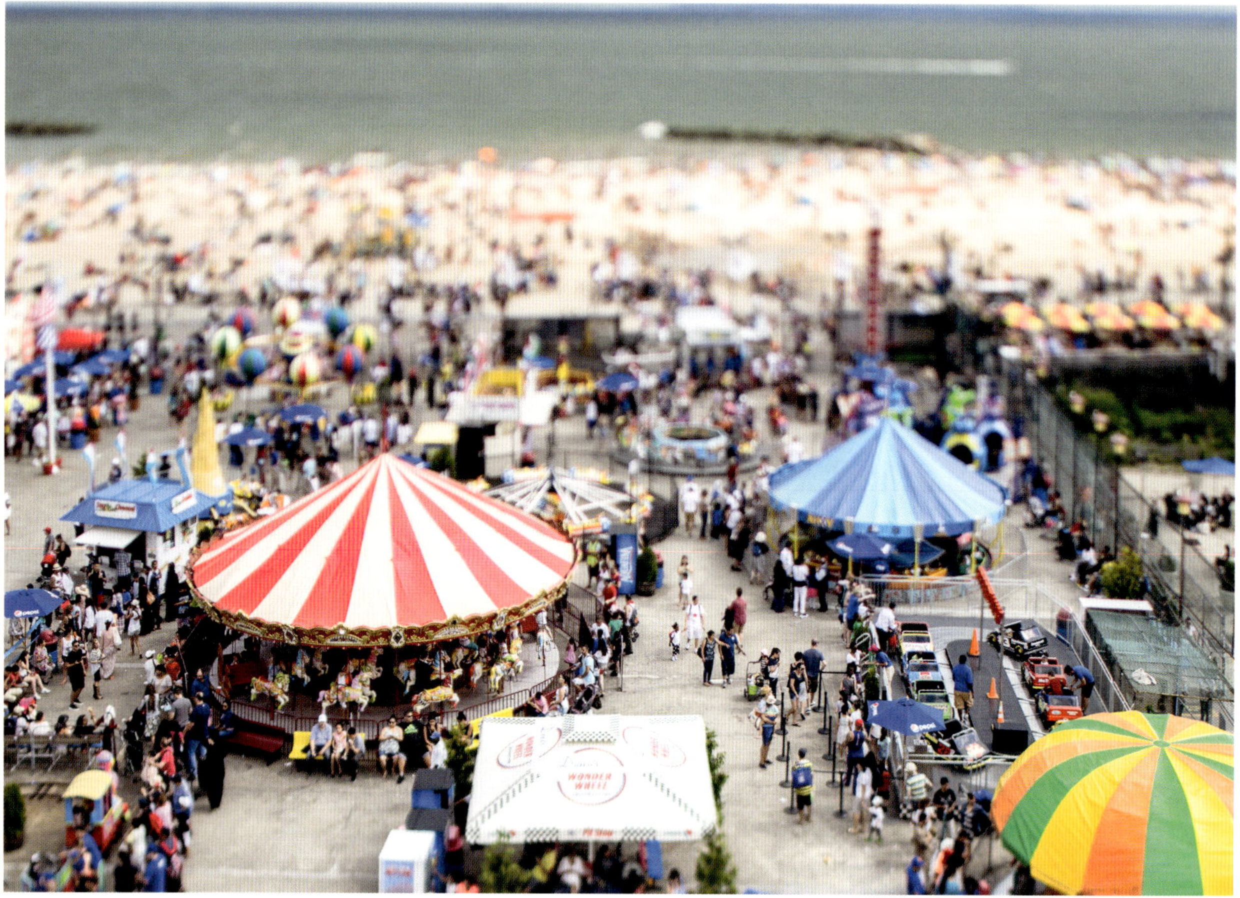

Coney Island, Brooklyn

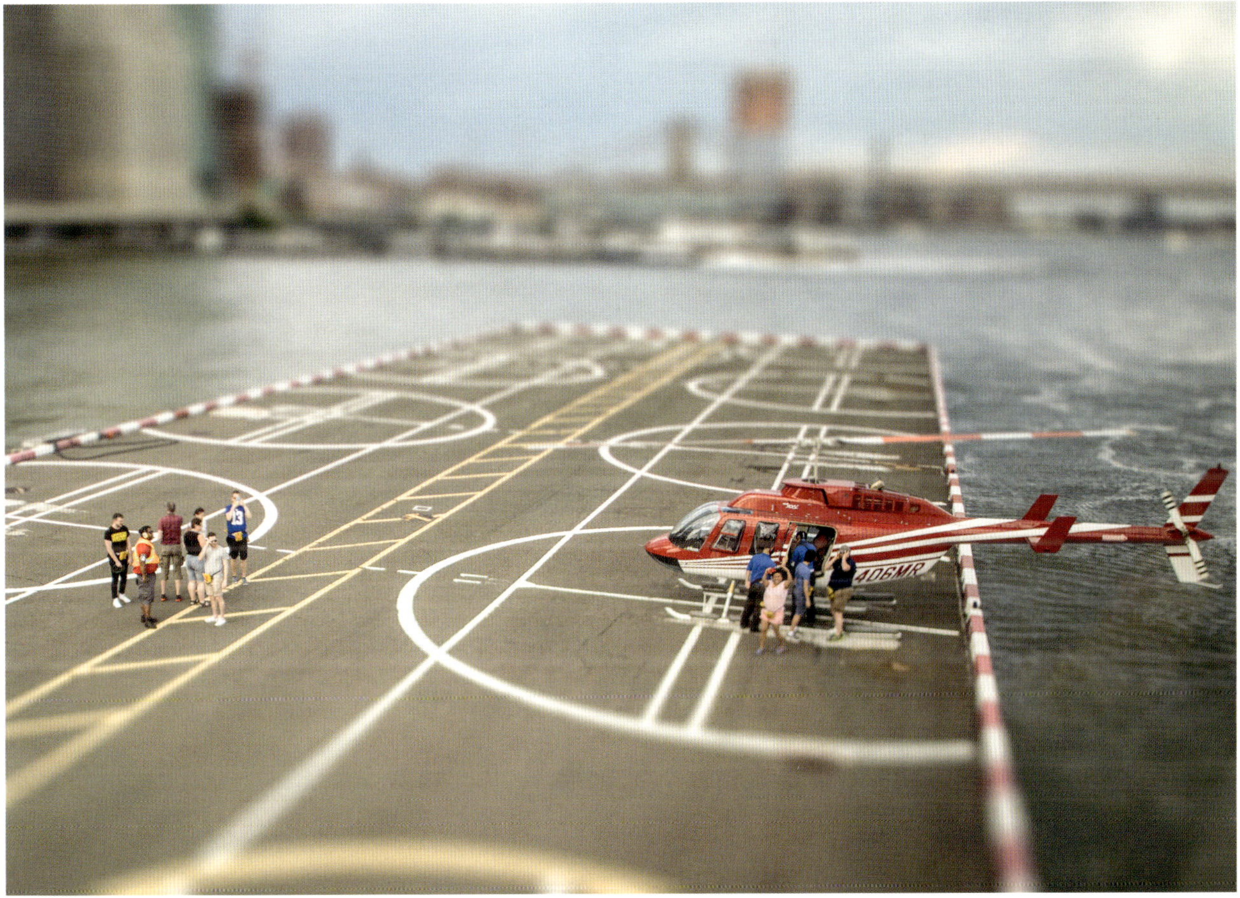

Manhattan Heliport

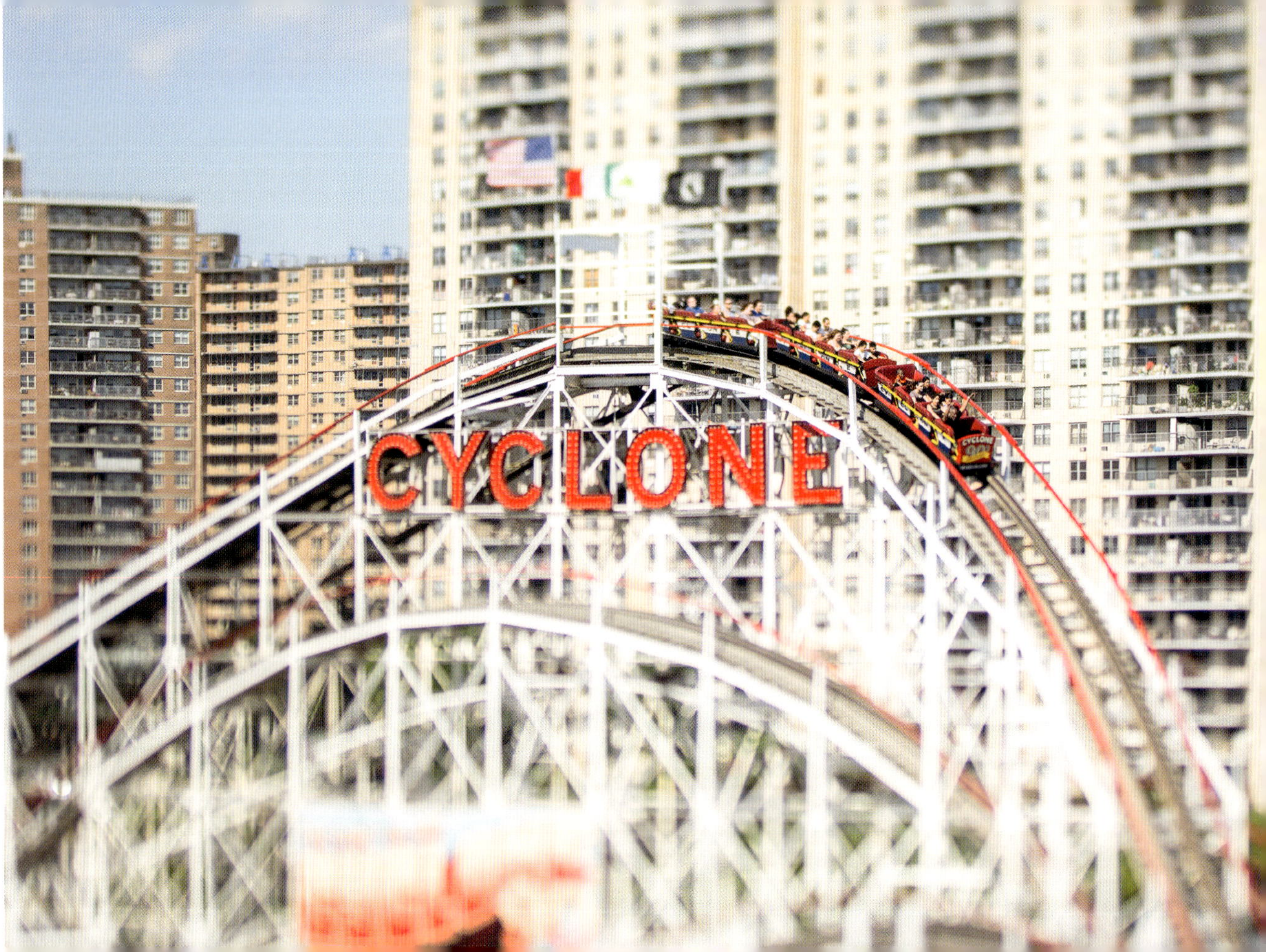

Coney Island, Brooklyn

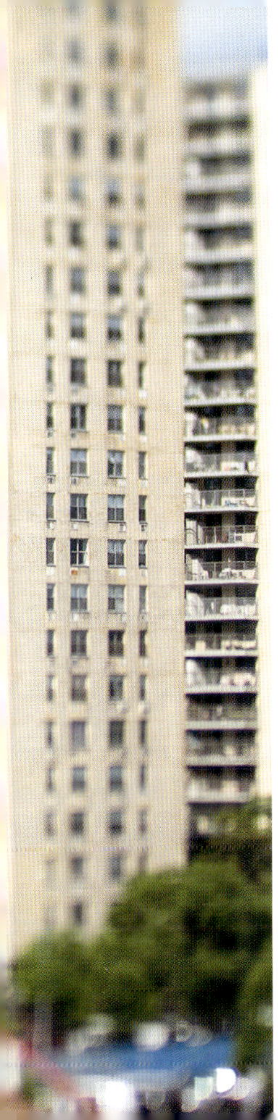

Silence? What can New York—noisy, roaring, rumbling, tumbling, bustling, story, turbulent New York—have to do with silence? Amid the universal clatter, the incessant din of business, the all swallowing vortex of the great money whirlpool—who has any, even distant, idea of the profound repose... of silence?

Walt Whitman

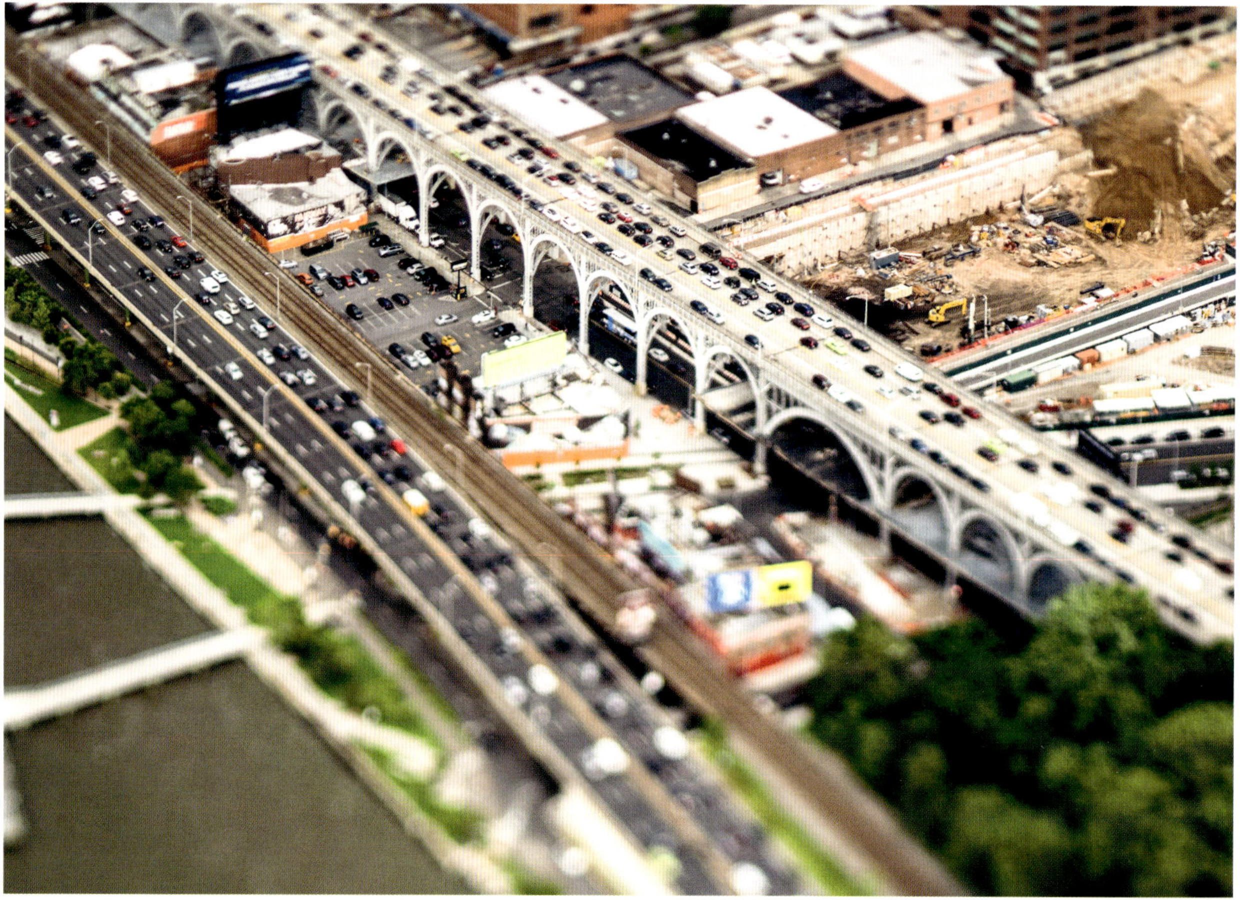

Riverside Drive Viaduct

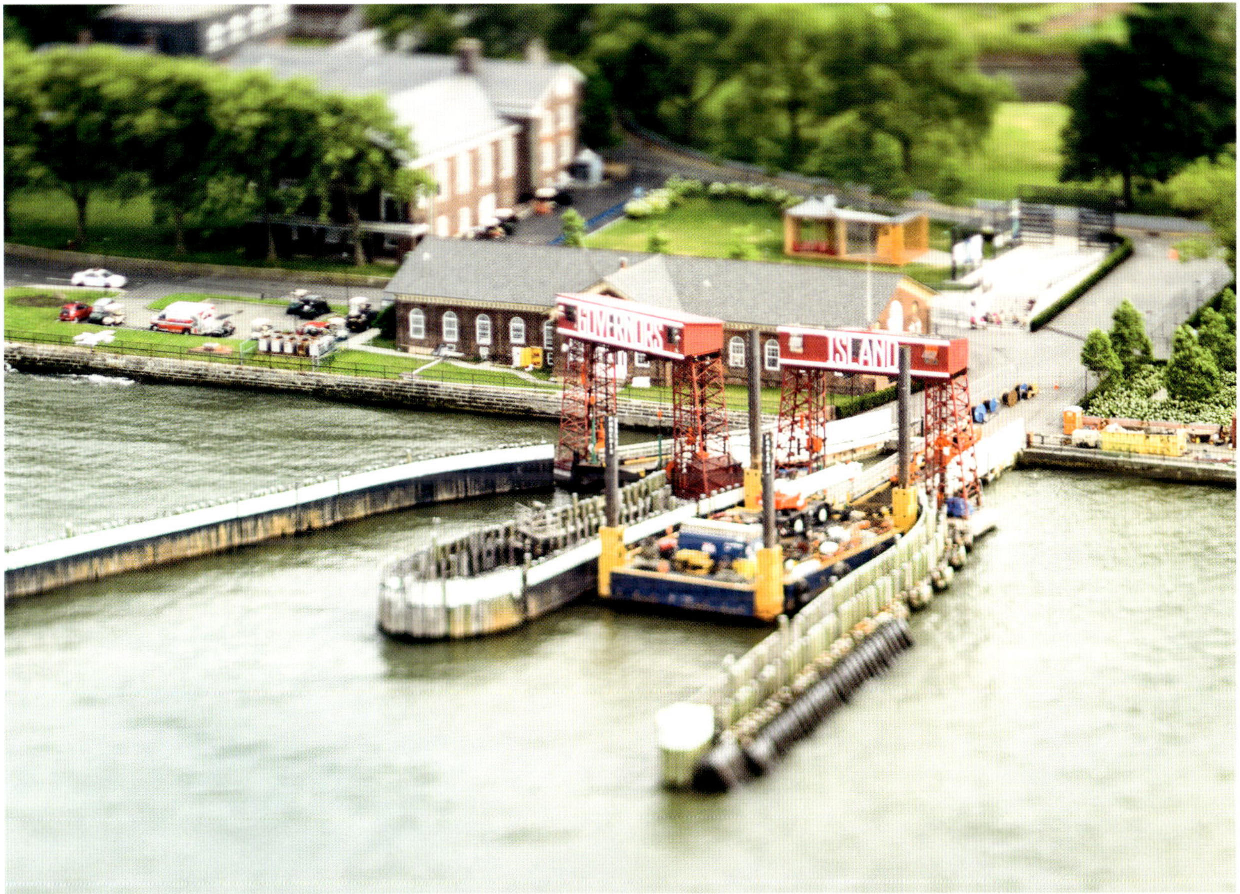

Governors Island

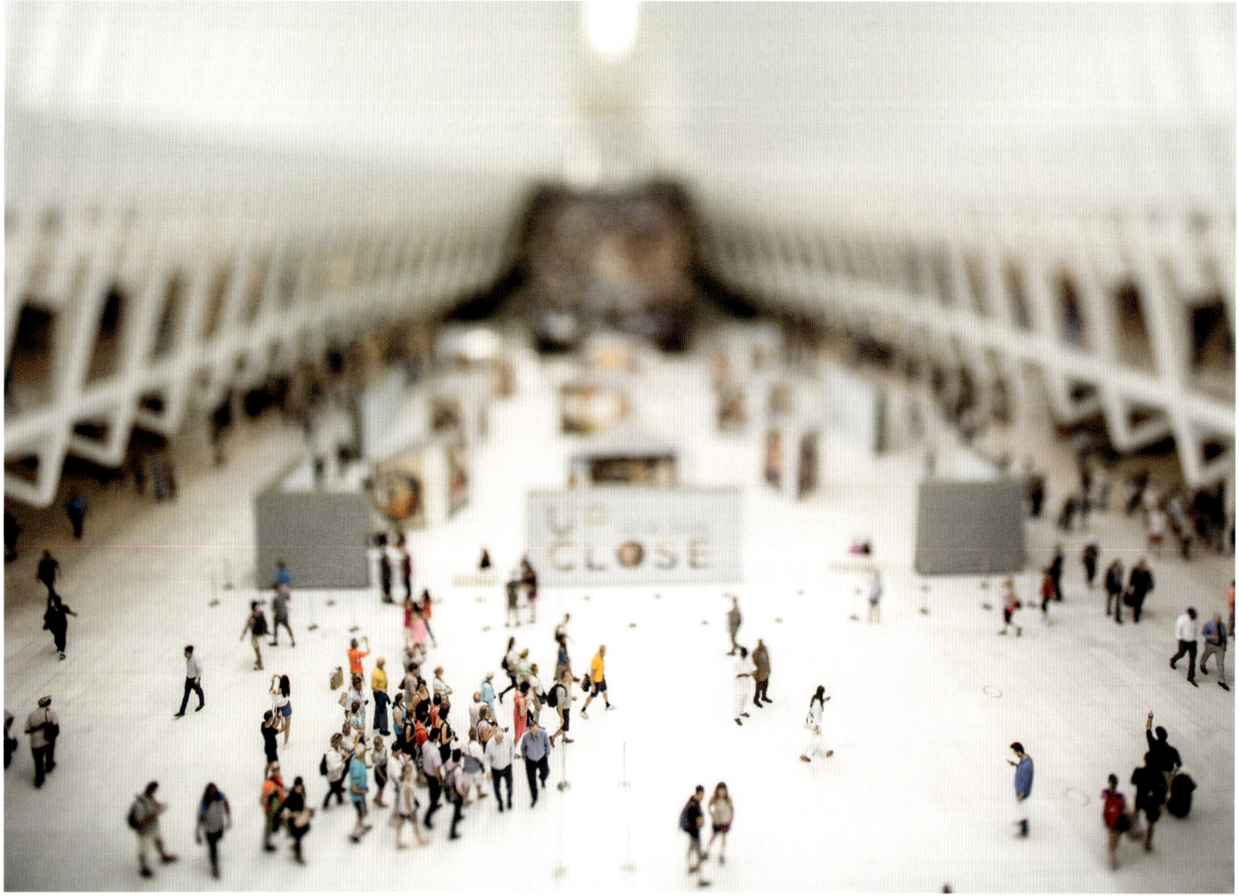

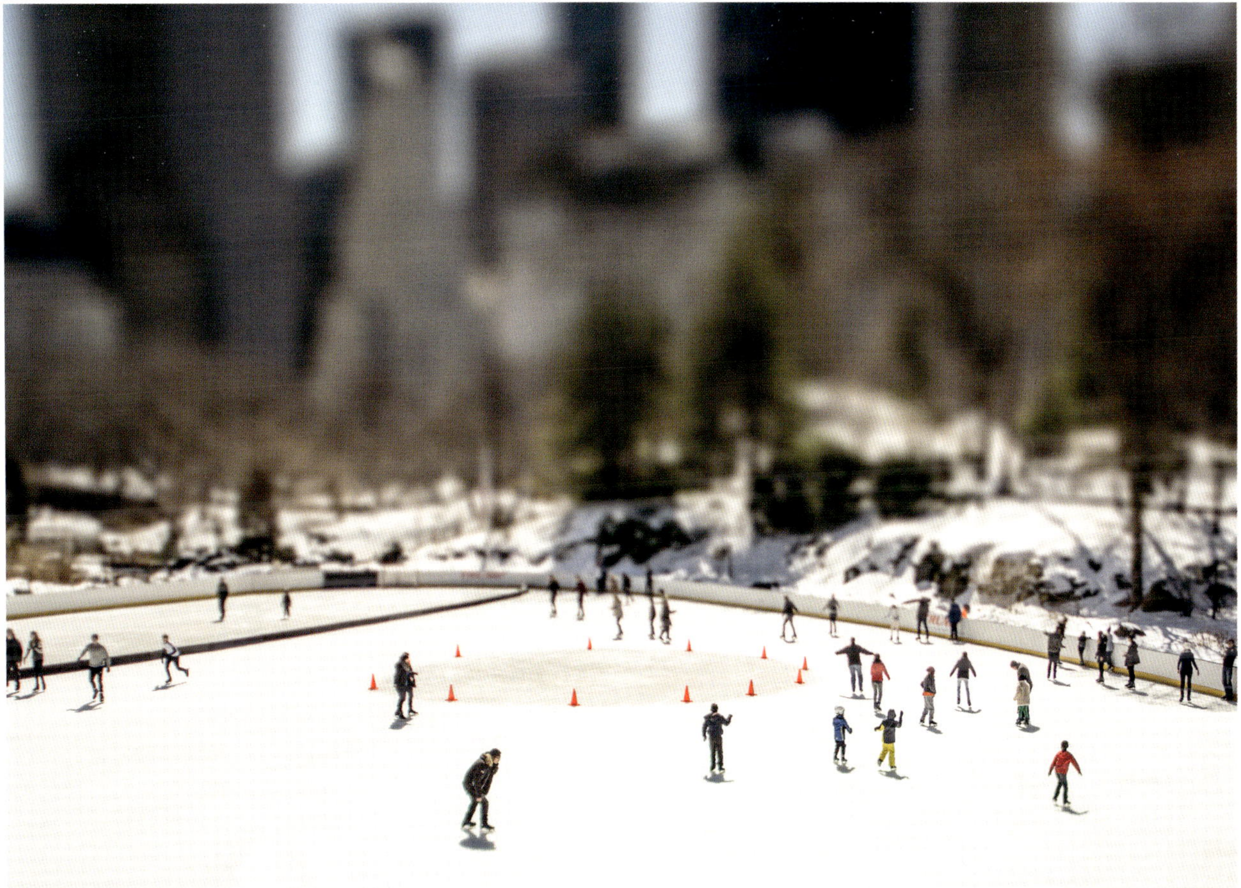

Central Park

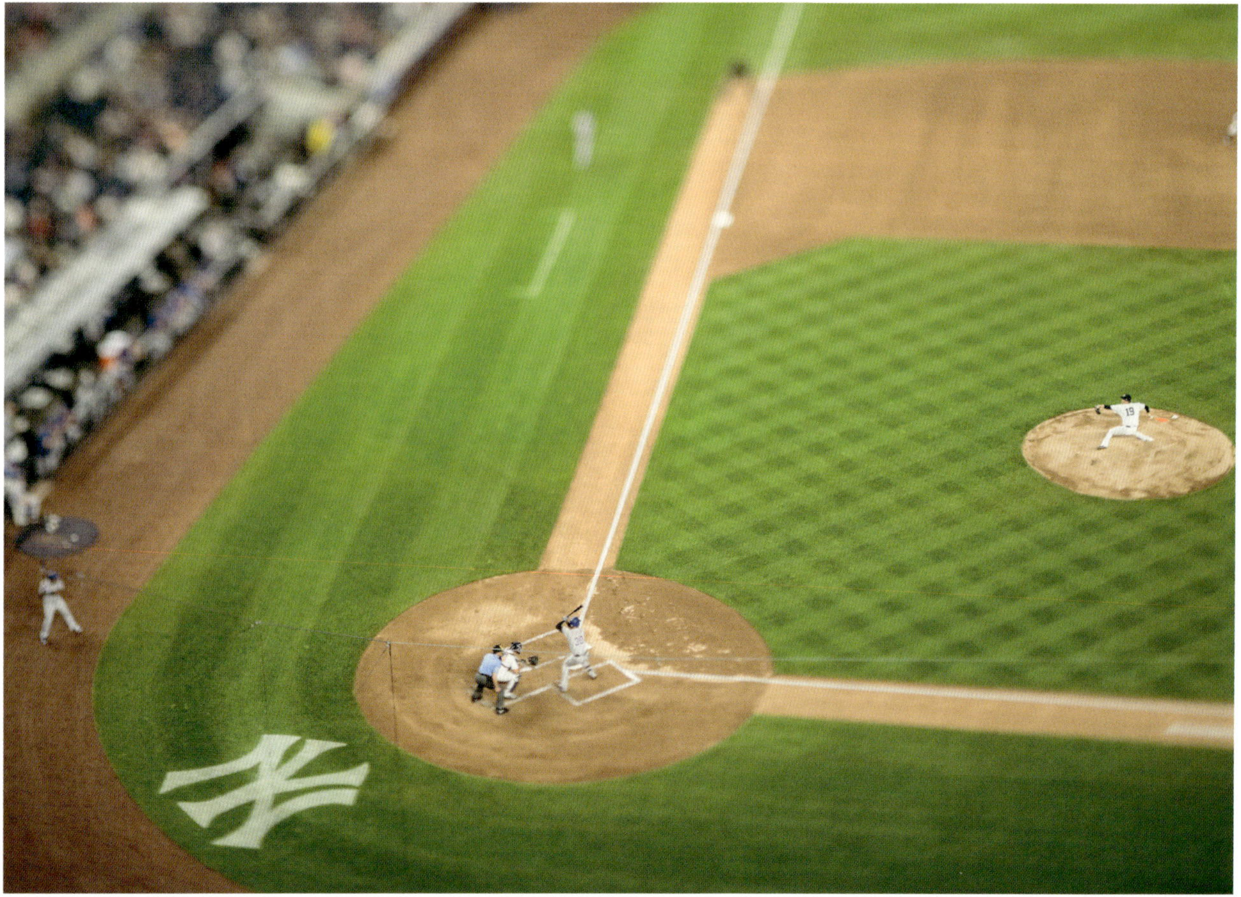

Yankee Stadium

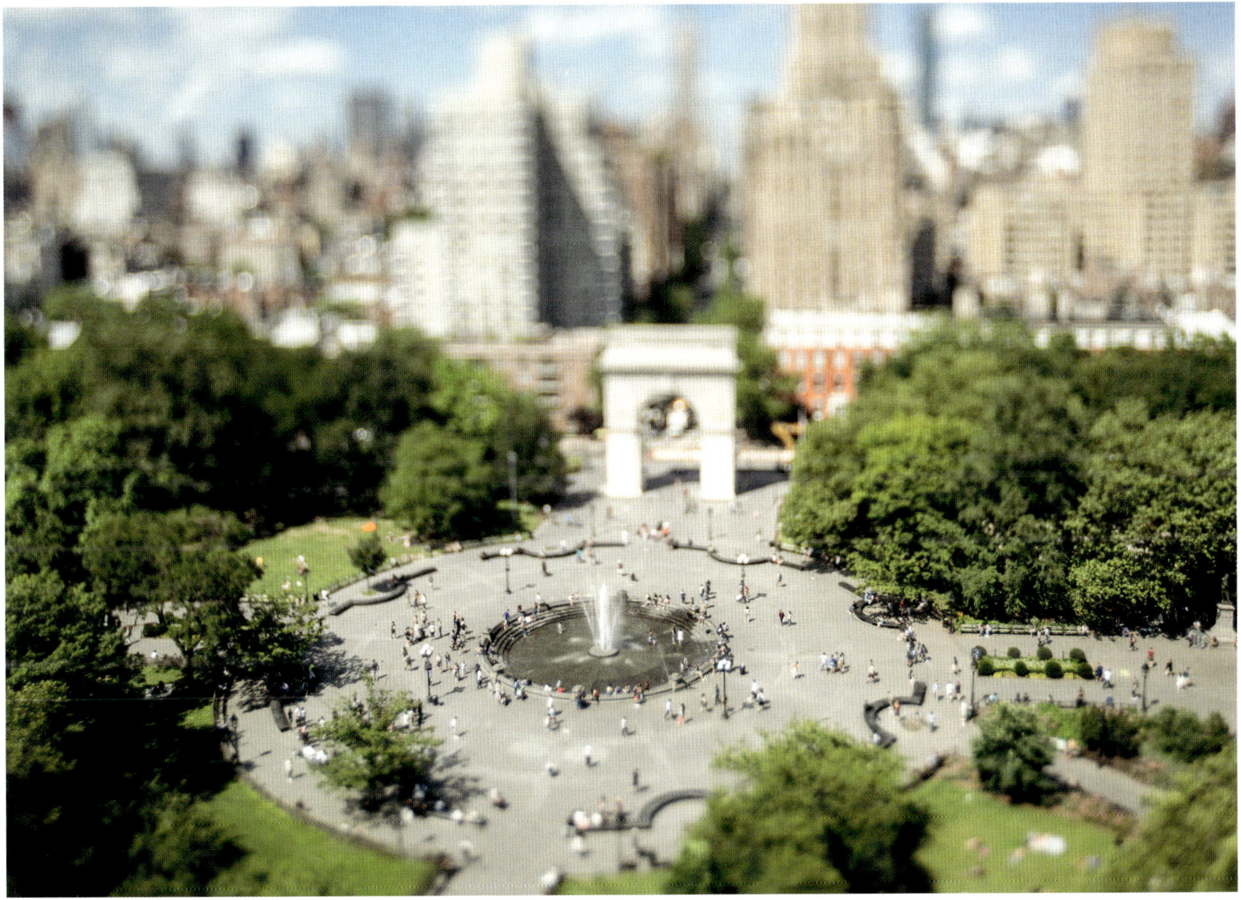

Washington Square Park

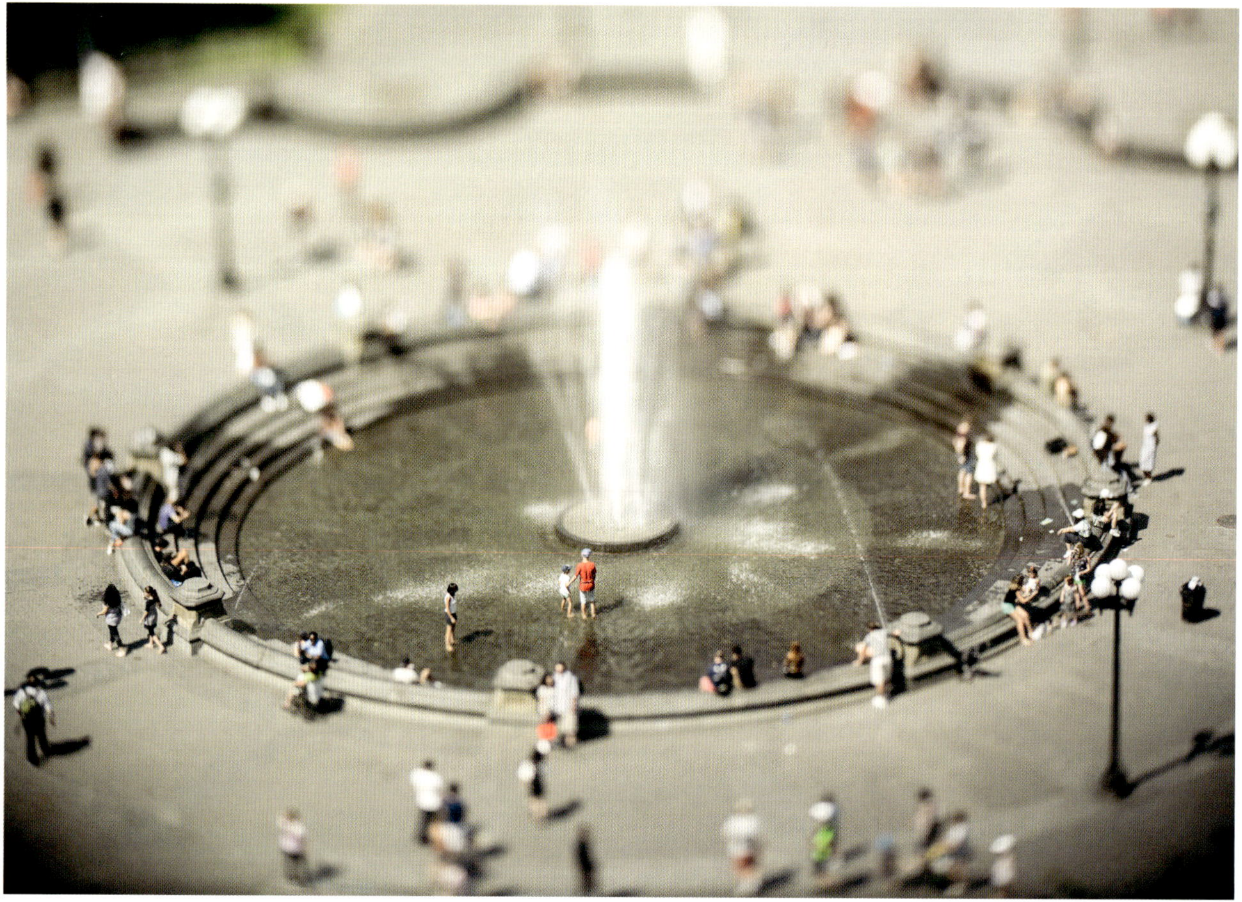

Washington Square Park

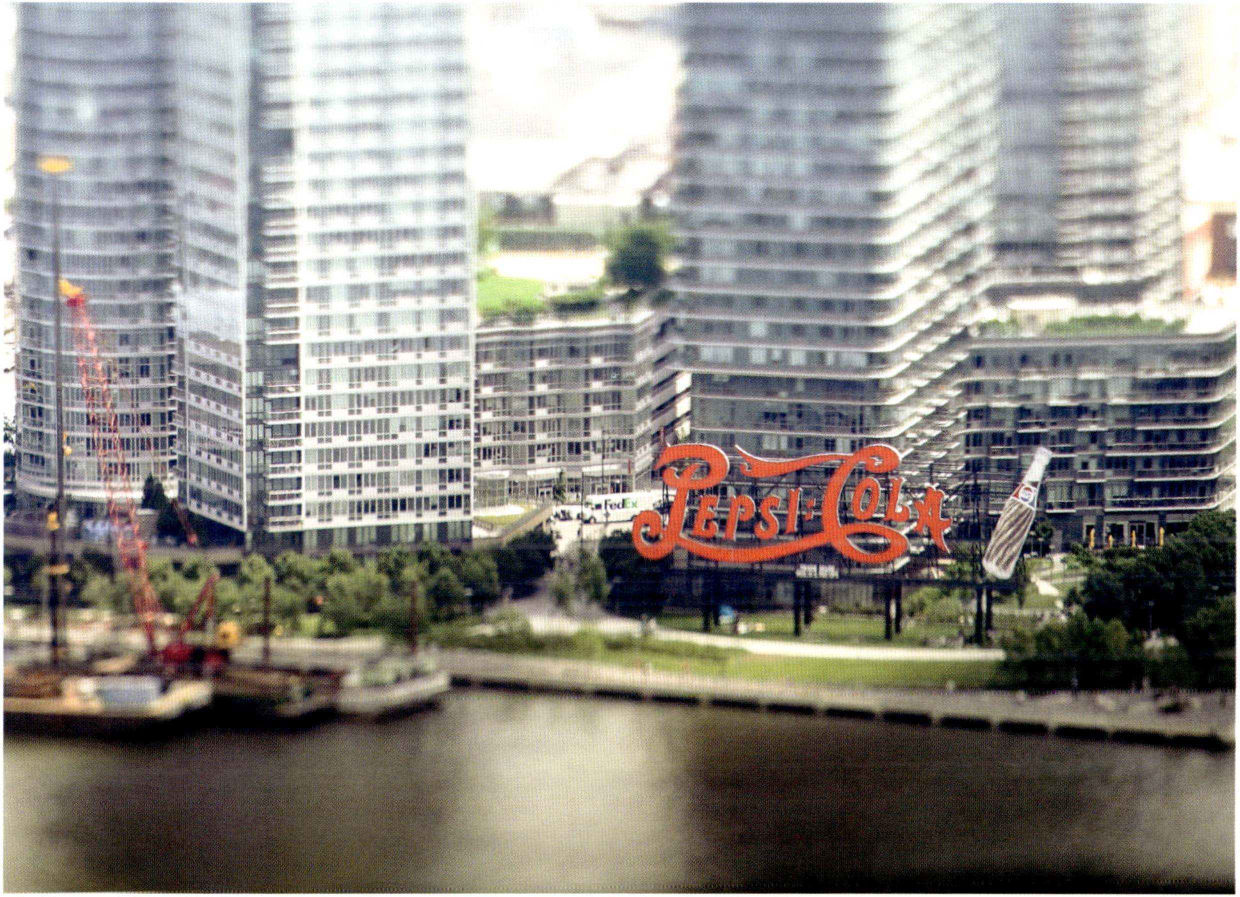

Pepsi Sign, Long Island City

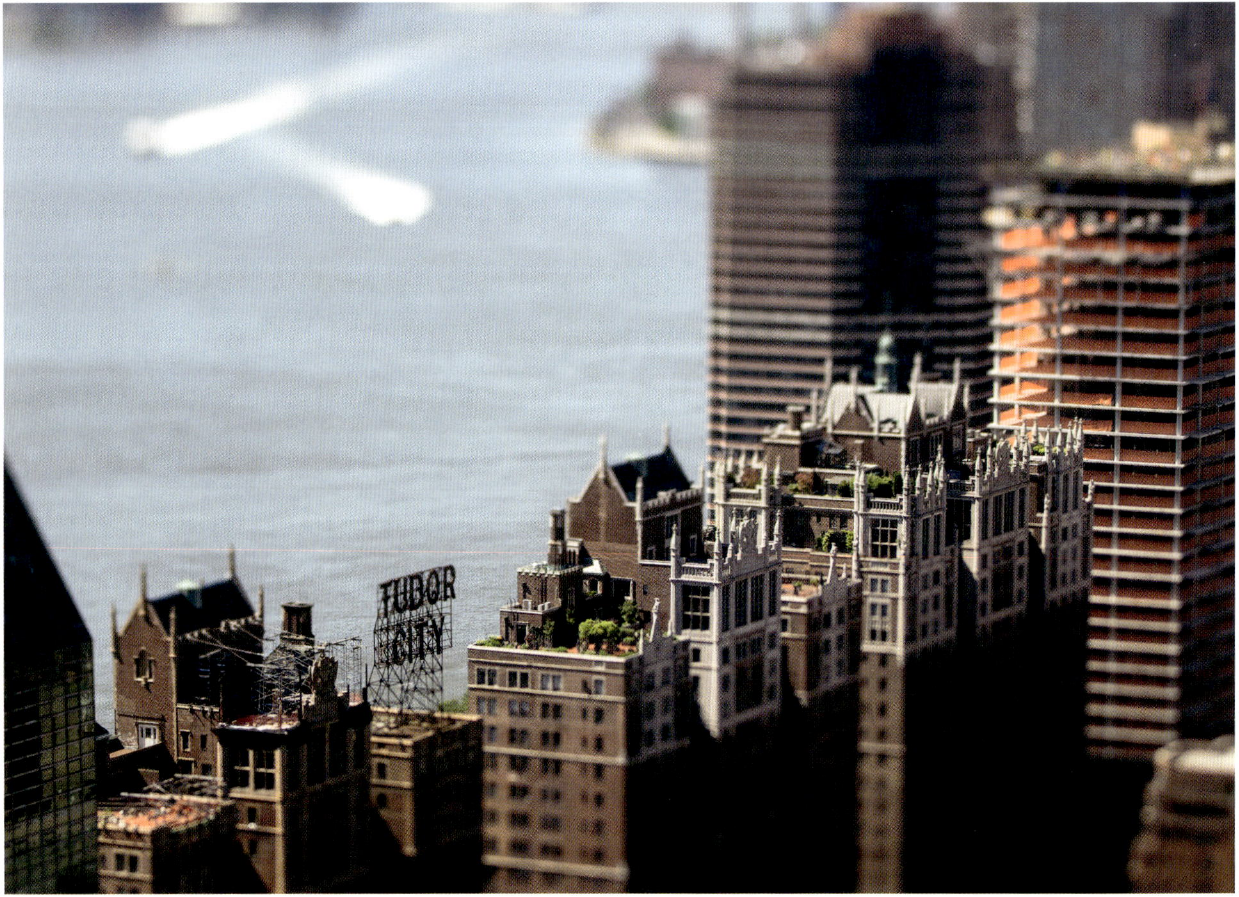
TUDOR
CITY

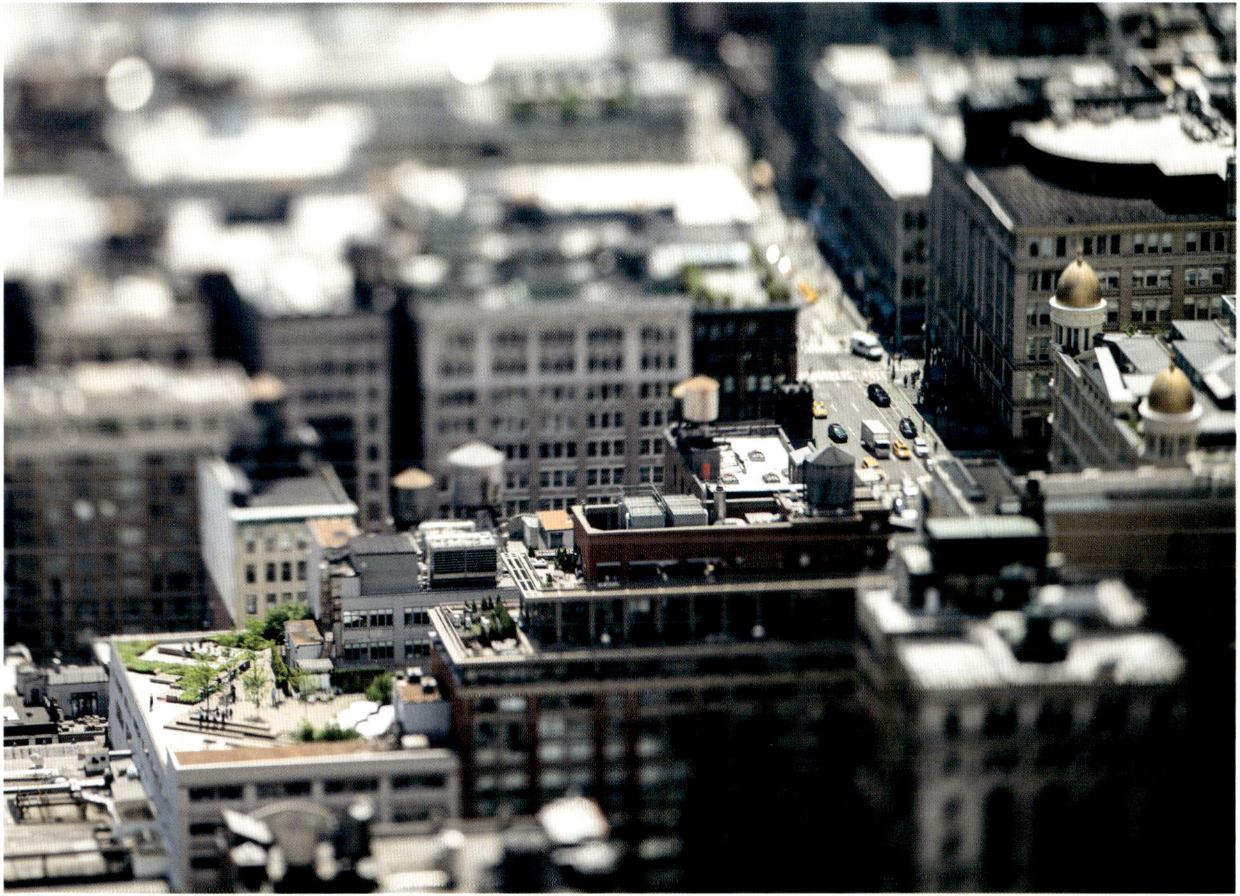

6th Ave

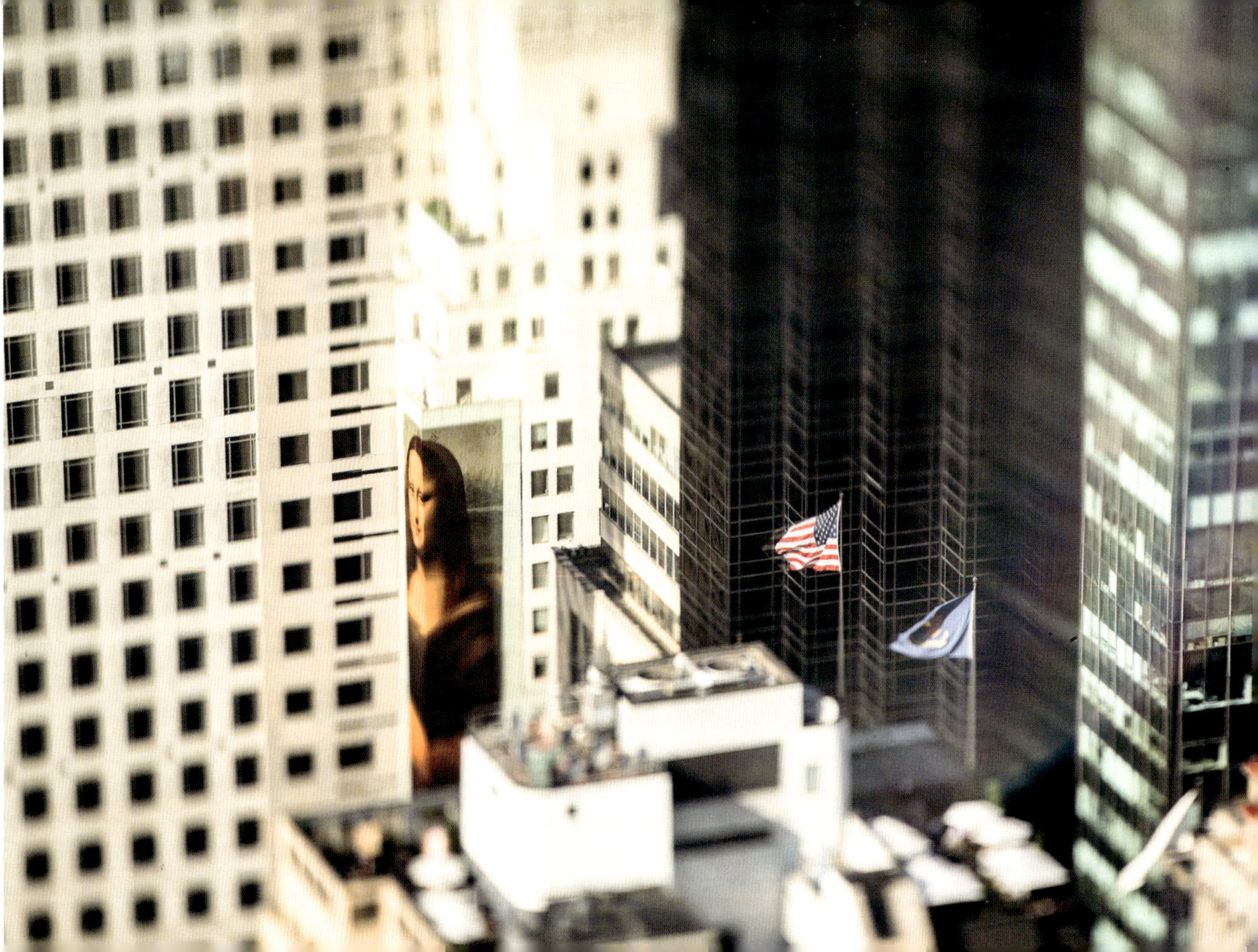

Midtown Manhattan

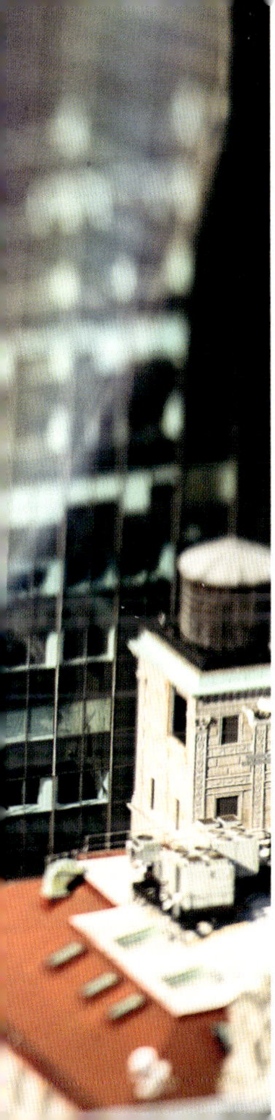

If London is a watercolor,

New York is an oil painting.

Peter Schaffer

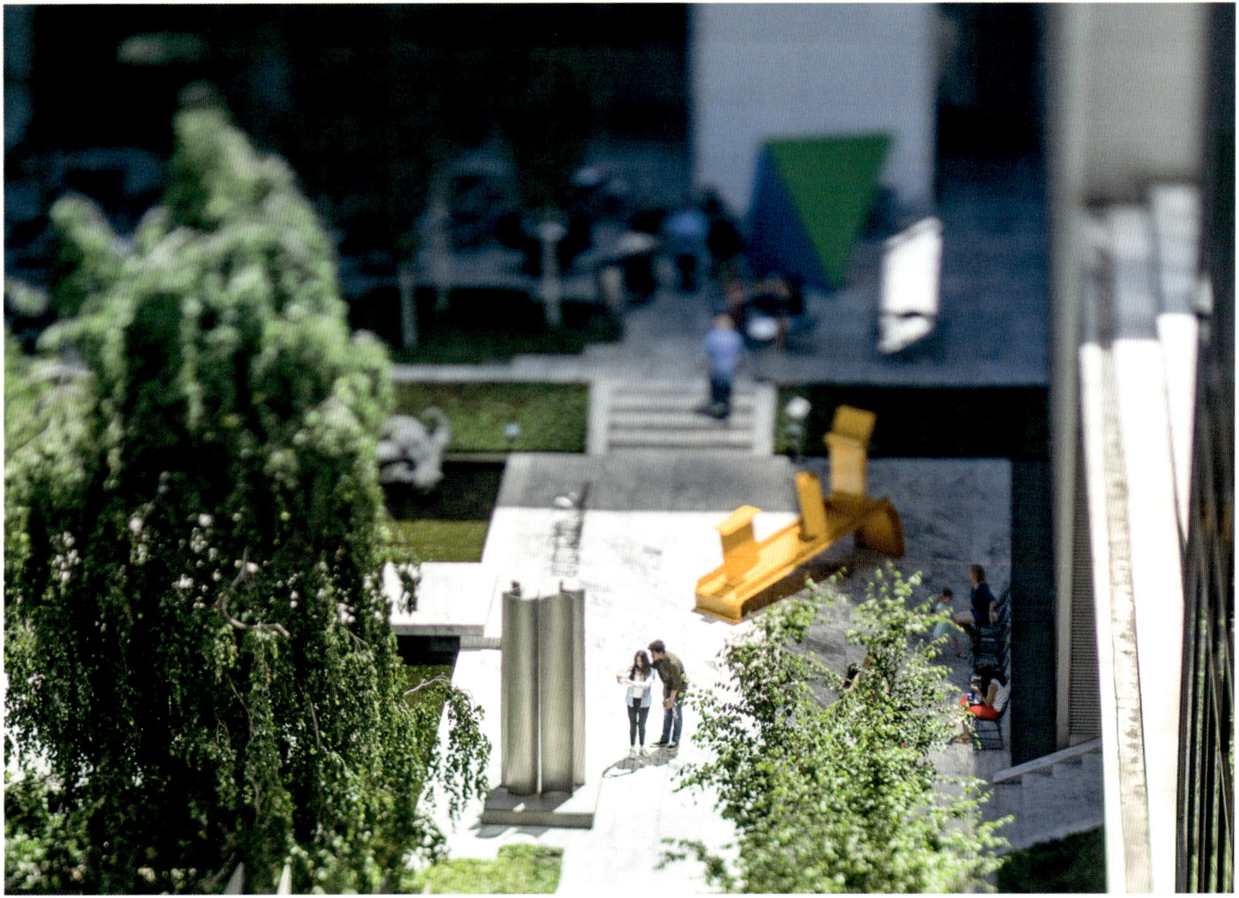

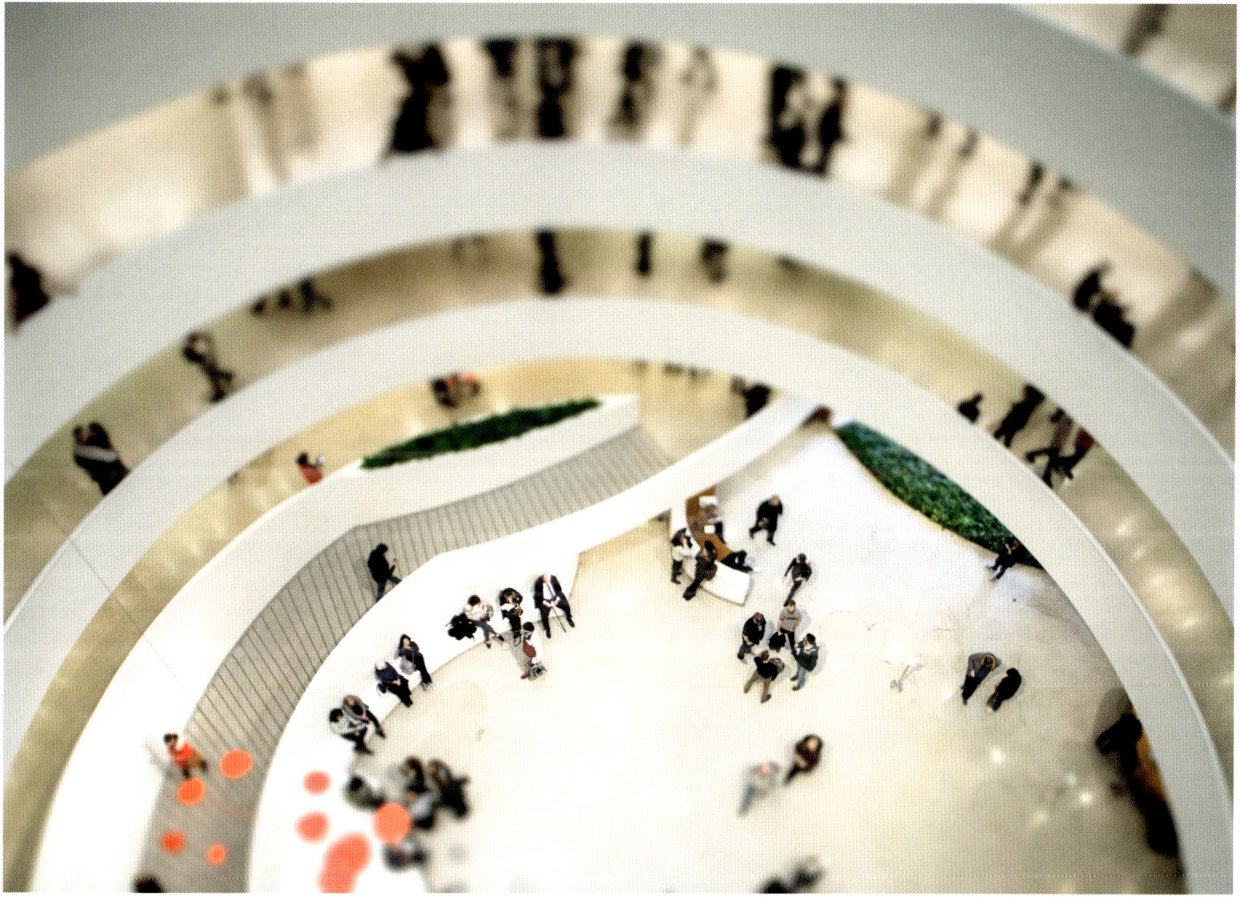

Guggenheim Museum

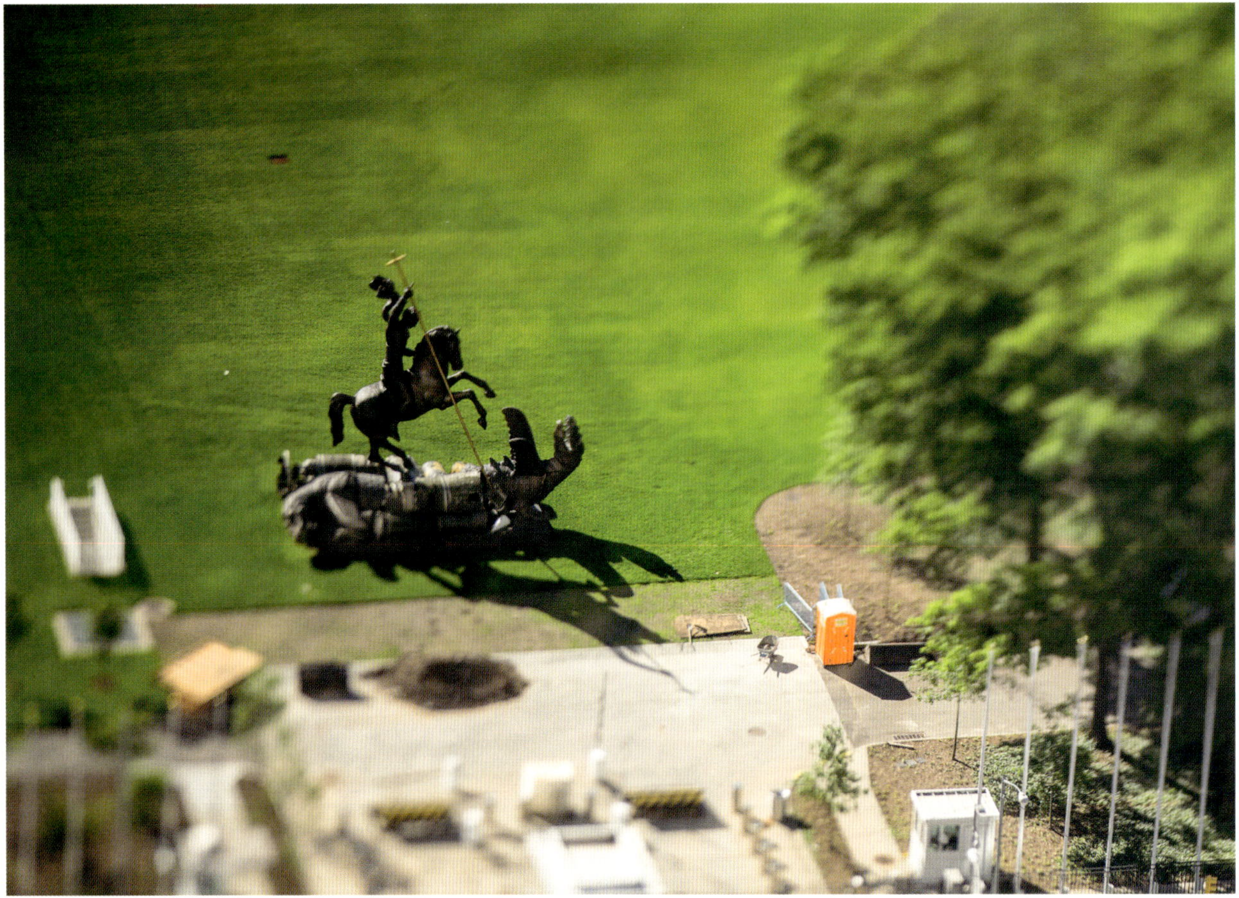

United Nations Plaza

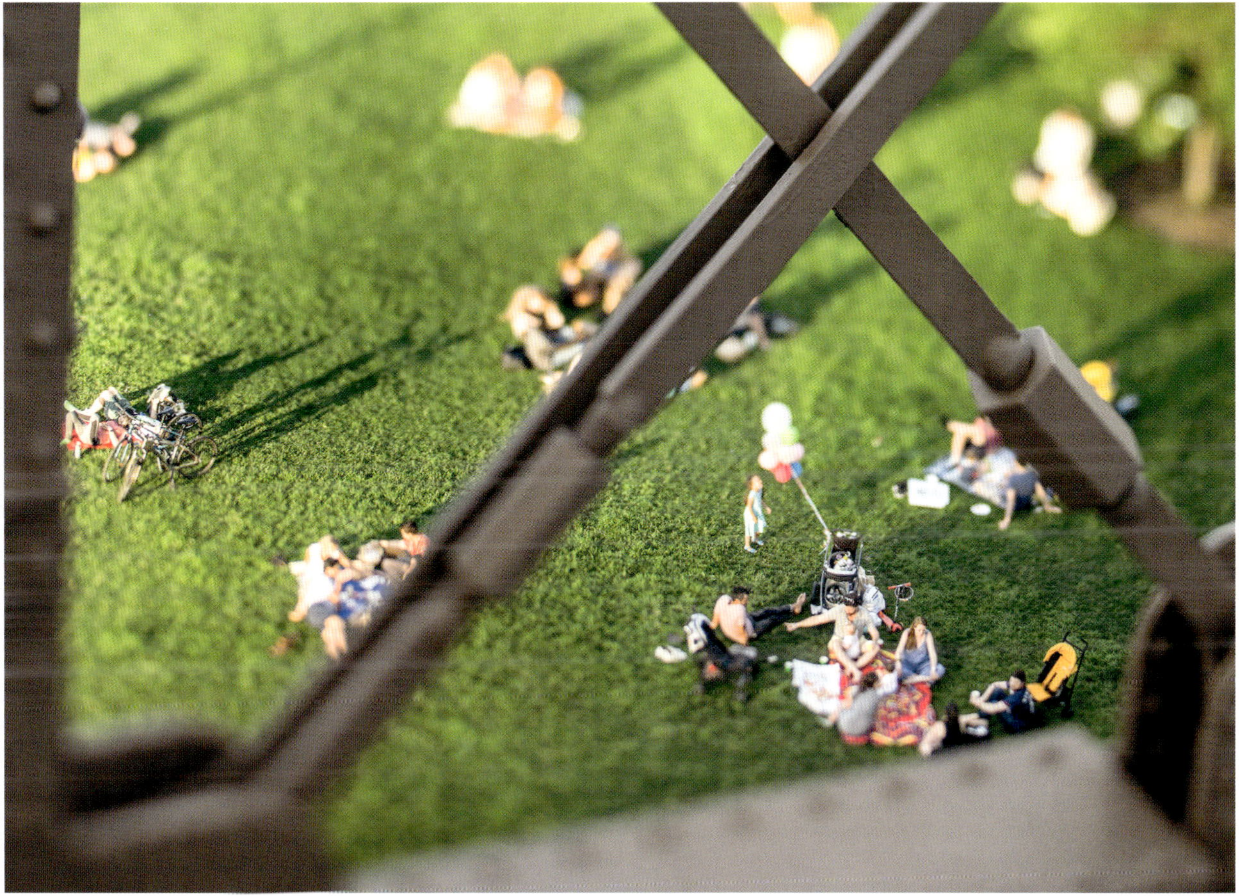

Brooklyn Bridge Park

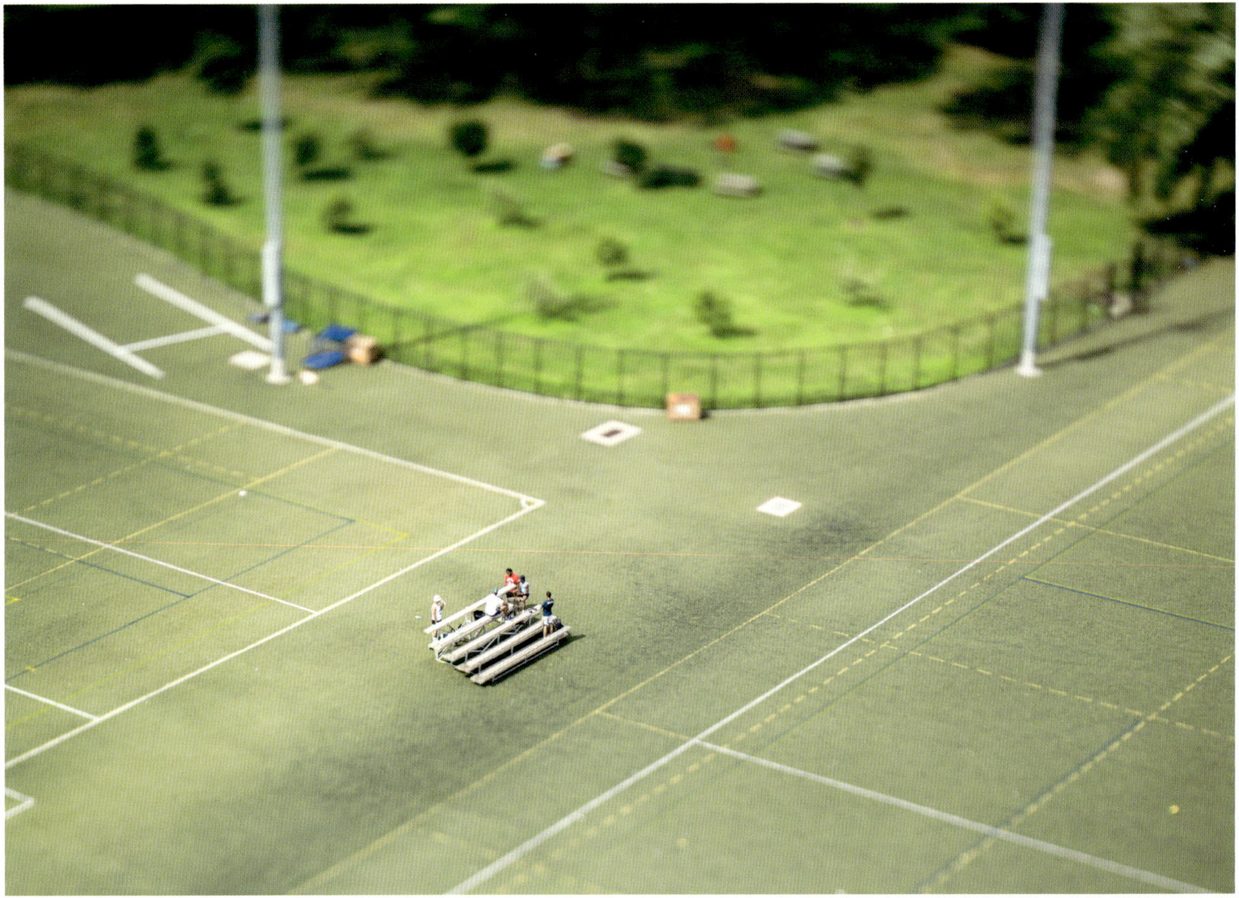

Wards Island Park

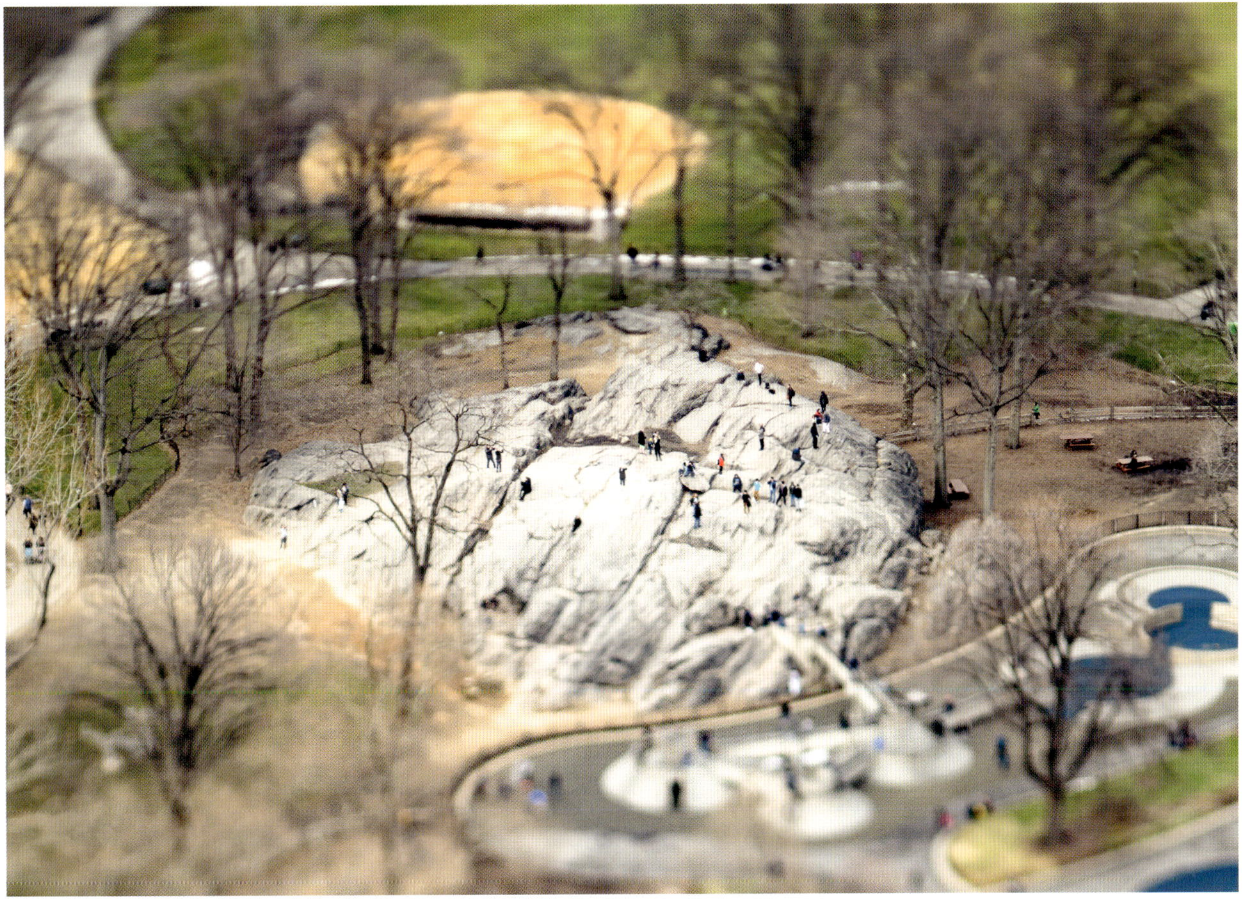

Central Park

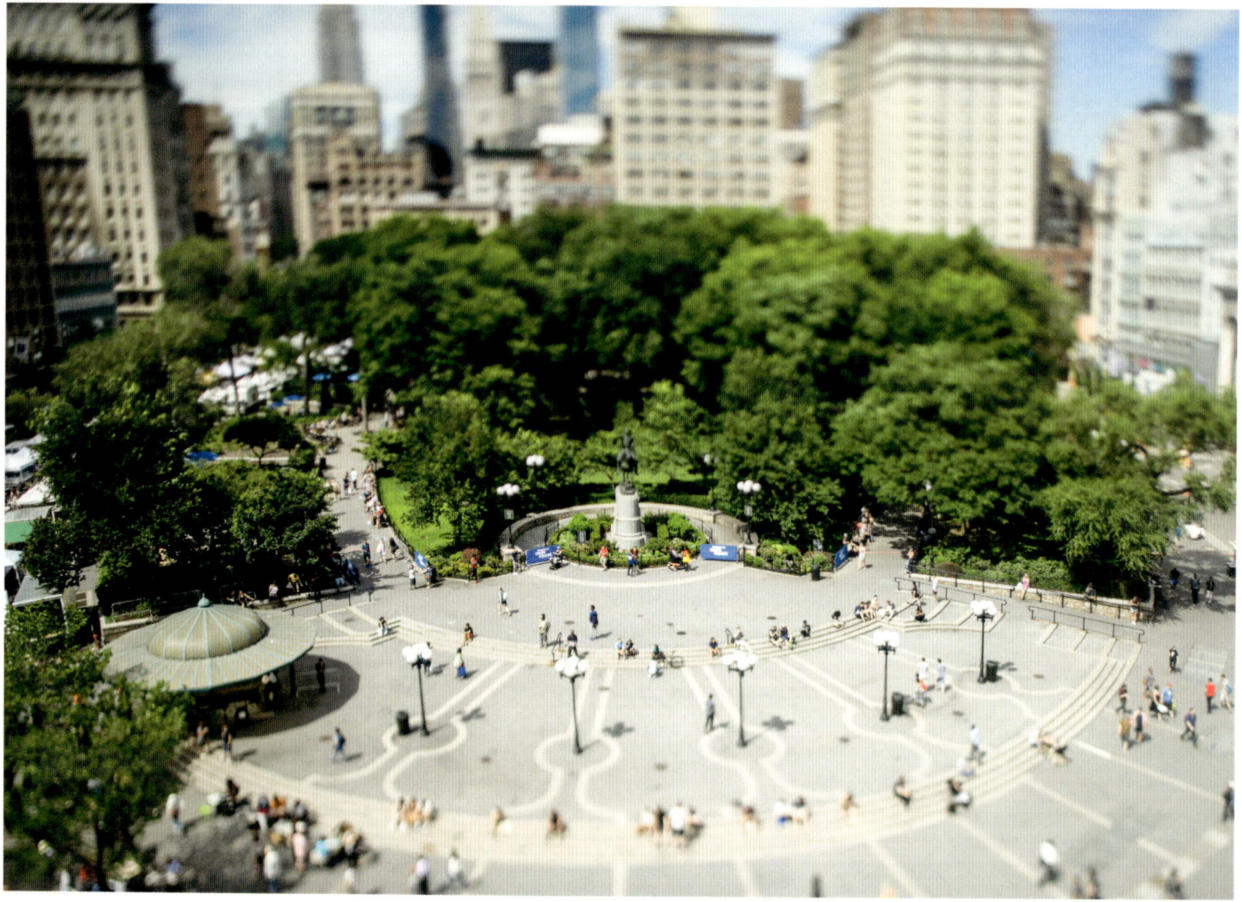

Union Square Park

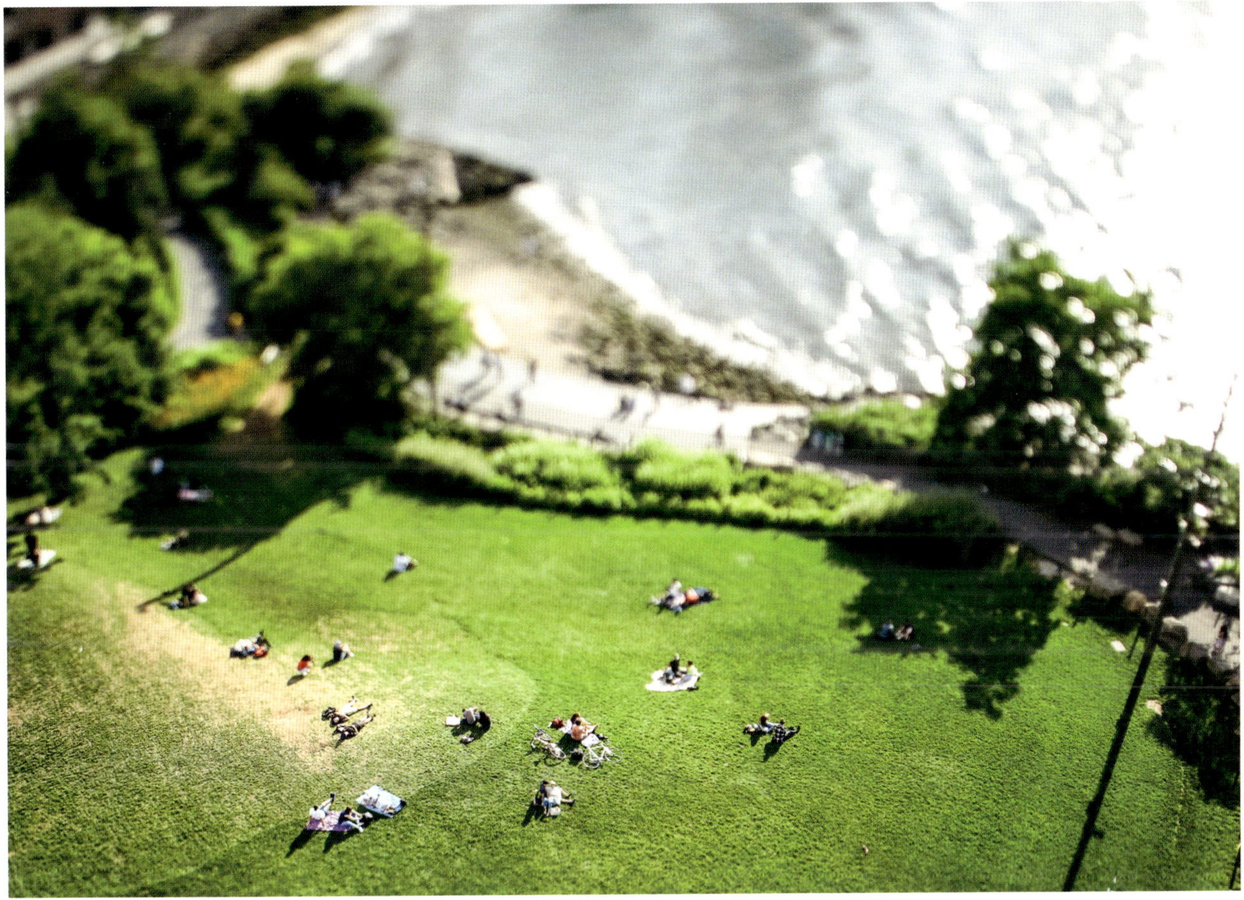

Brooklyn Bridge Park

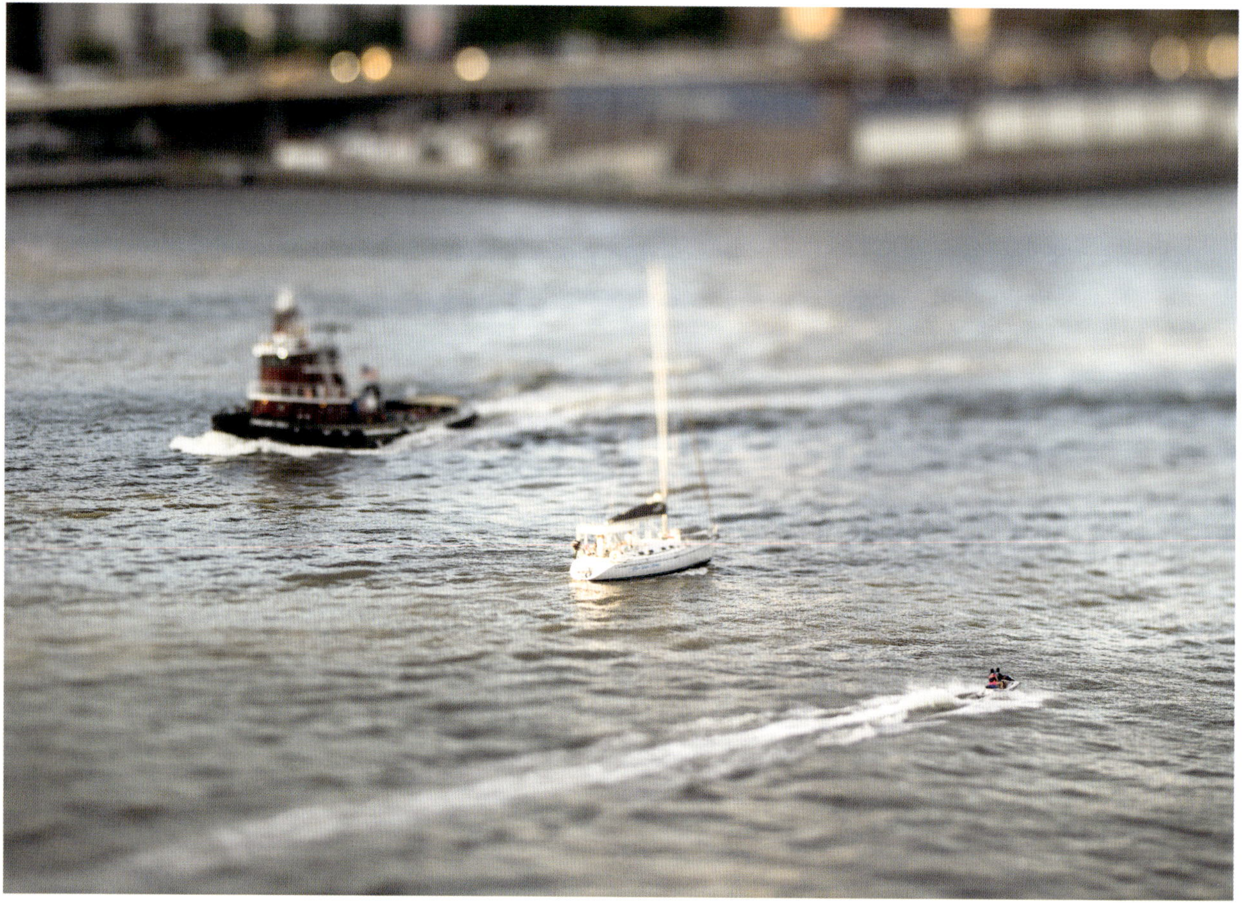

East River

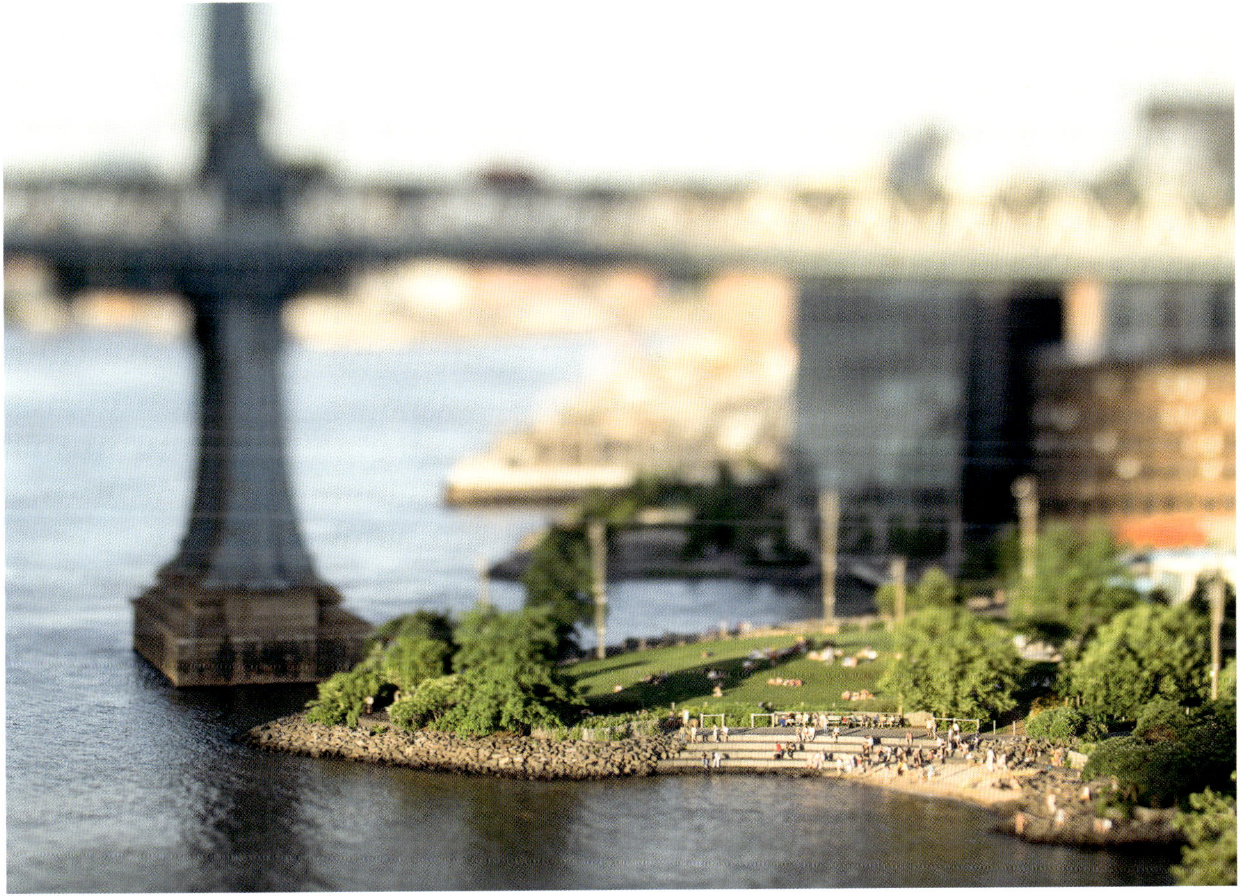

Brooklyn Bridge Park

Central Park is the grandiose symbol of the front yard each child in New York hasn't got.

Robert Benchley

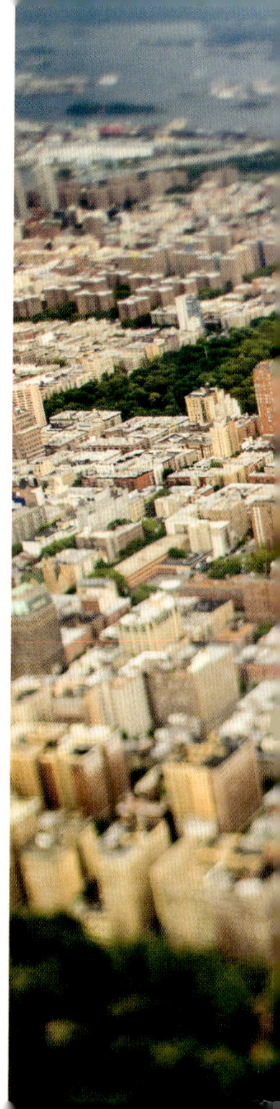

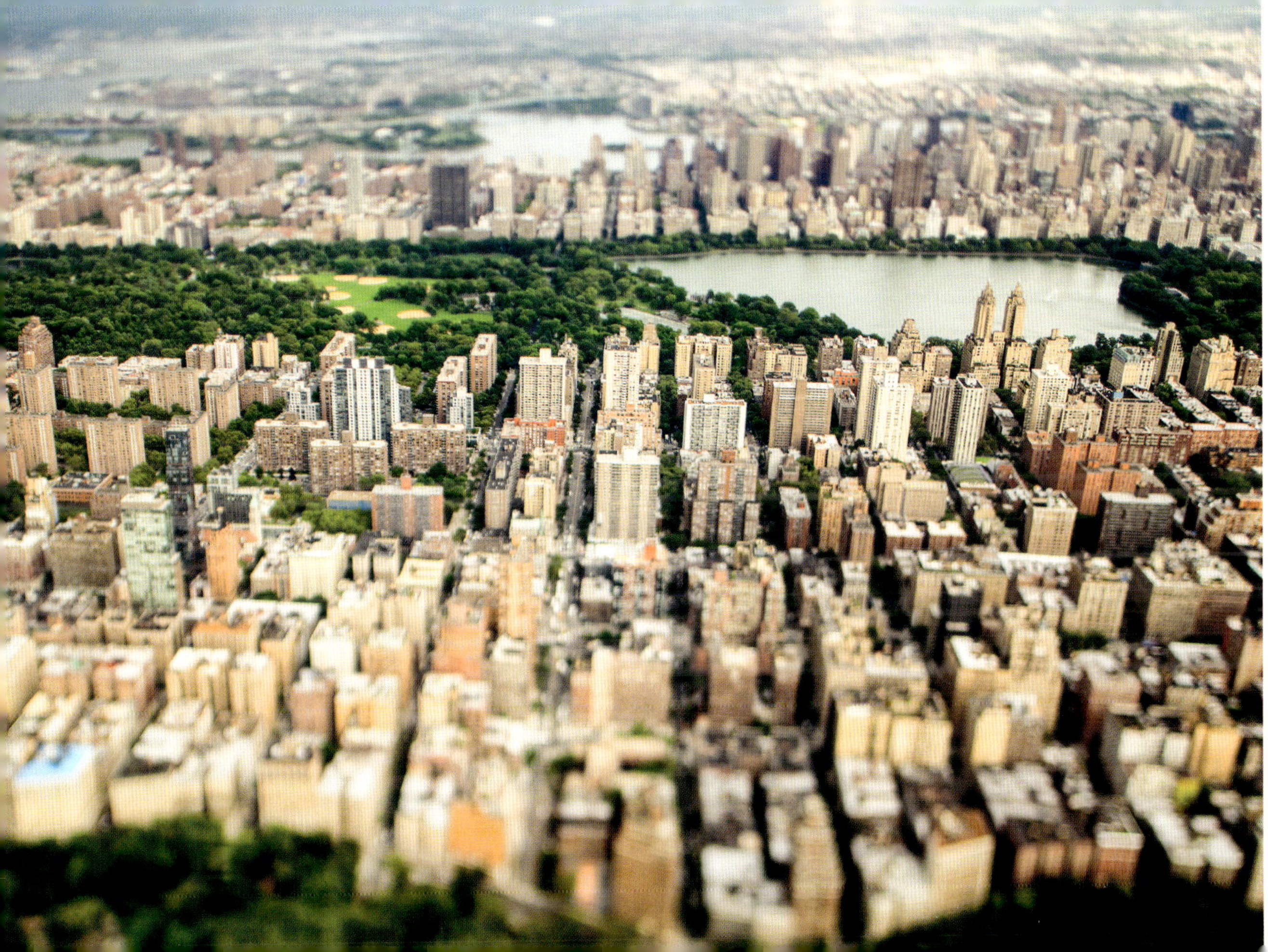

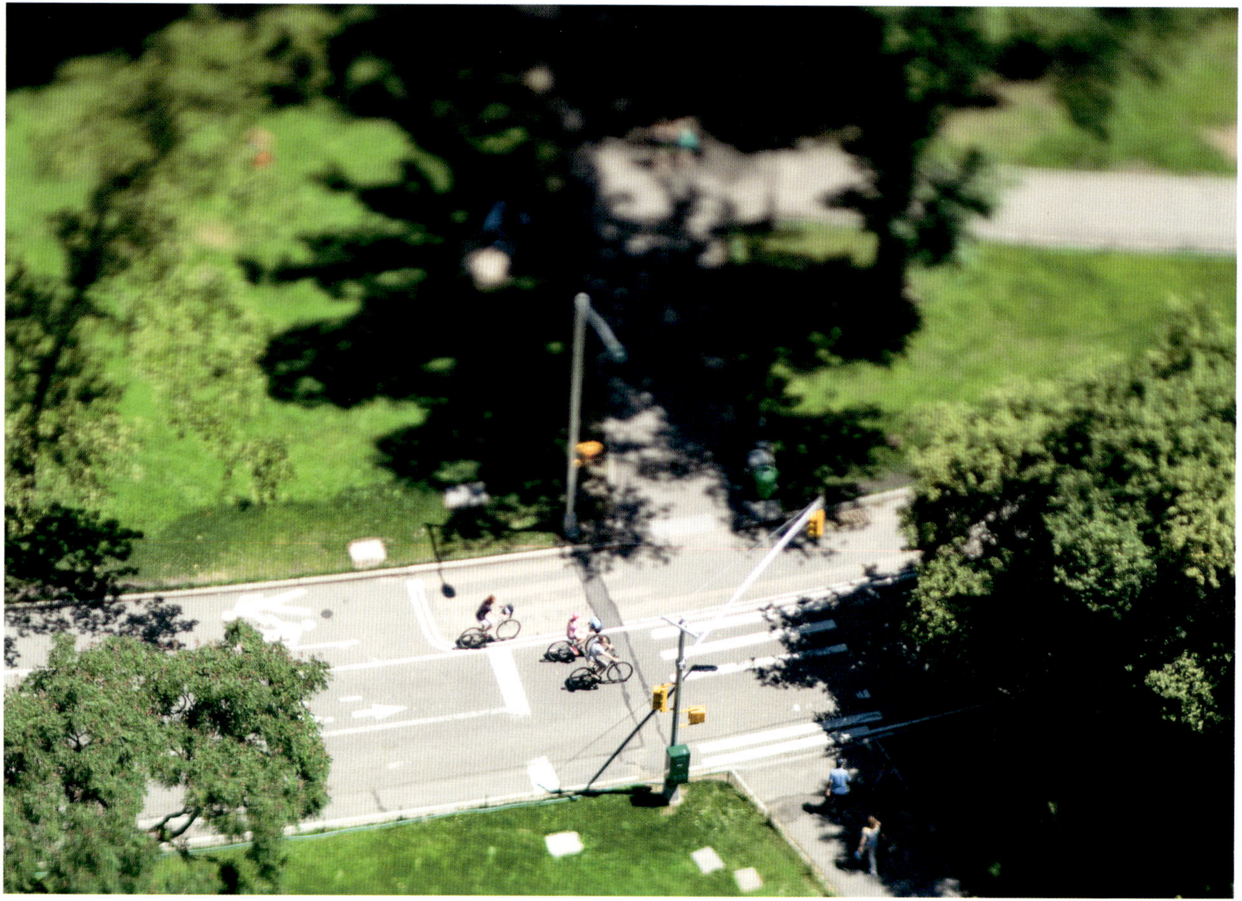

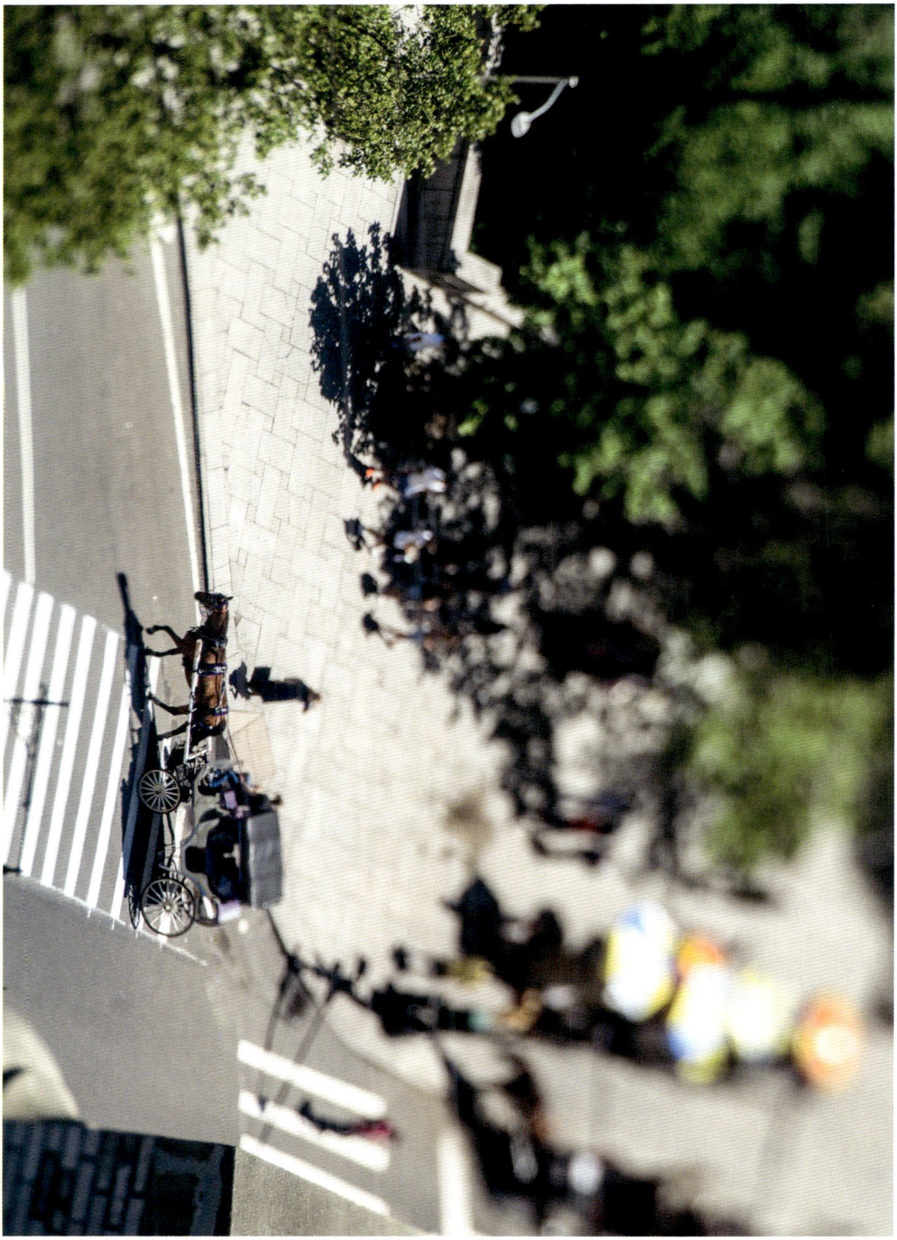

Central Park

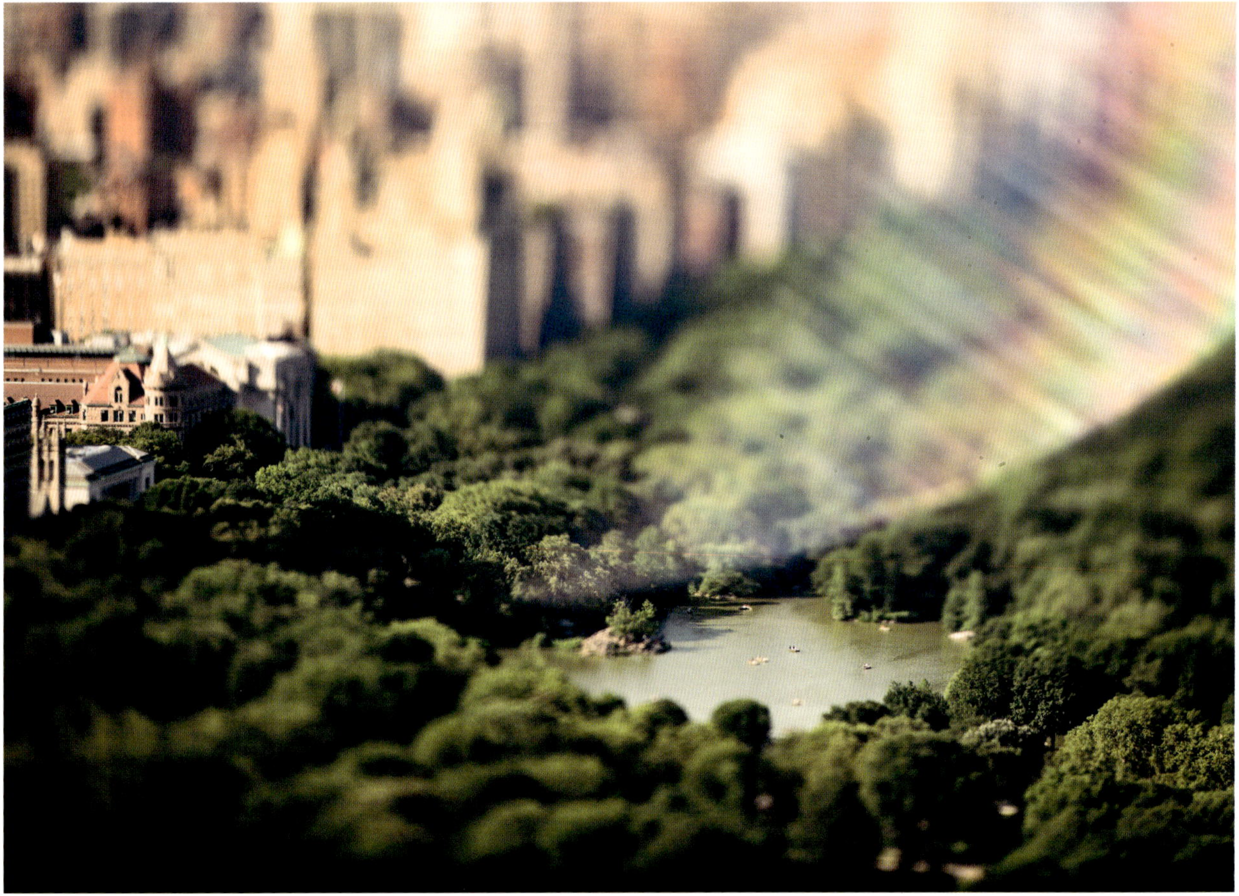

Central Park

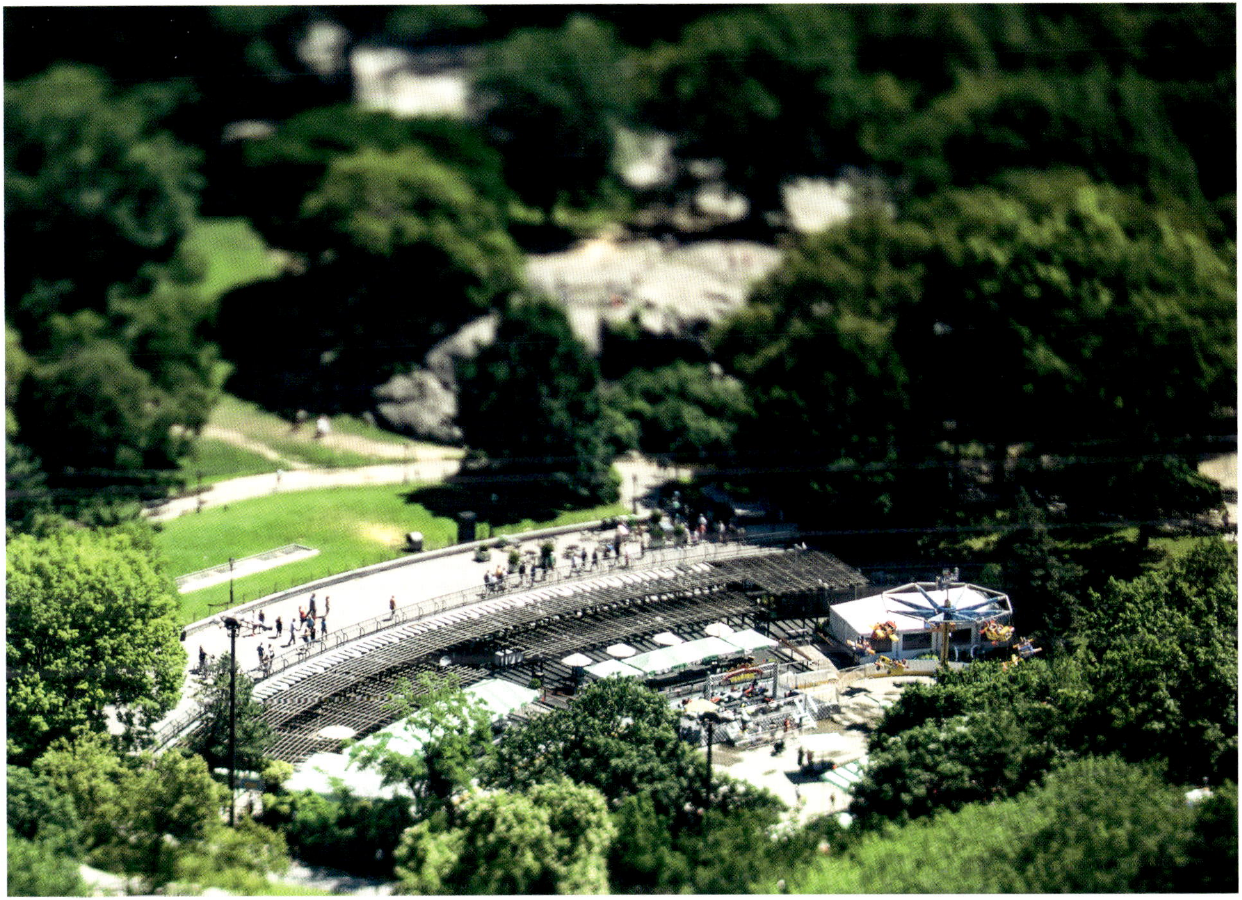

Central Park

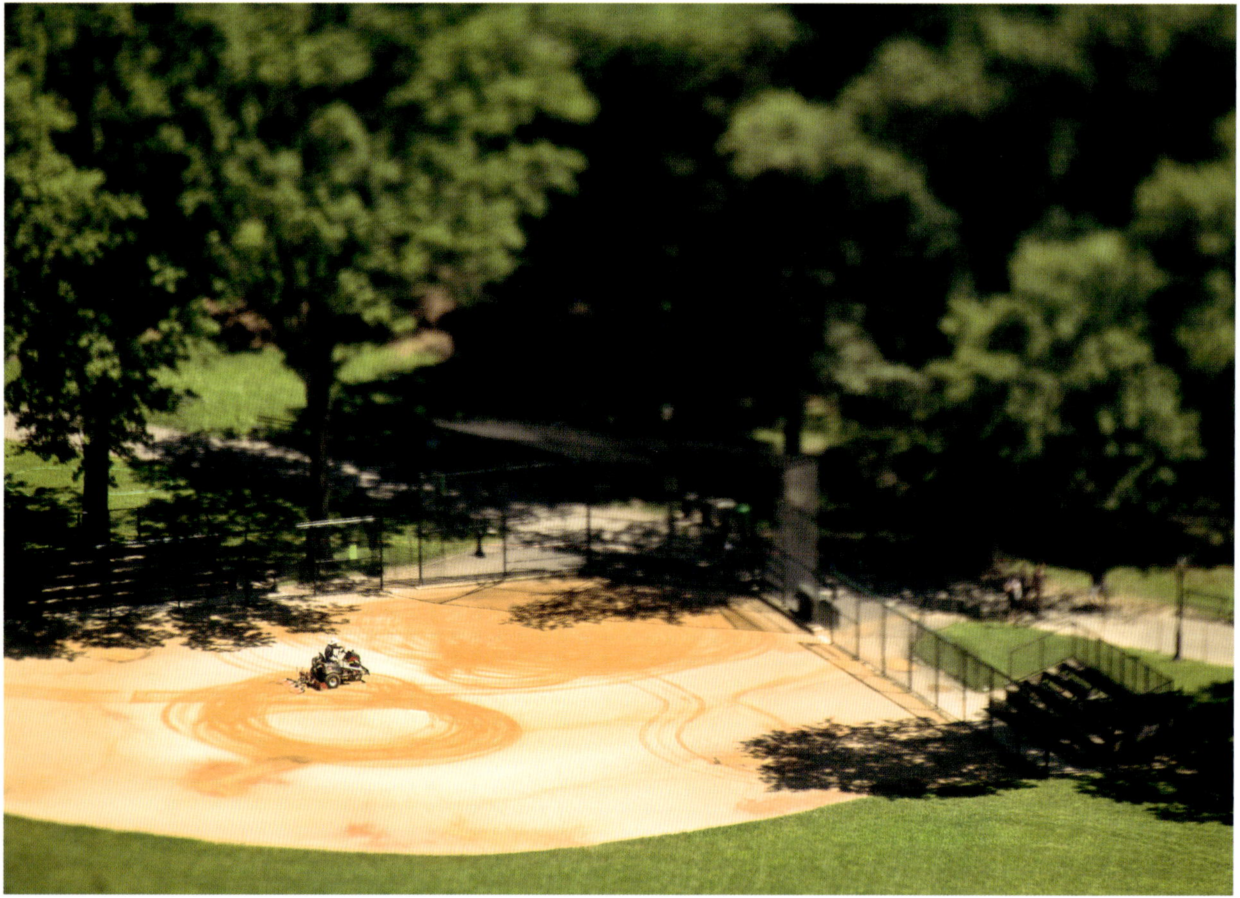

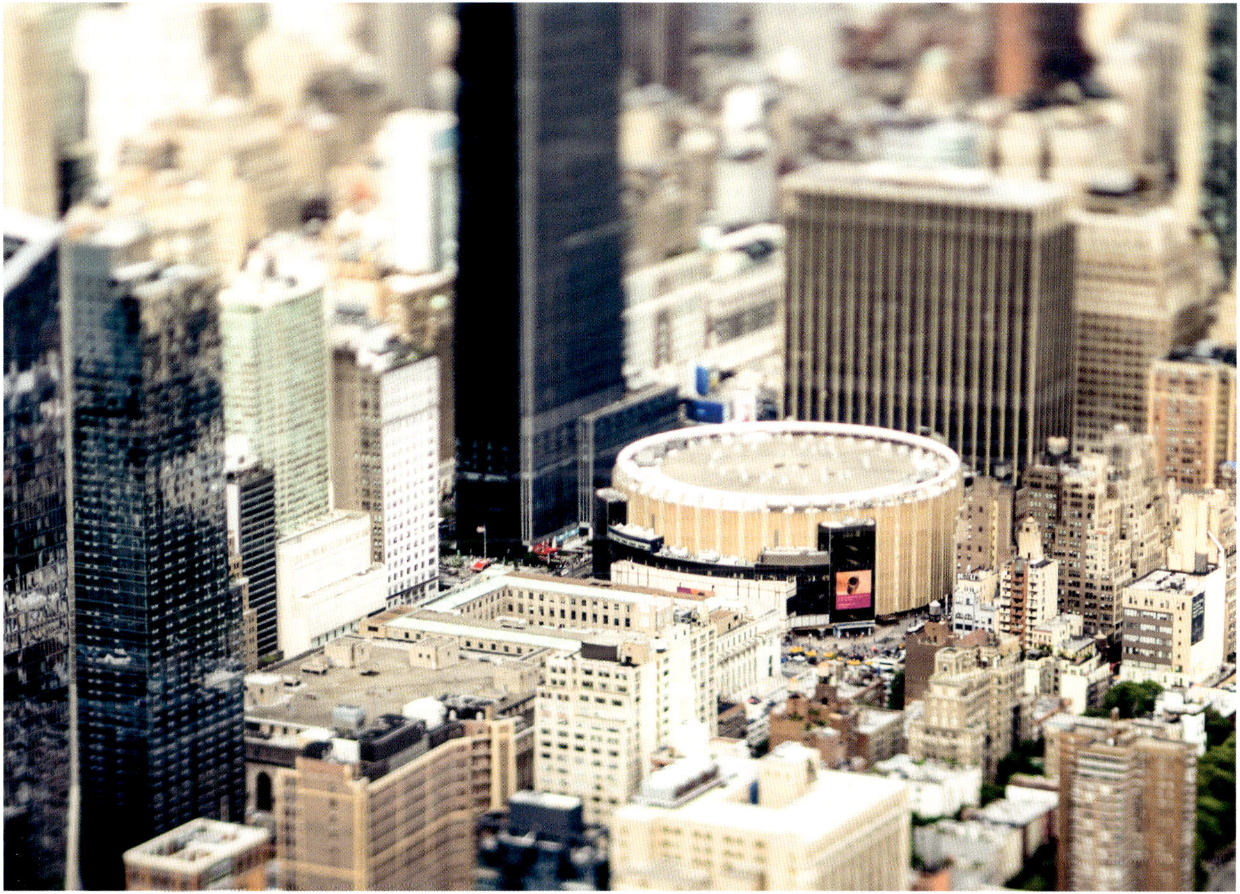

Madison Square Garden

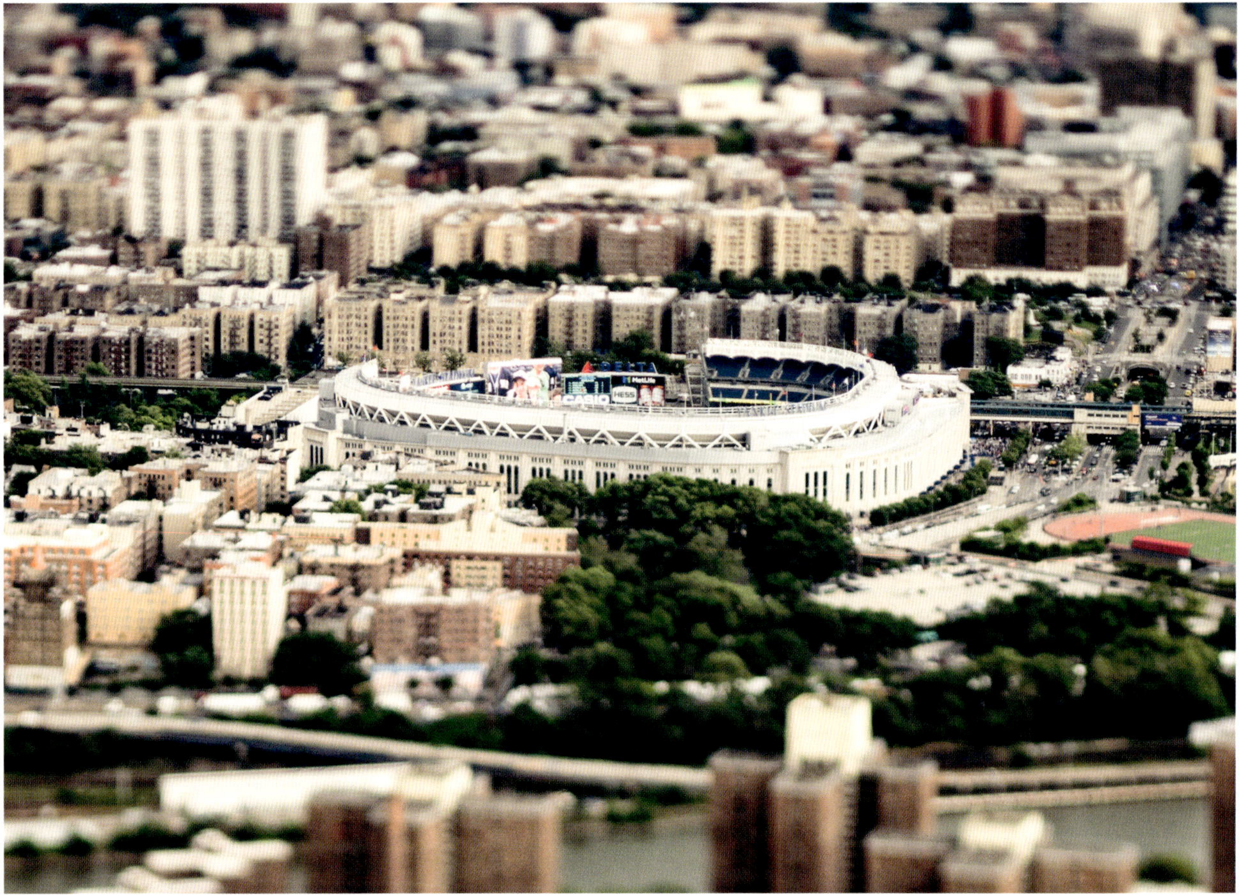

Yankee Stadium

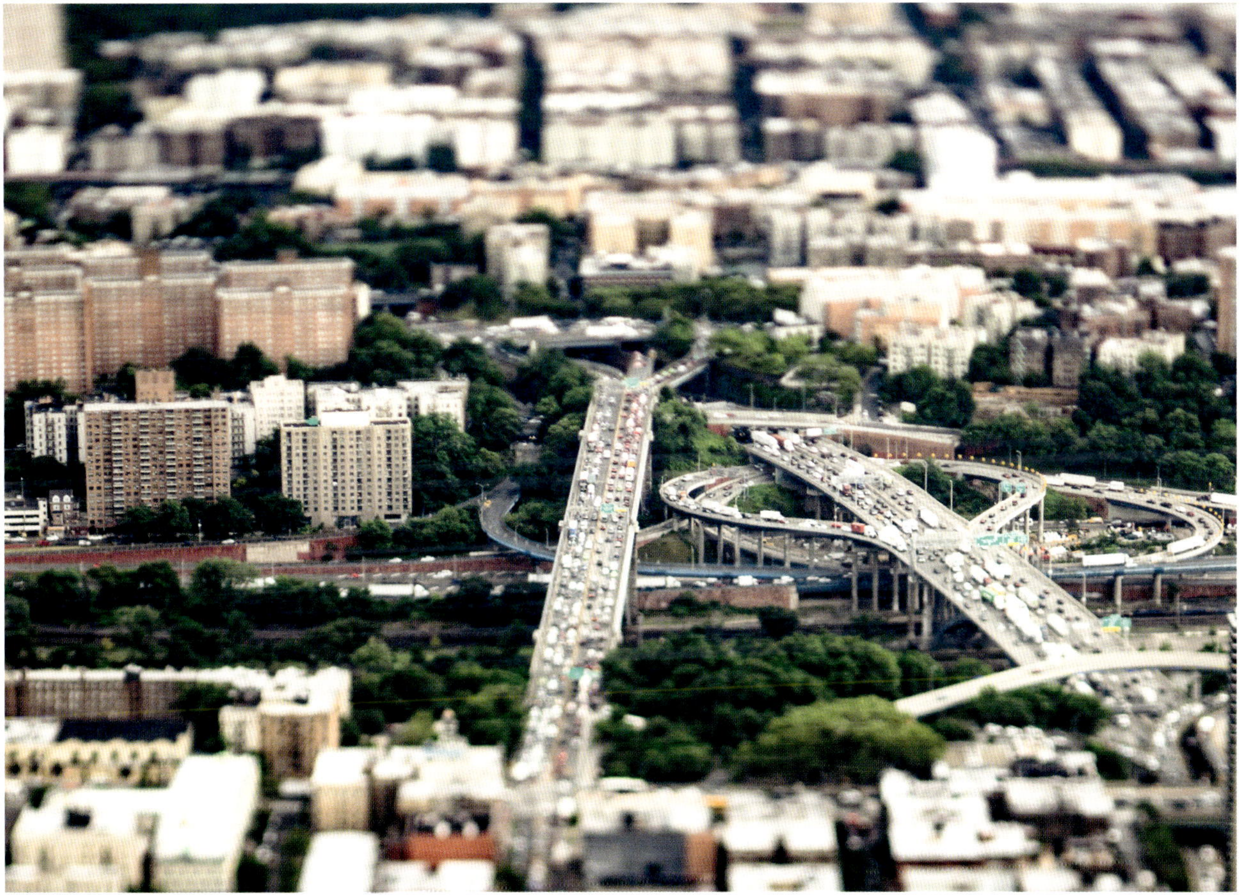

Alexander Hamilton Bridge

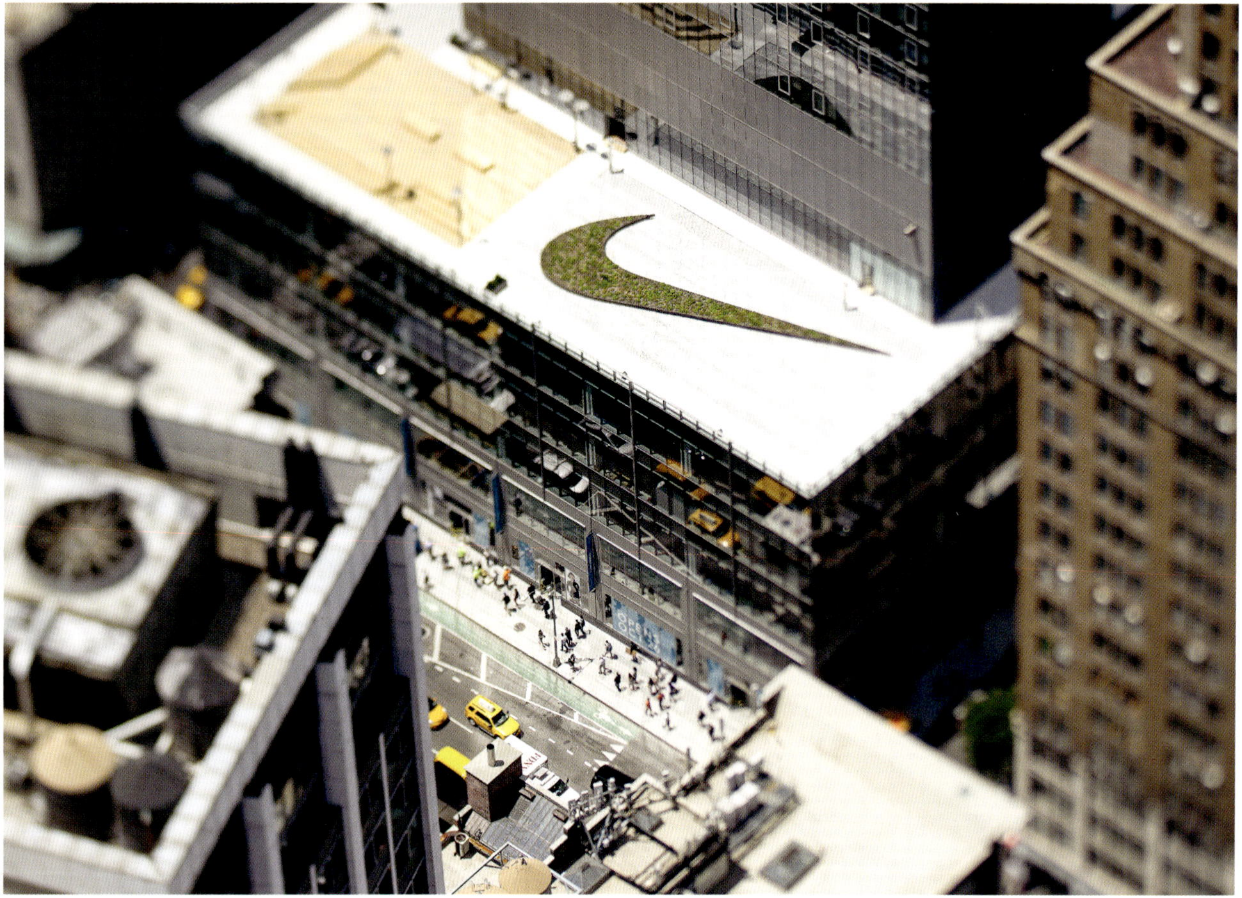

6th Ave

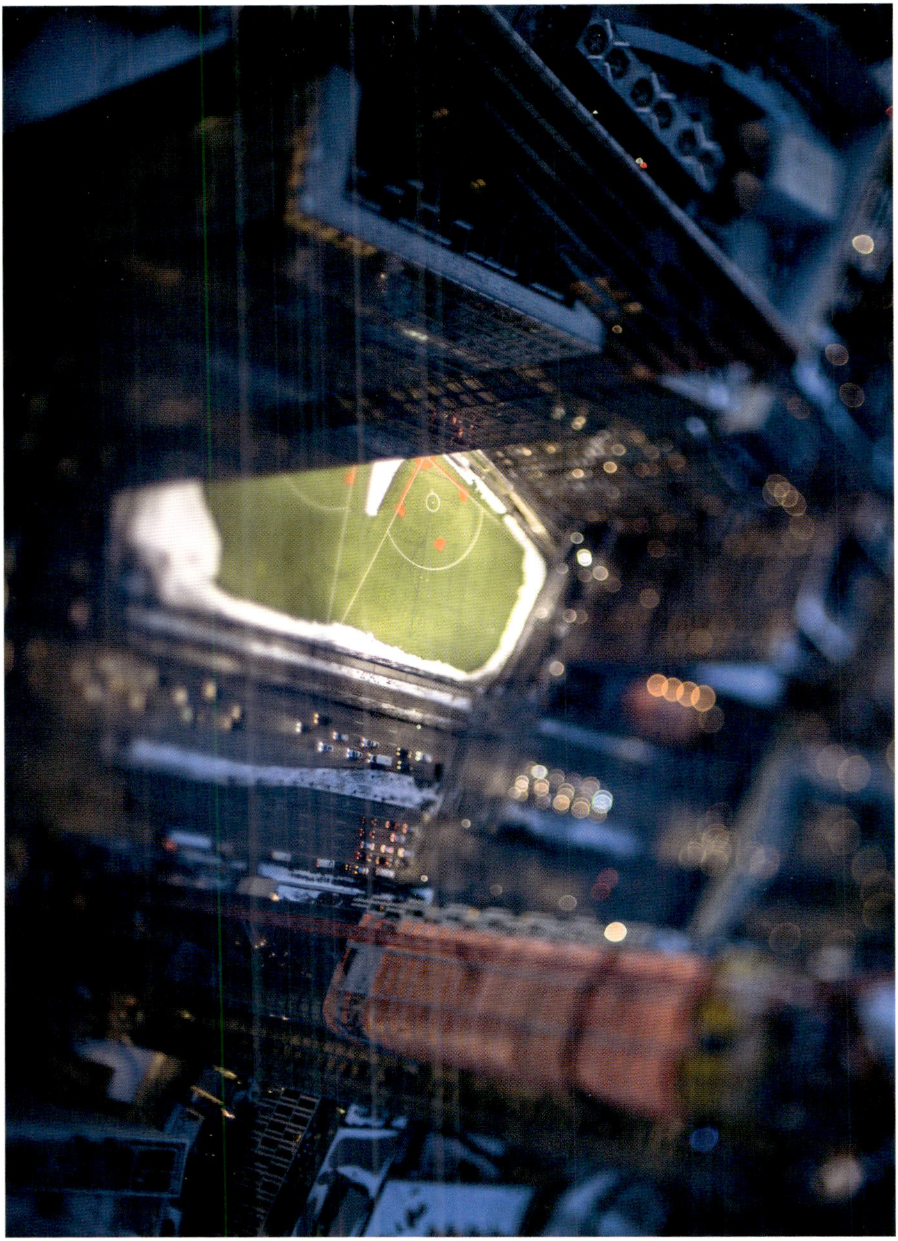

Battery Park City Ball Fields

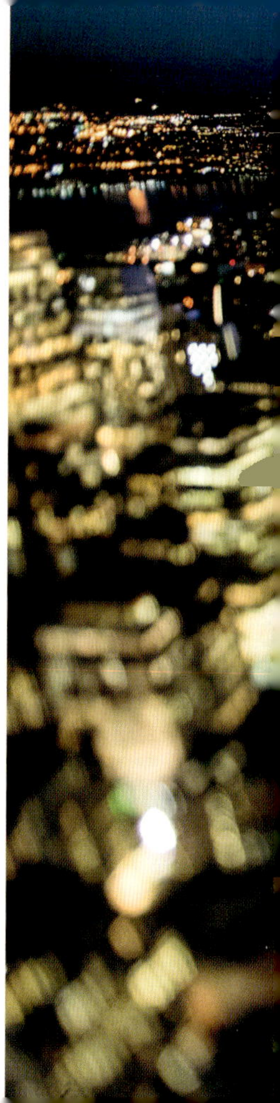

And New York is the most beautiful city in the world? It is not far from it. No urban night is like the night there... Squares after squares of flame, set up and cut into the aether. Here is our poetry, for we have pulled down the stars to our will.

Ezra Pound

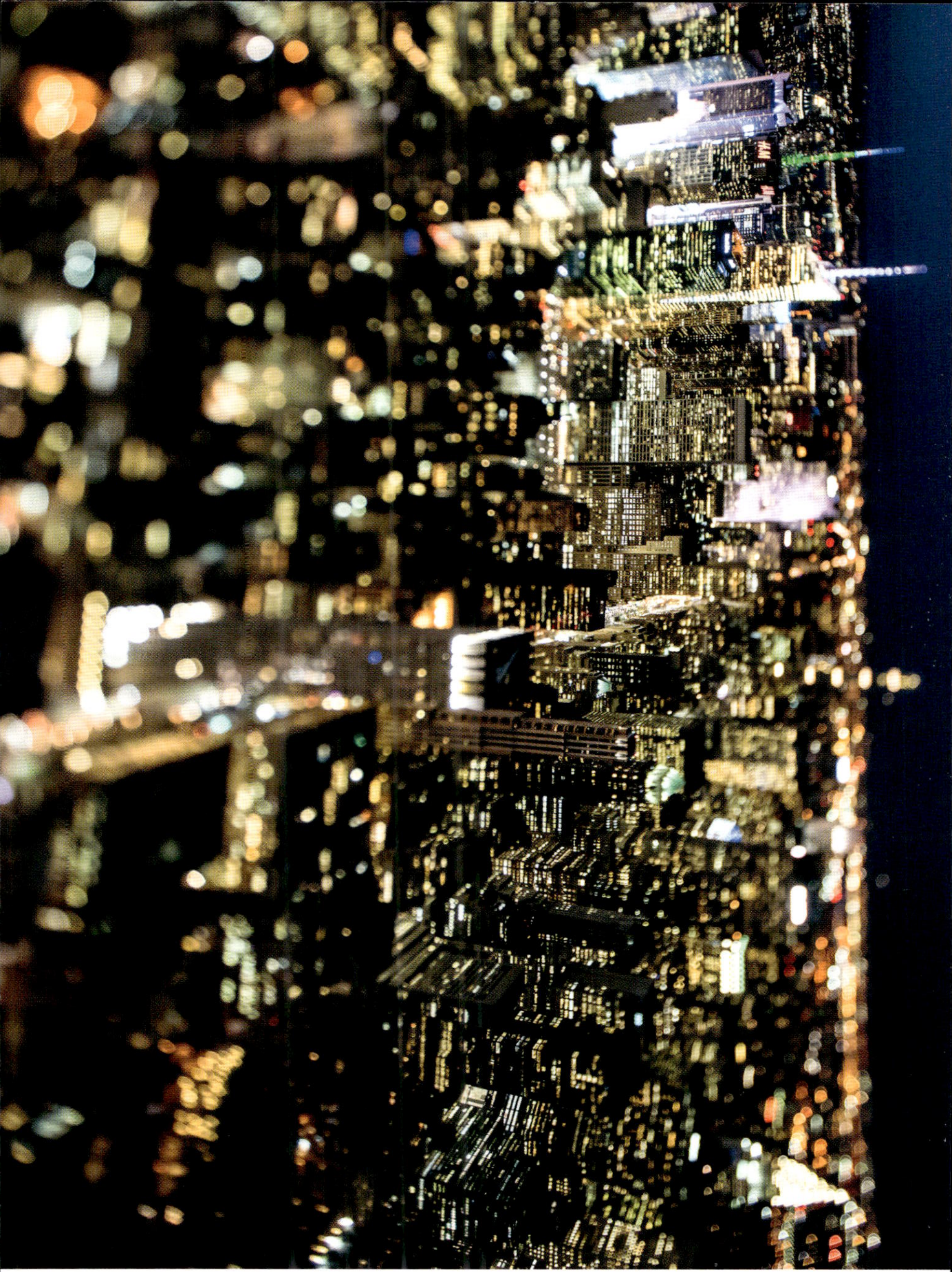

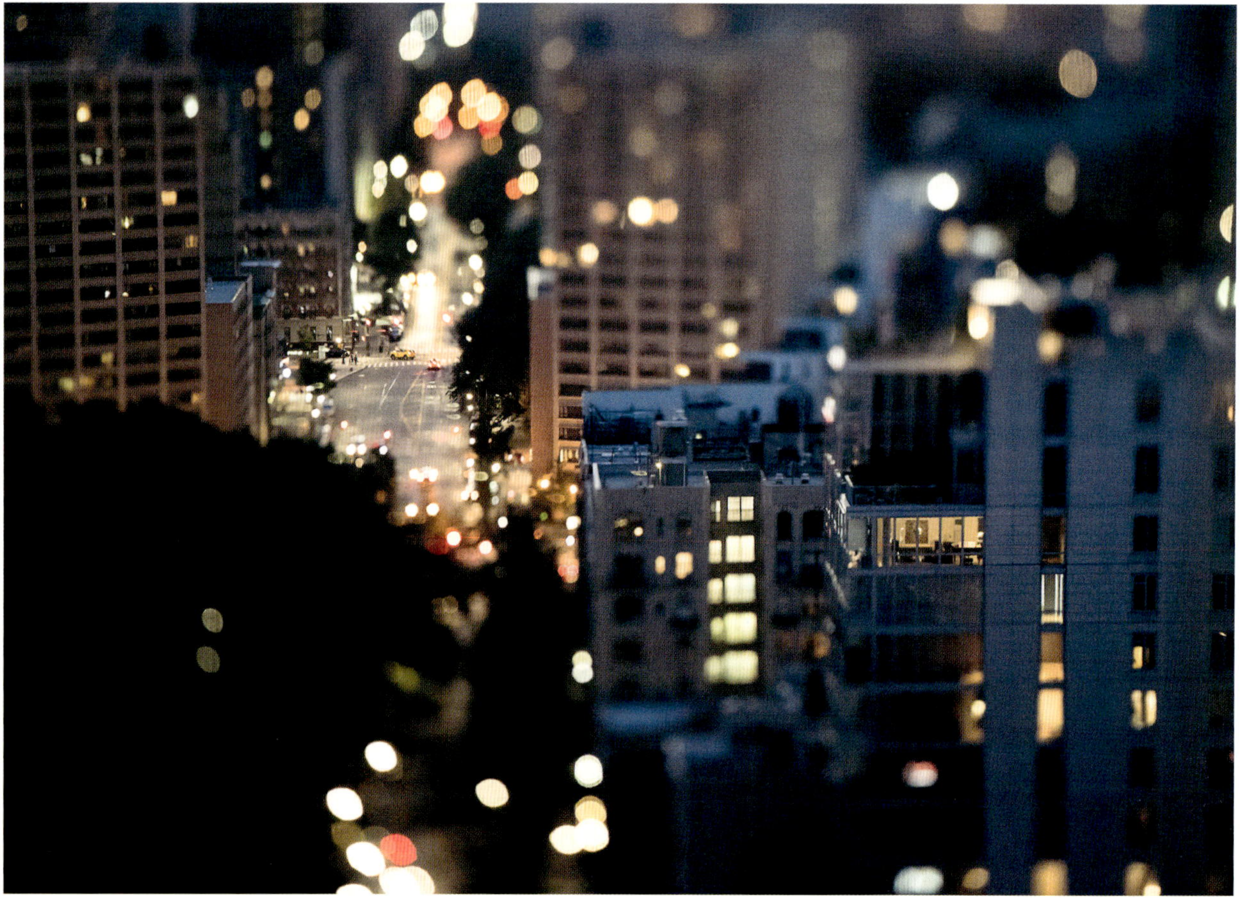

110th Street

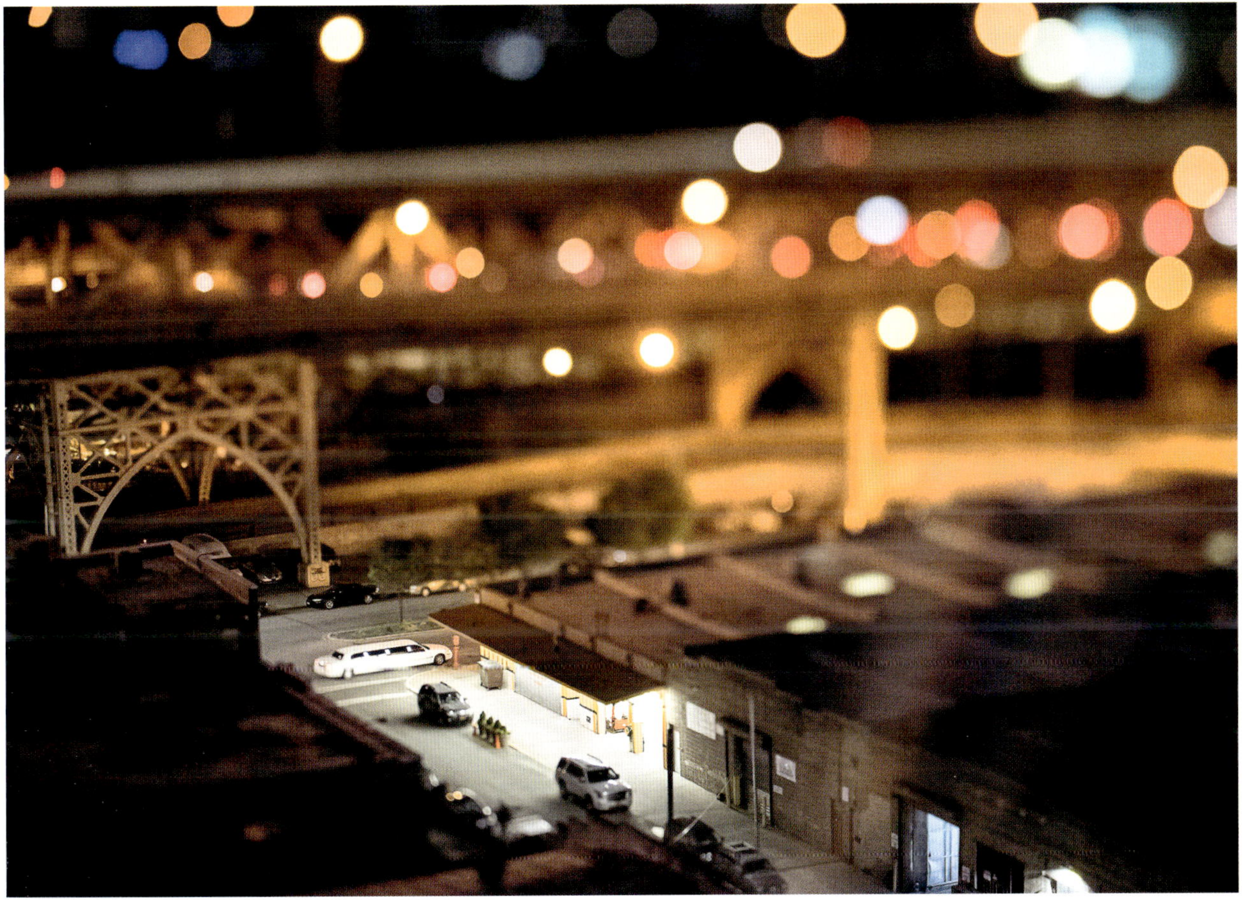

Queens Plaza, Long Island City

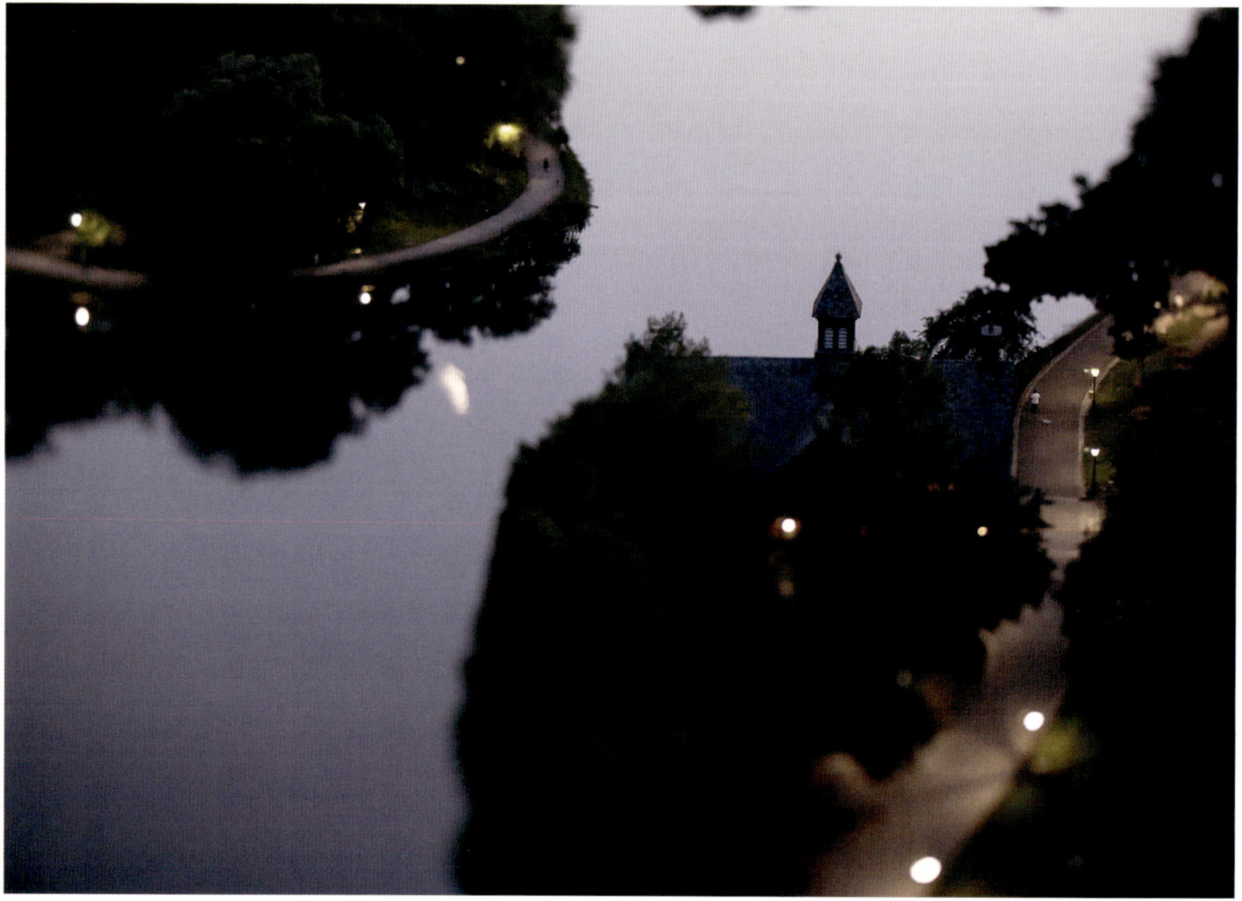

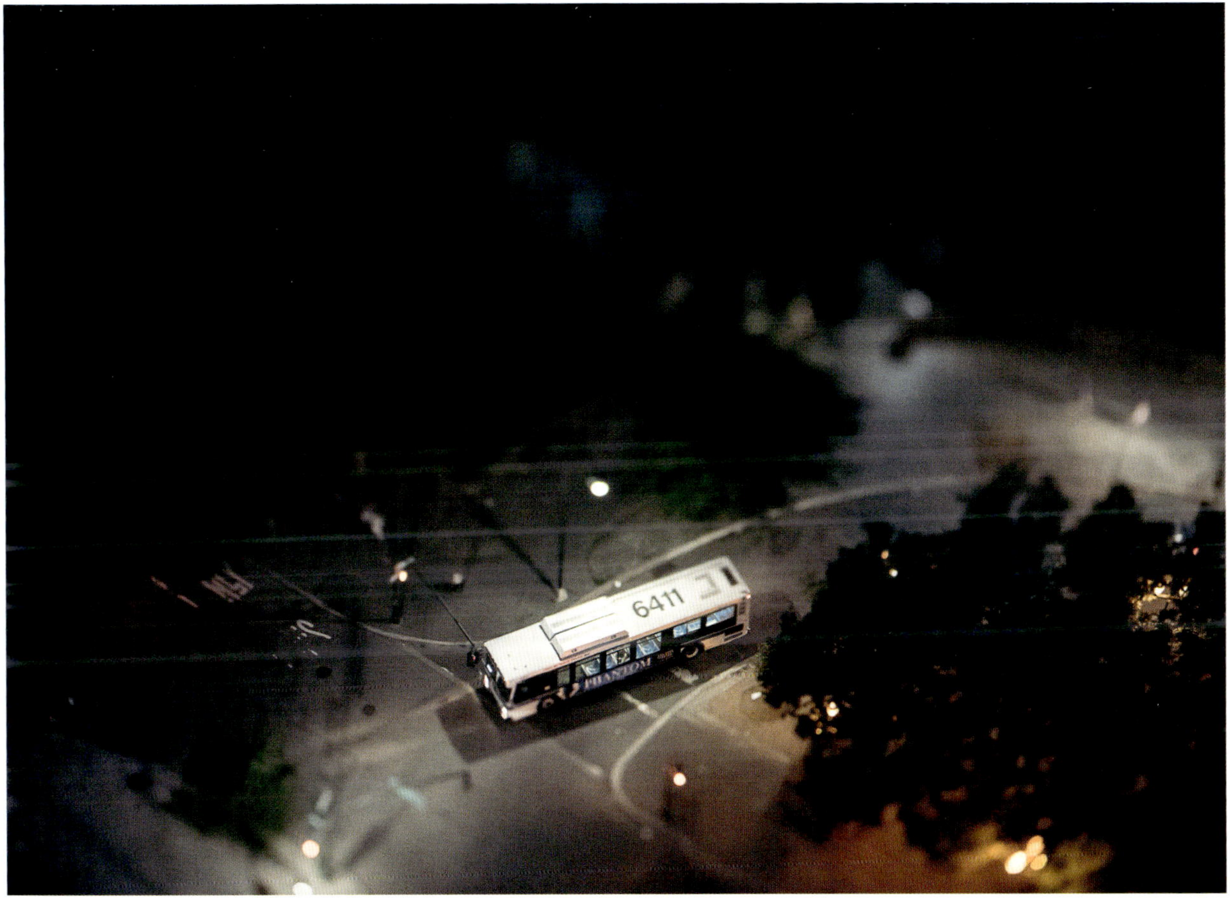

Duke Ellington Circle

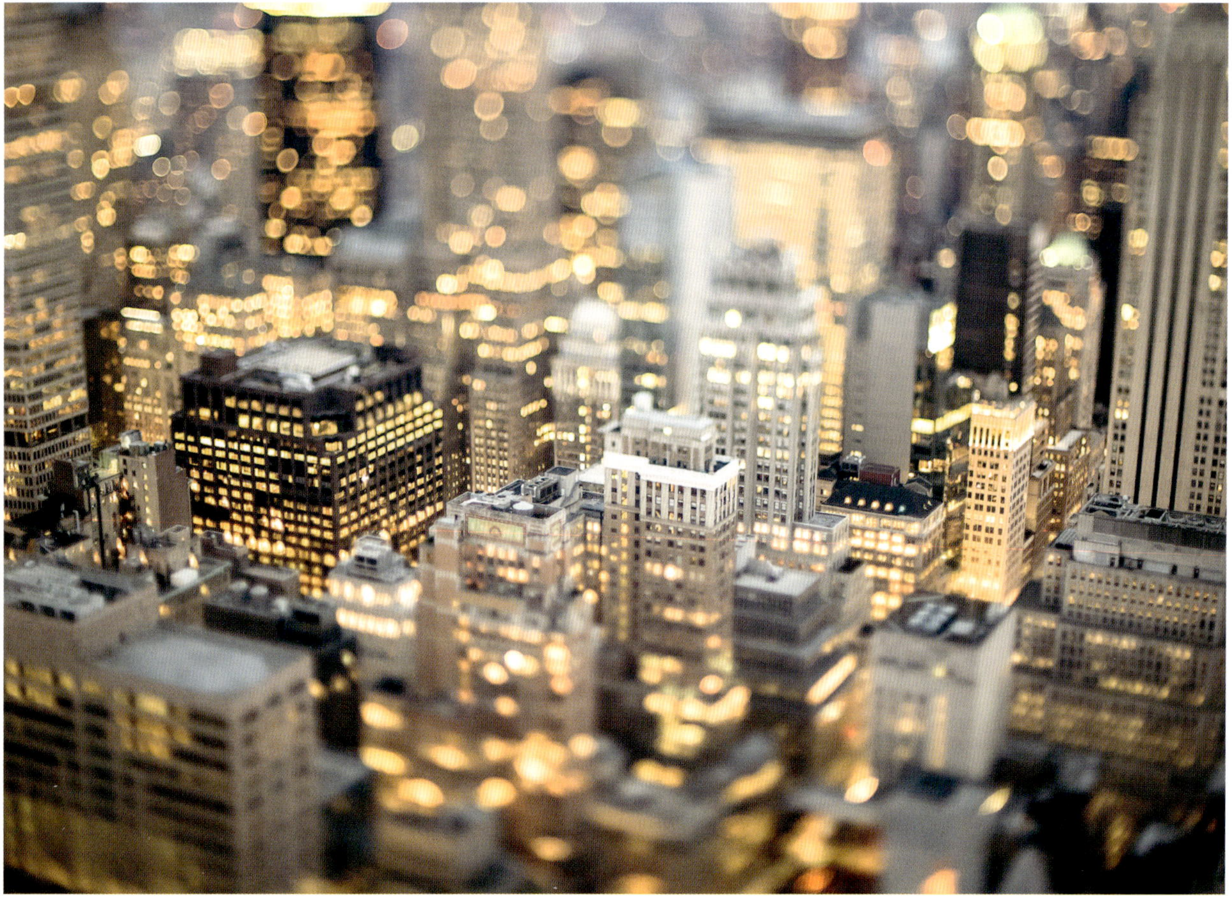

Midtown Manhattan

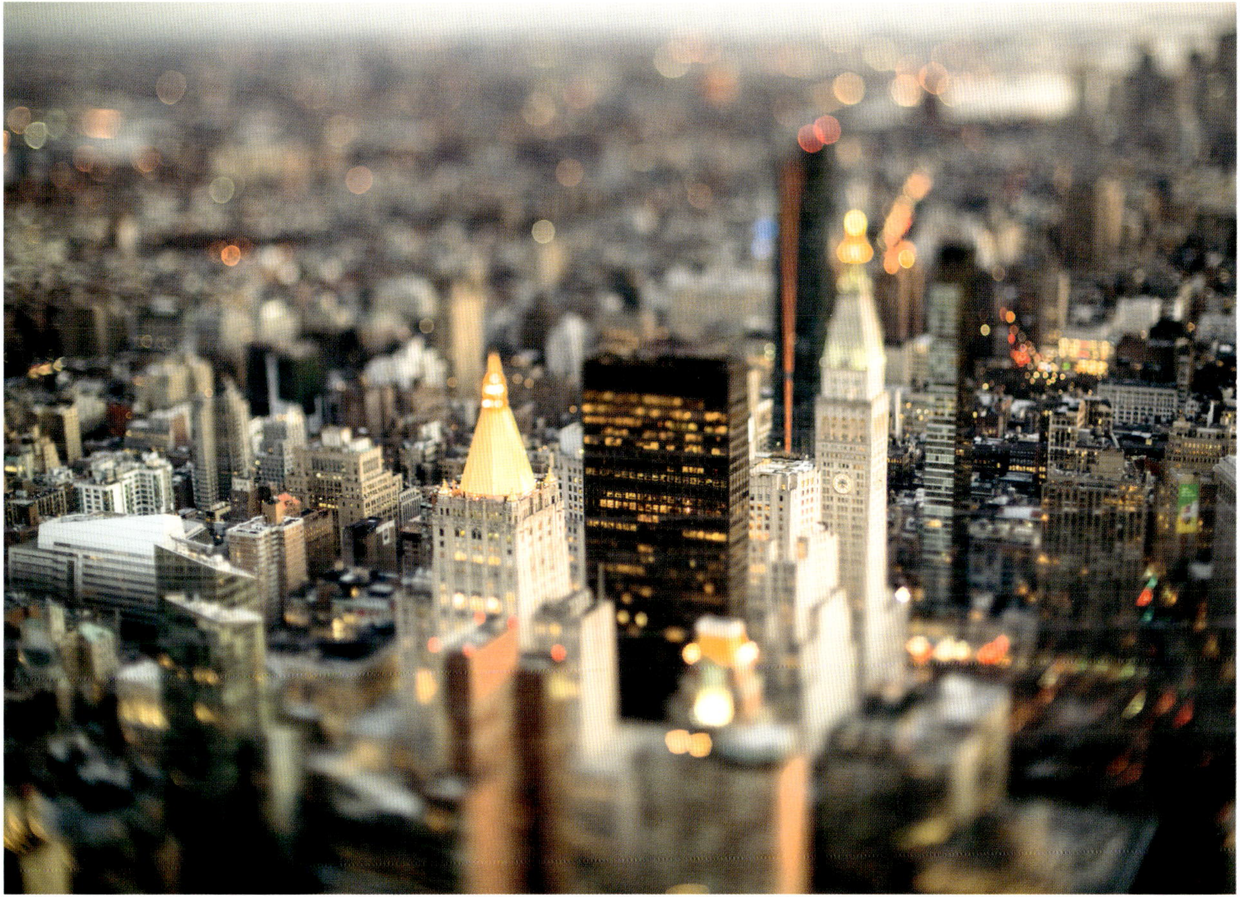

Midtown Manhattan

Everybody ought to have a Lower East Side in their life.

Irving Berlin

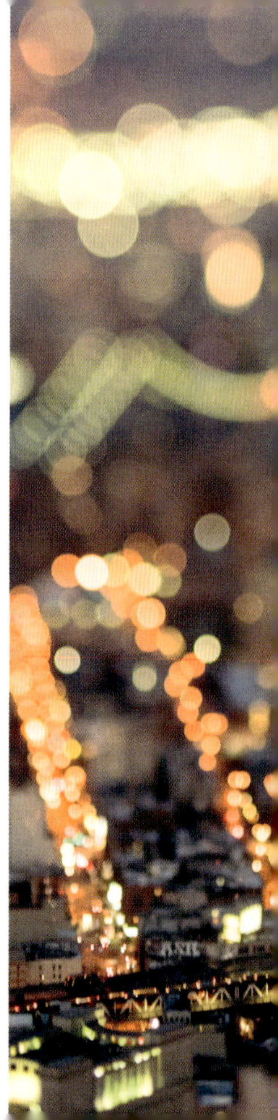

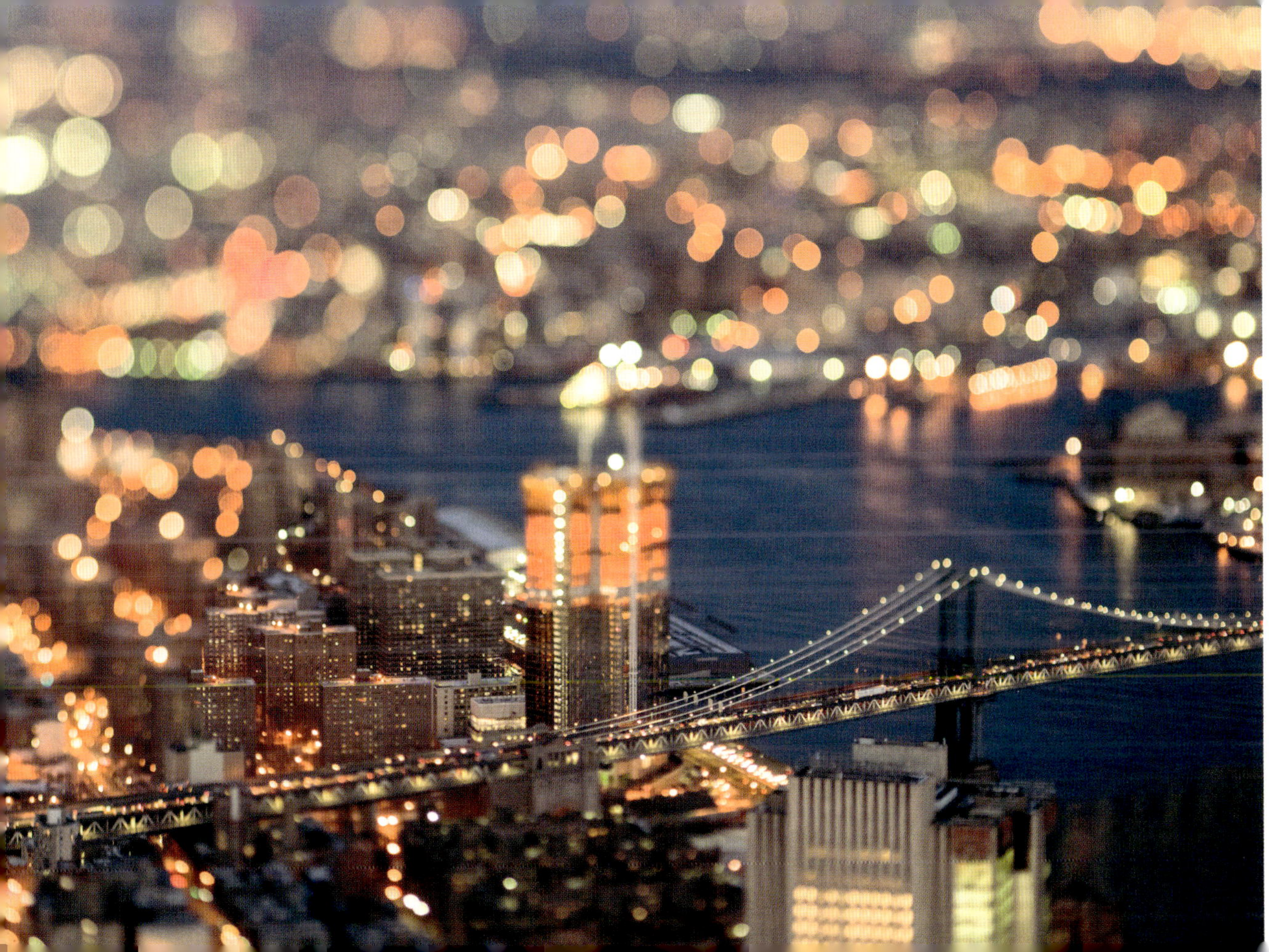

Manhattan Bridge, Lower East Side

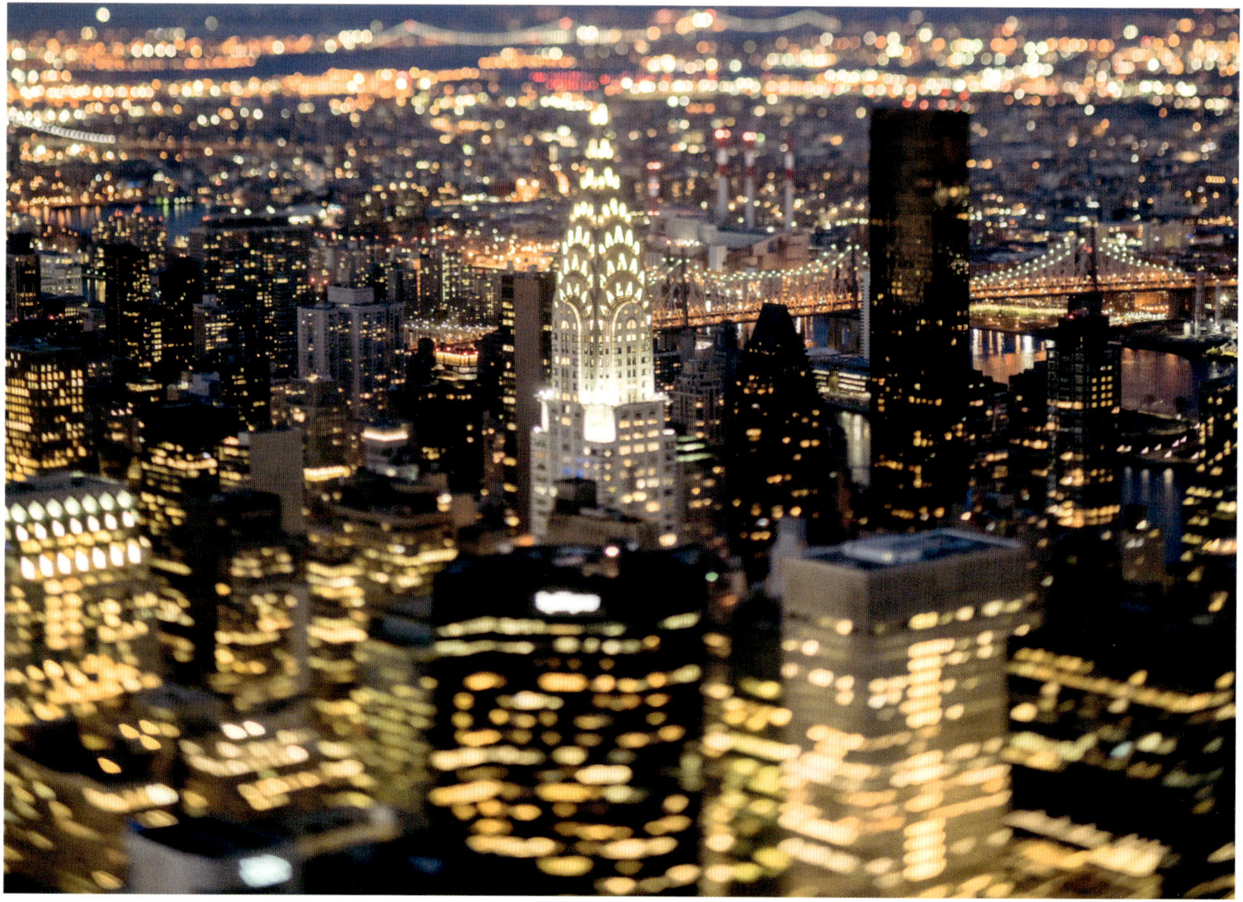

Chrysler Building

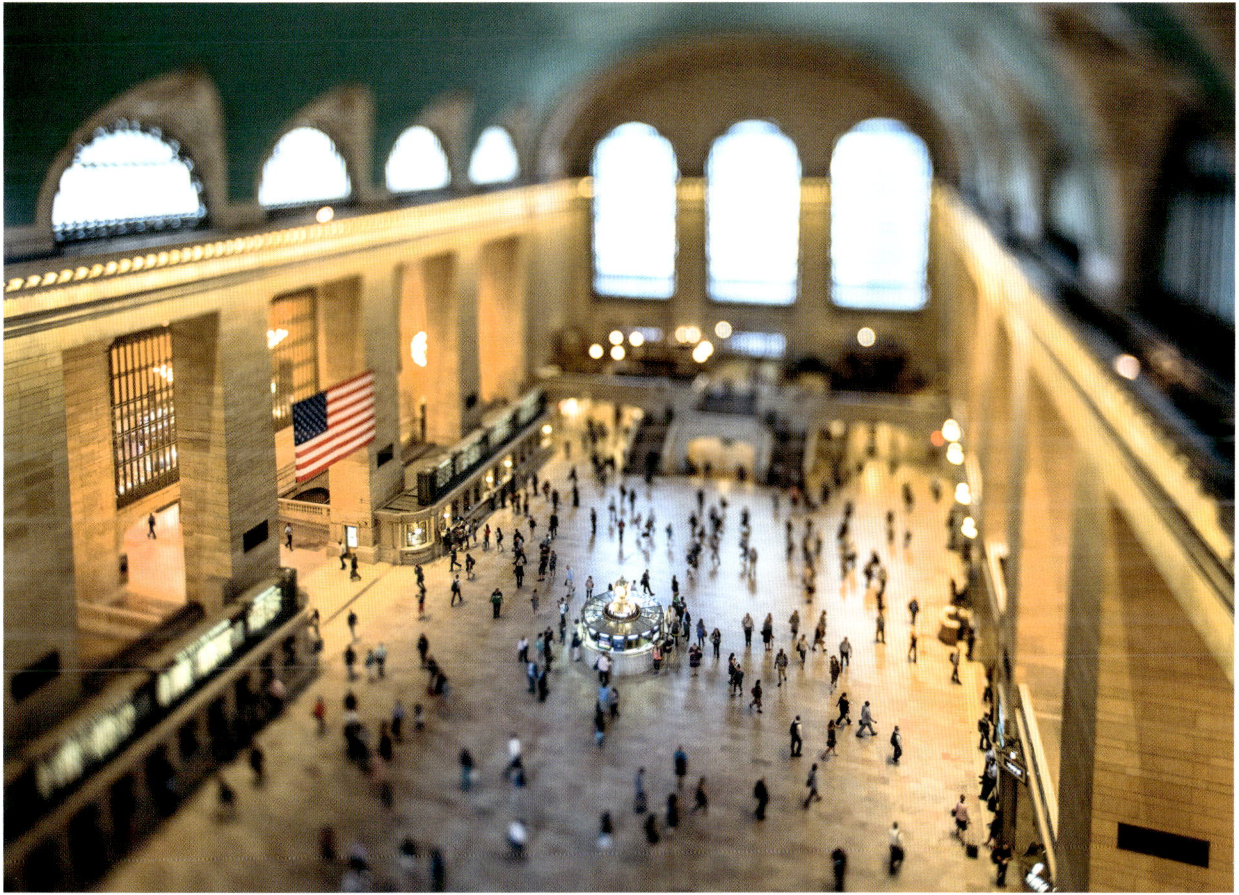

Grand Central Terminal

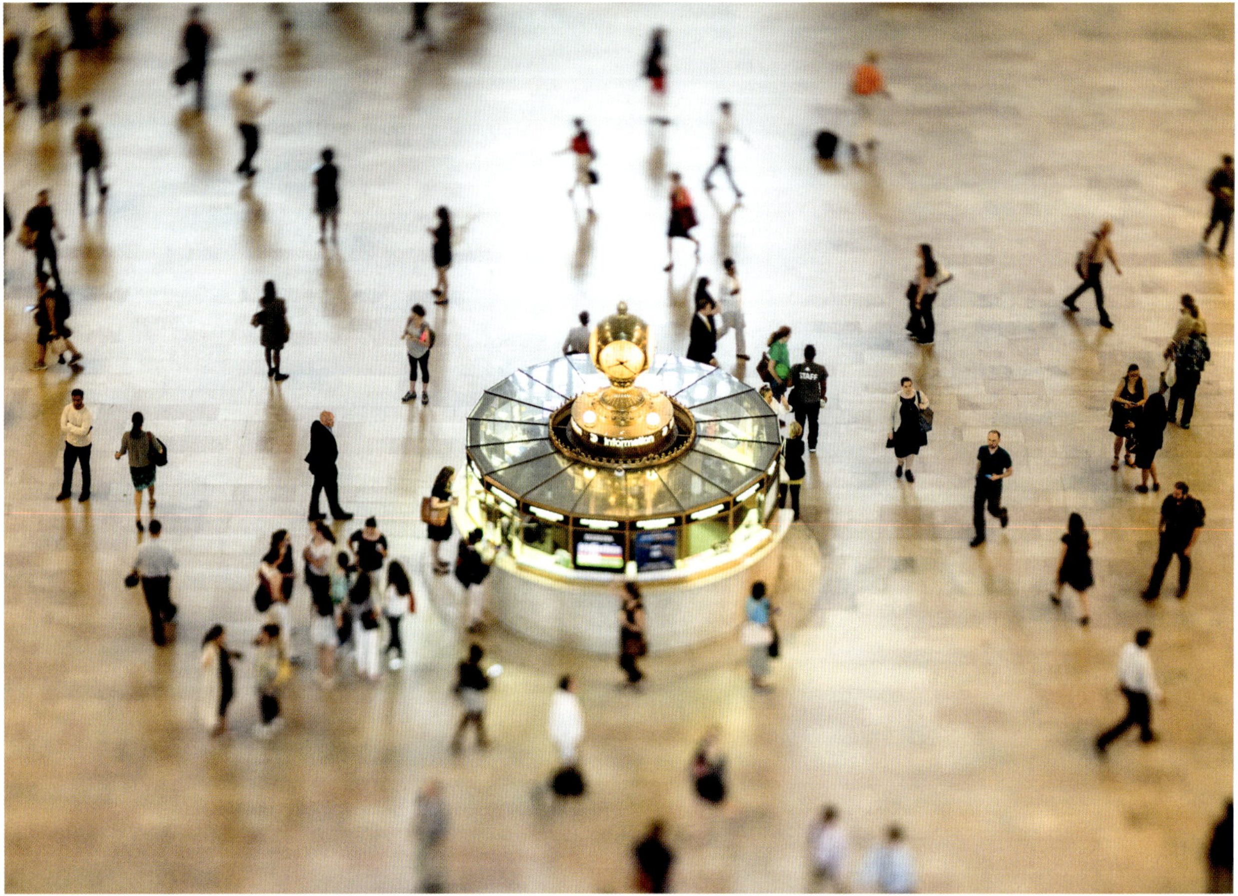
Information

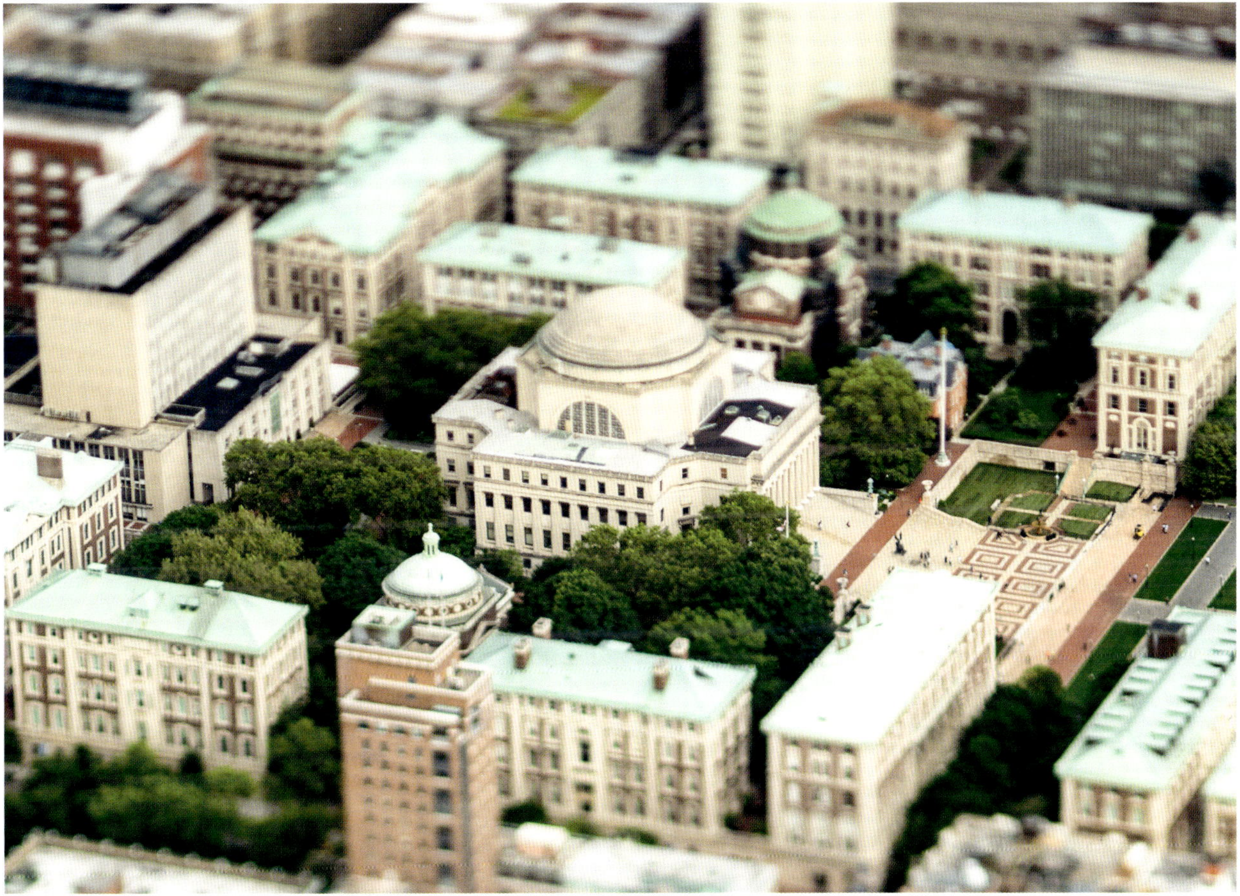

Columbia University

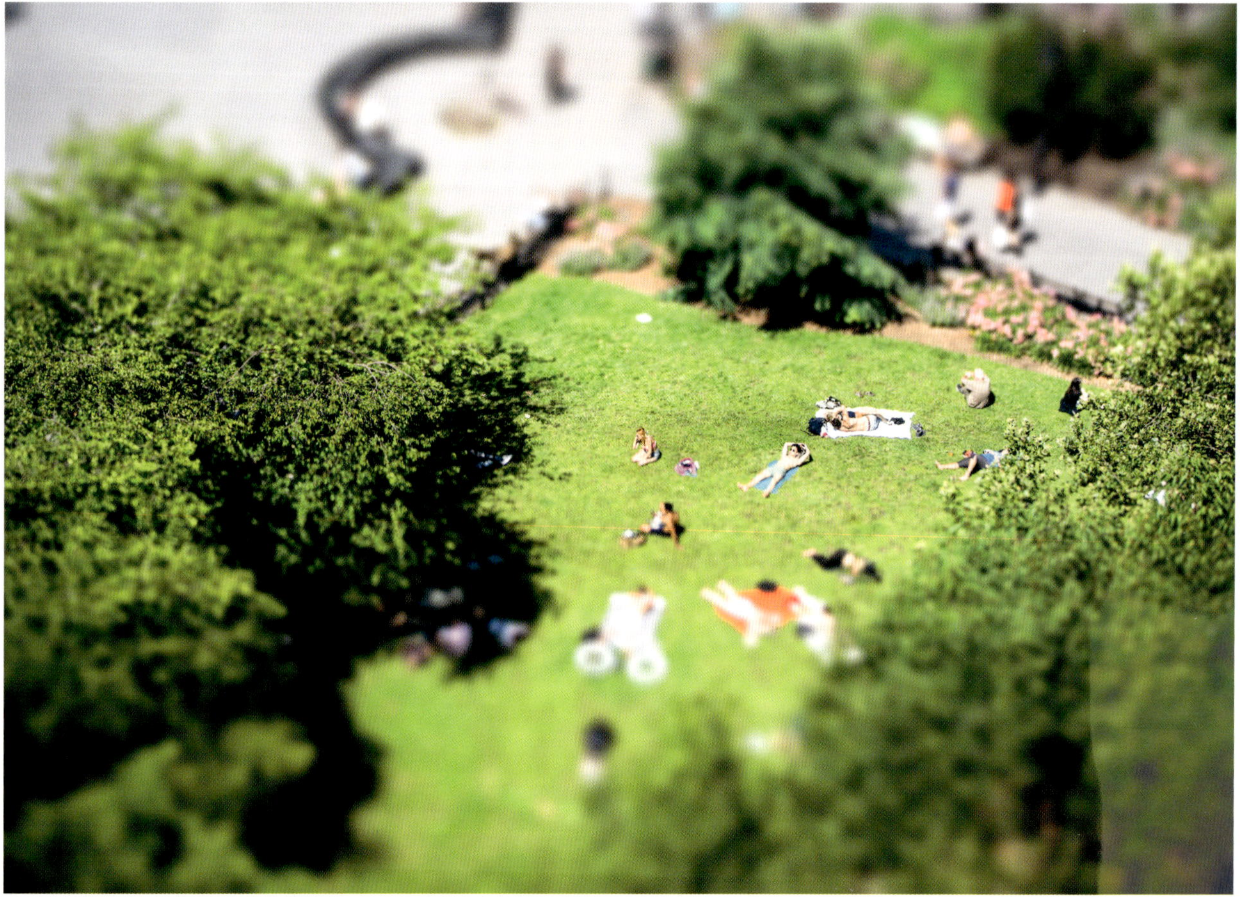

Washington Square Park

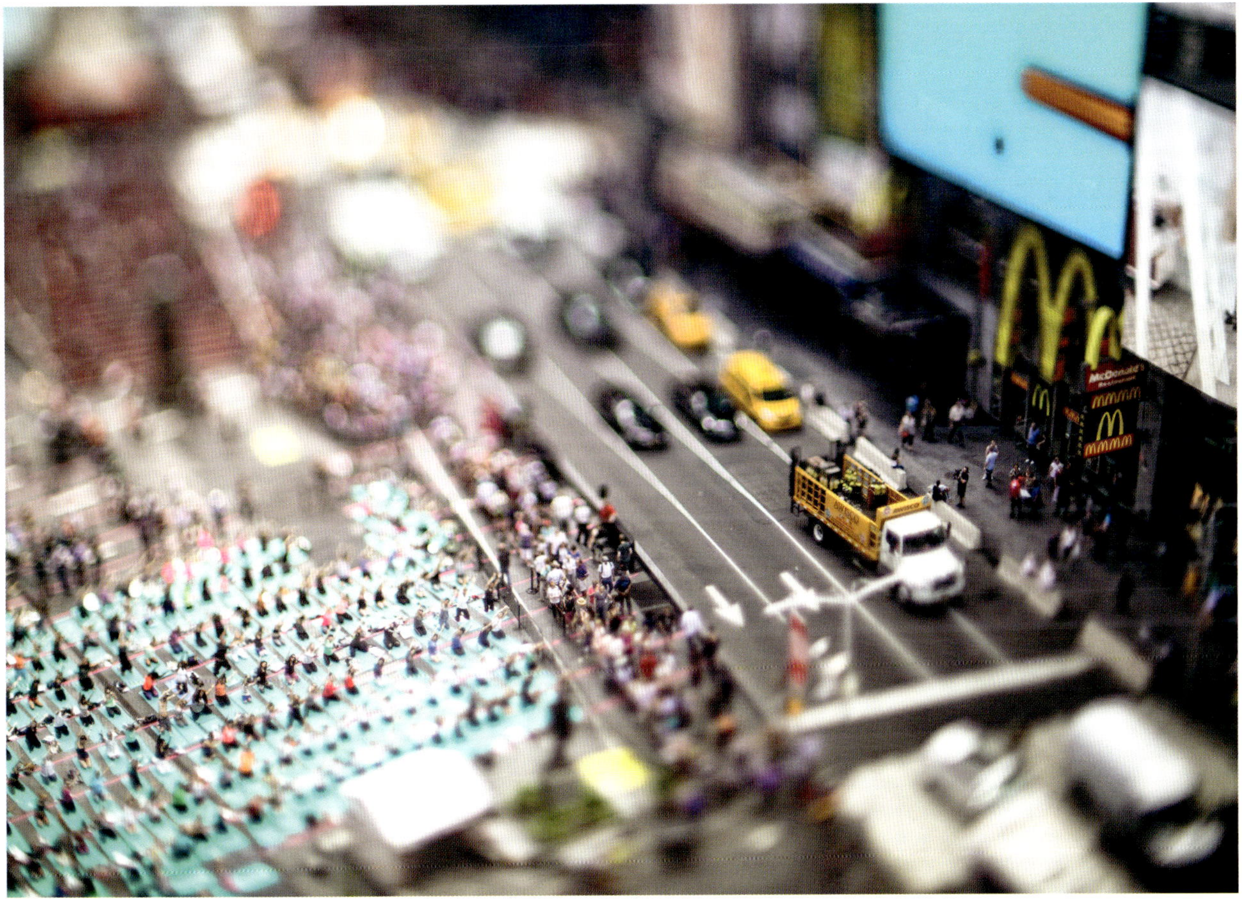

Times Square

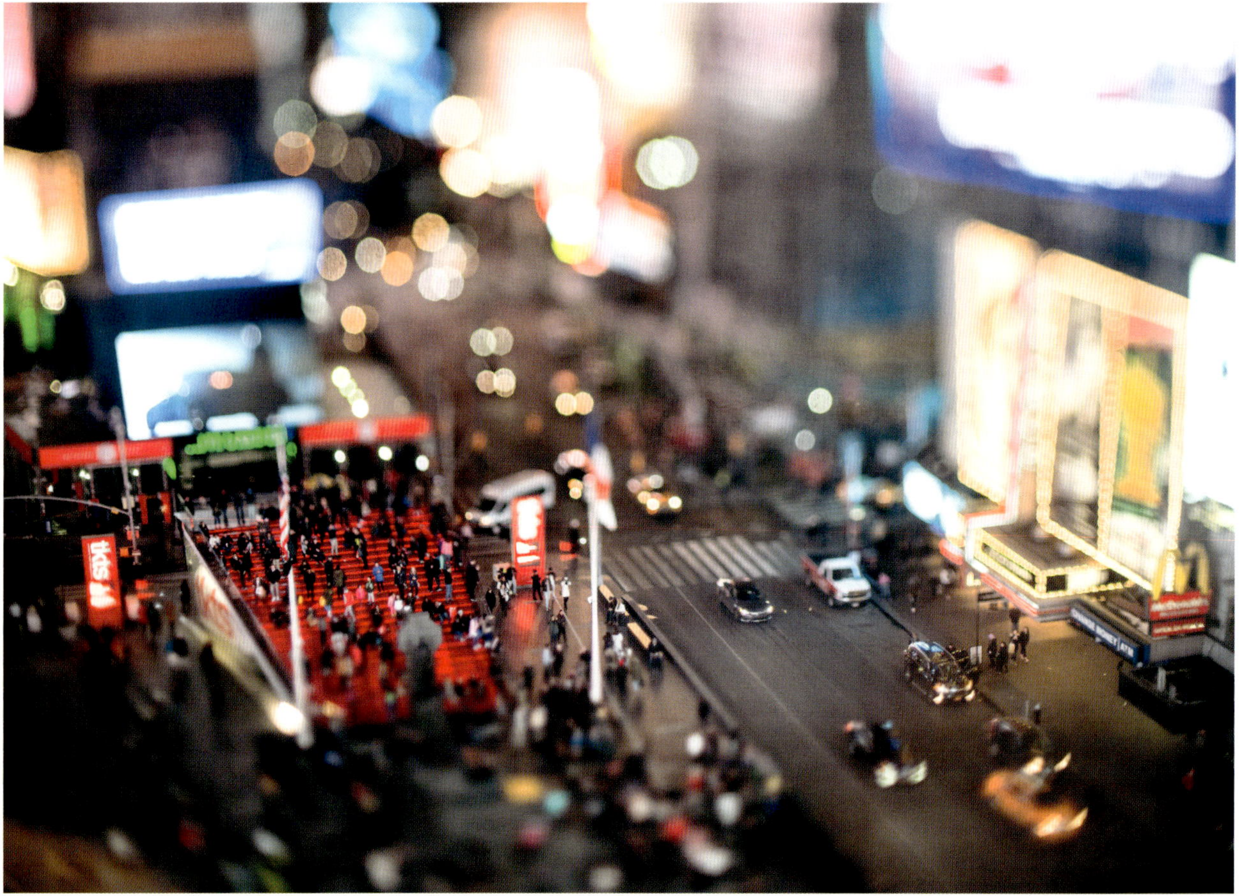

Times Square

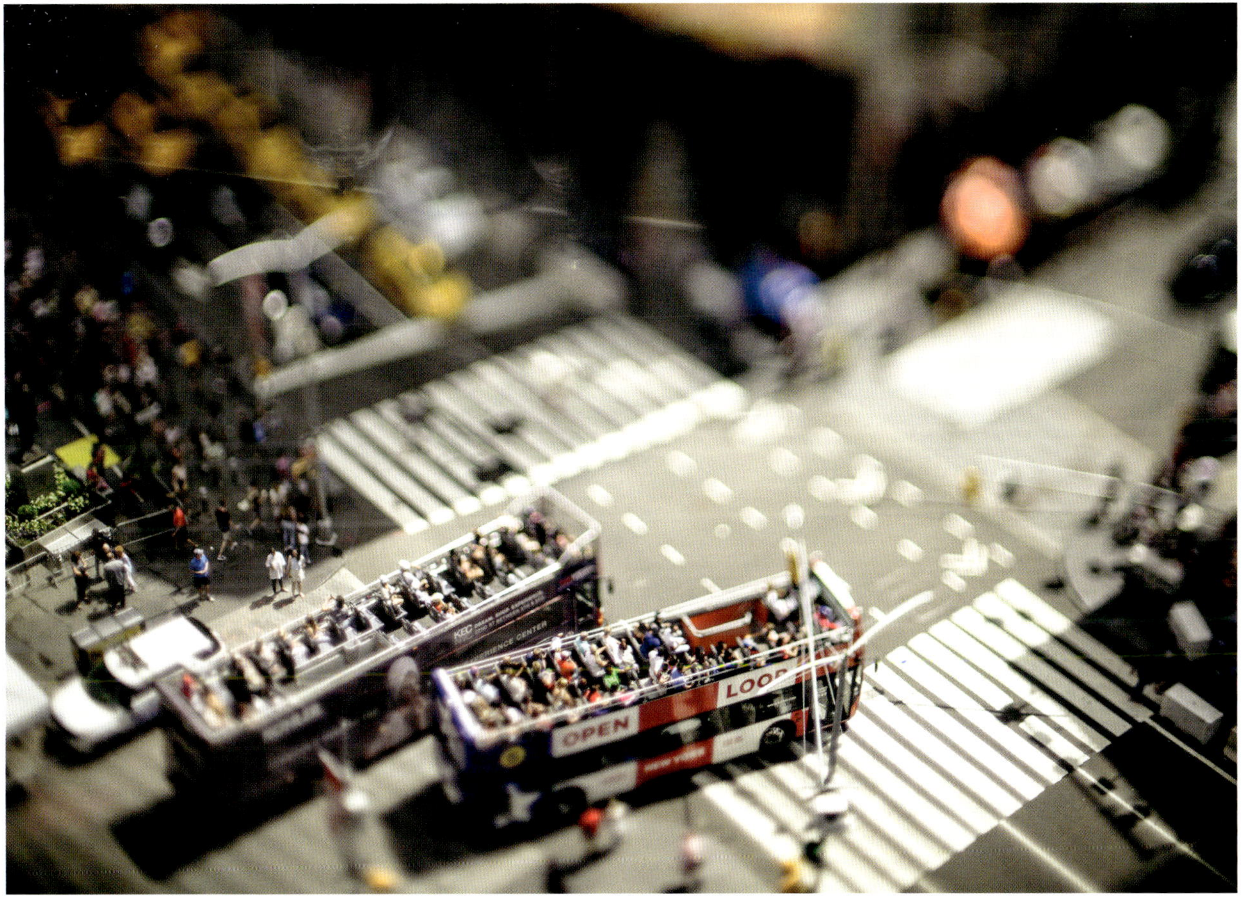

Times Square

New York is like a disco,

but without the music.

Elaine Stritch

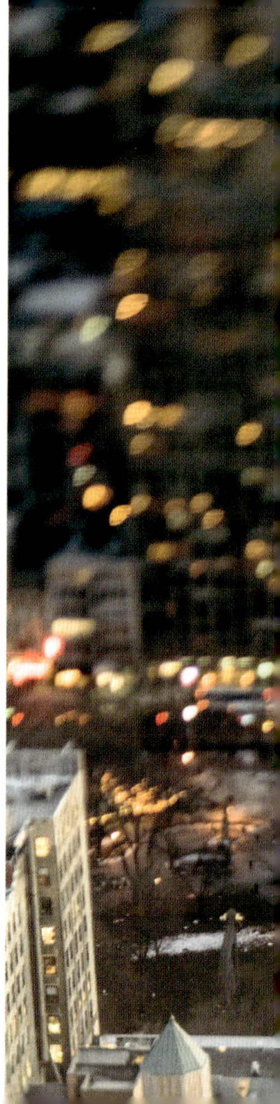

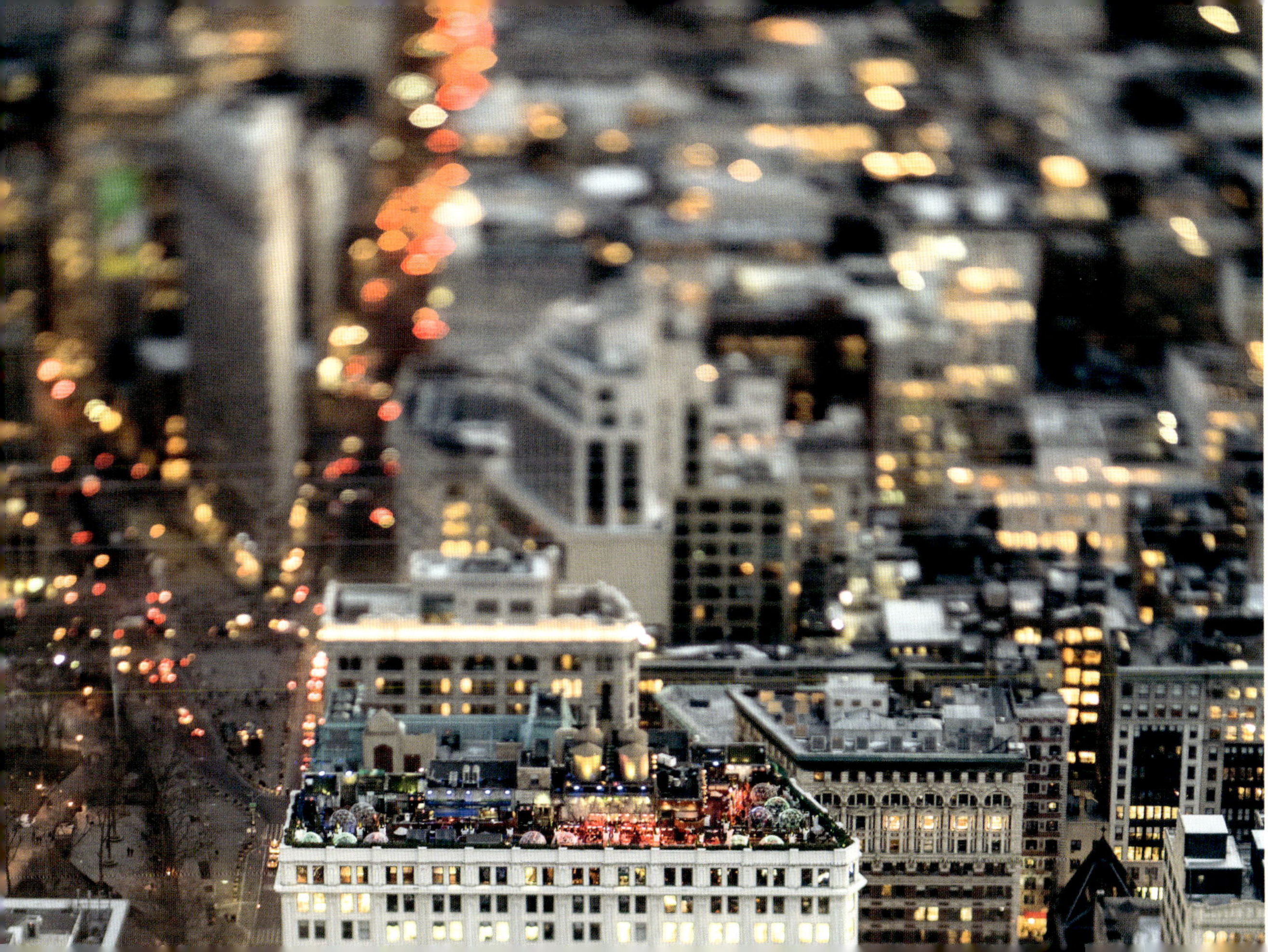

230 Fifth Rooftop Bar

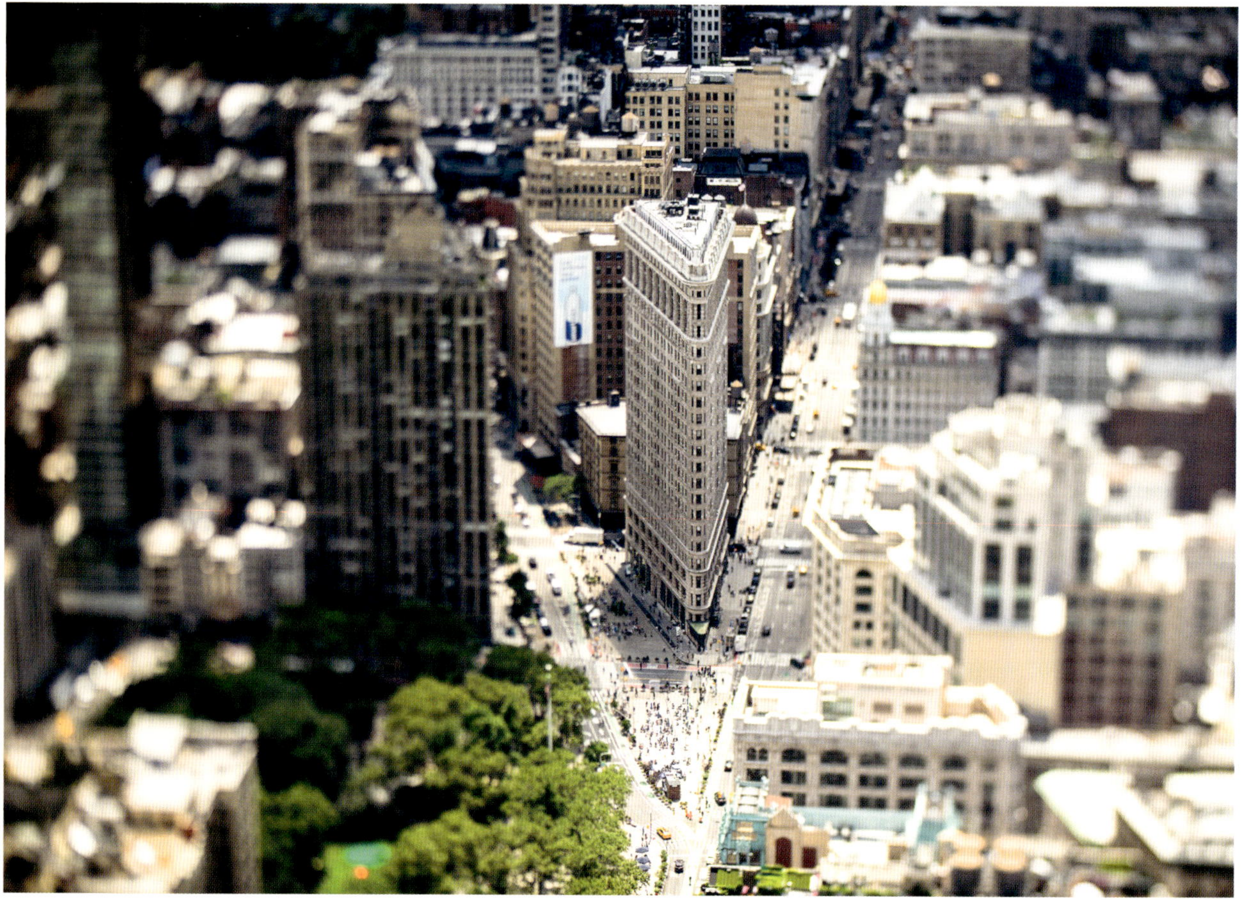

Flatiron Building

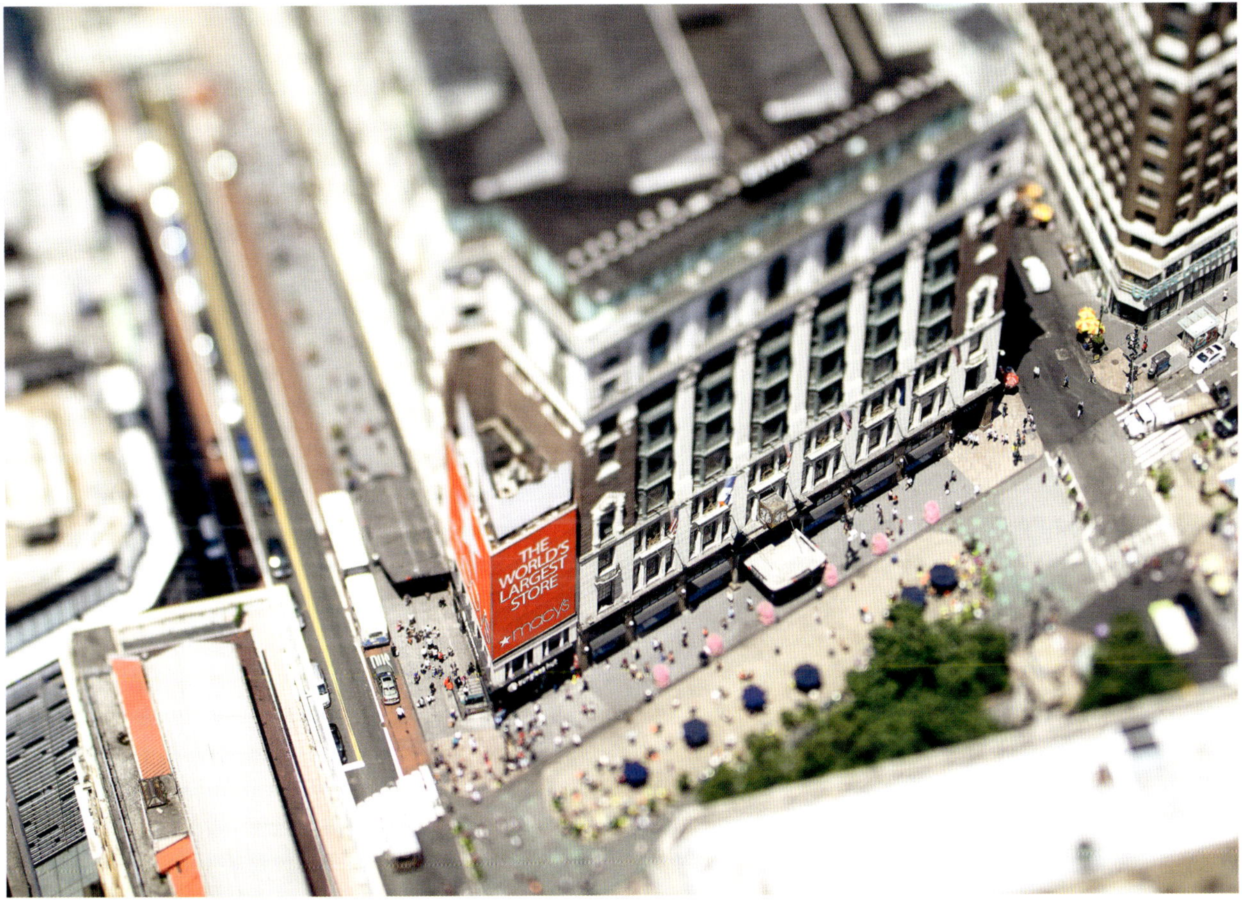

Herald Square

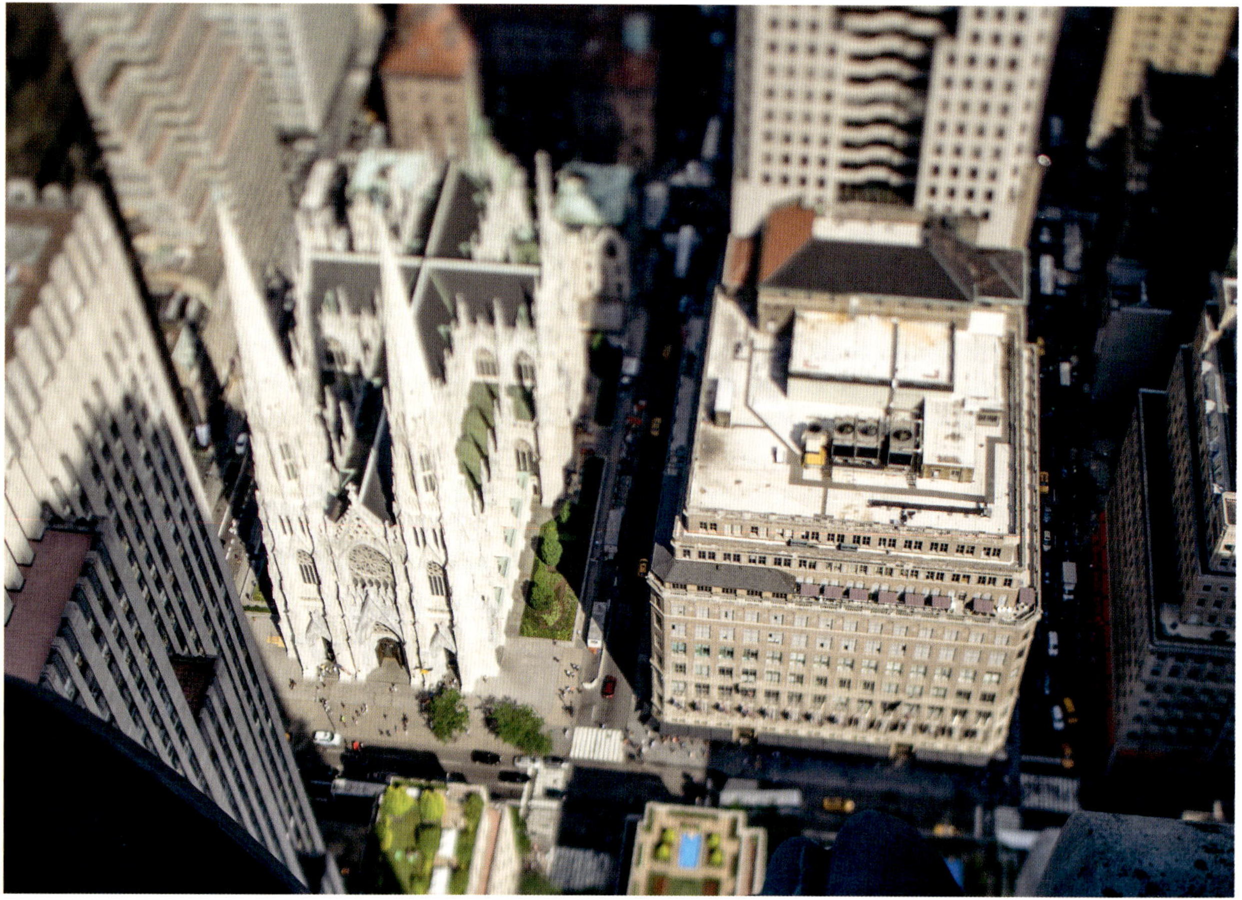

Saint Patrick's Cathedral

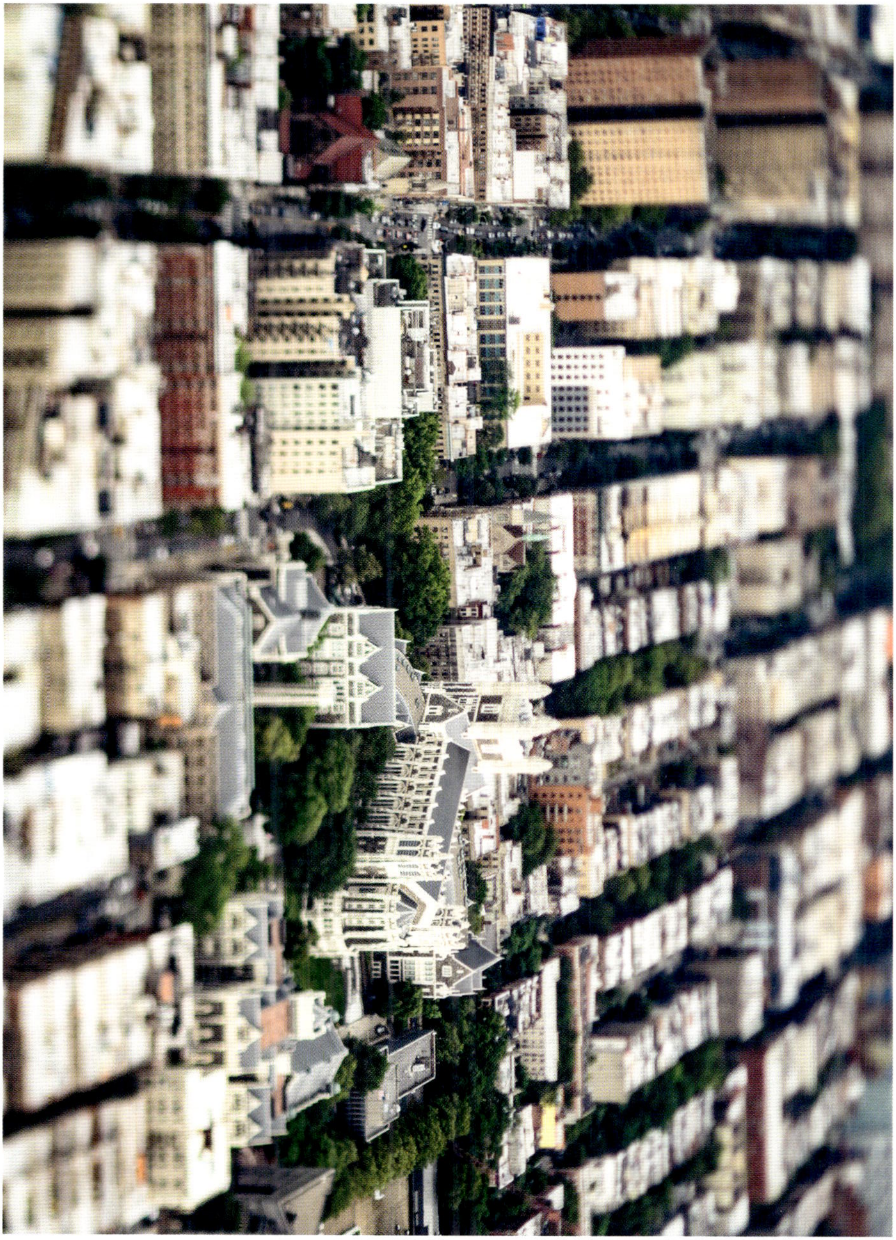

Shepard Hall

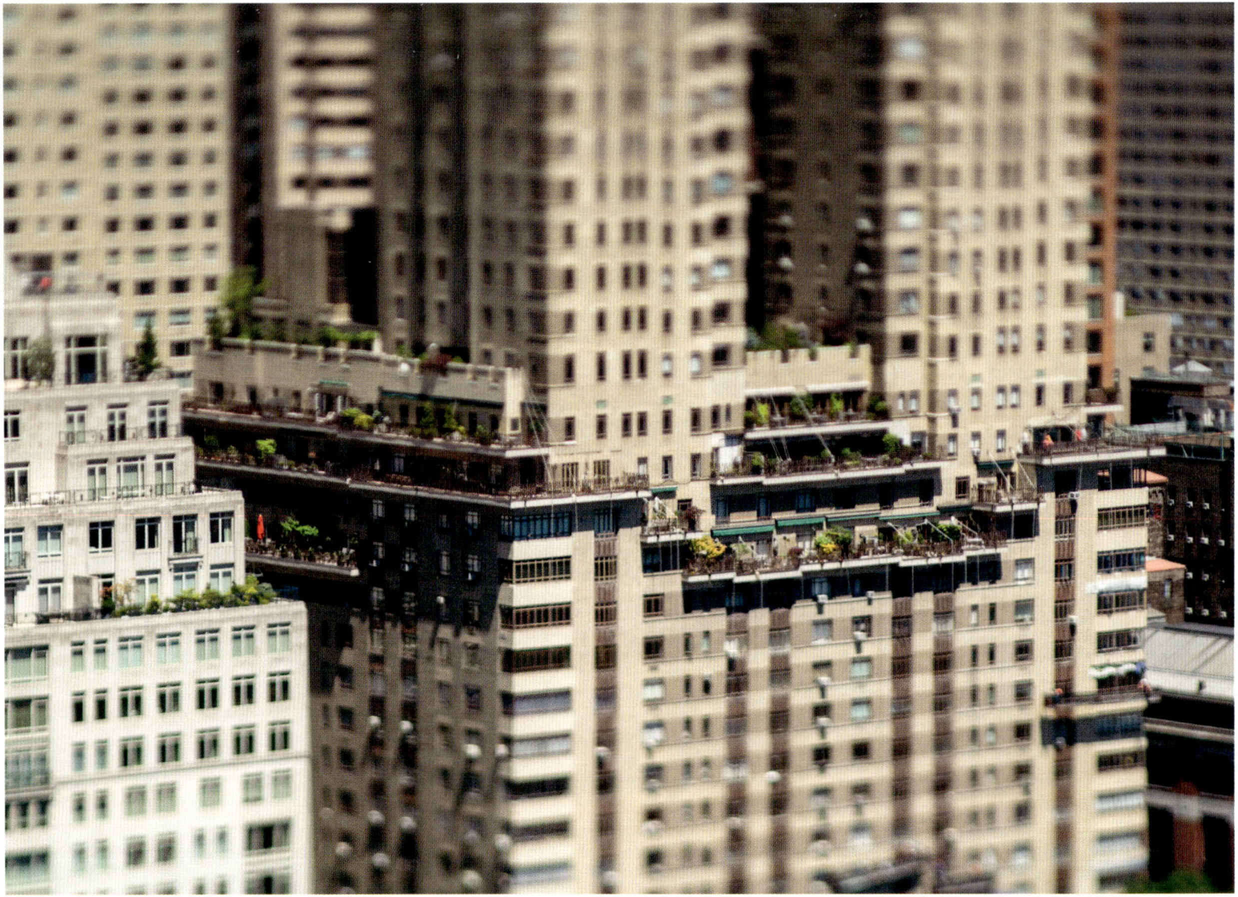

Central Park West

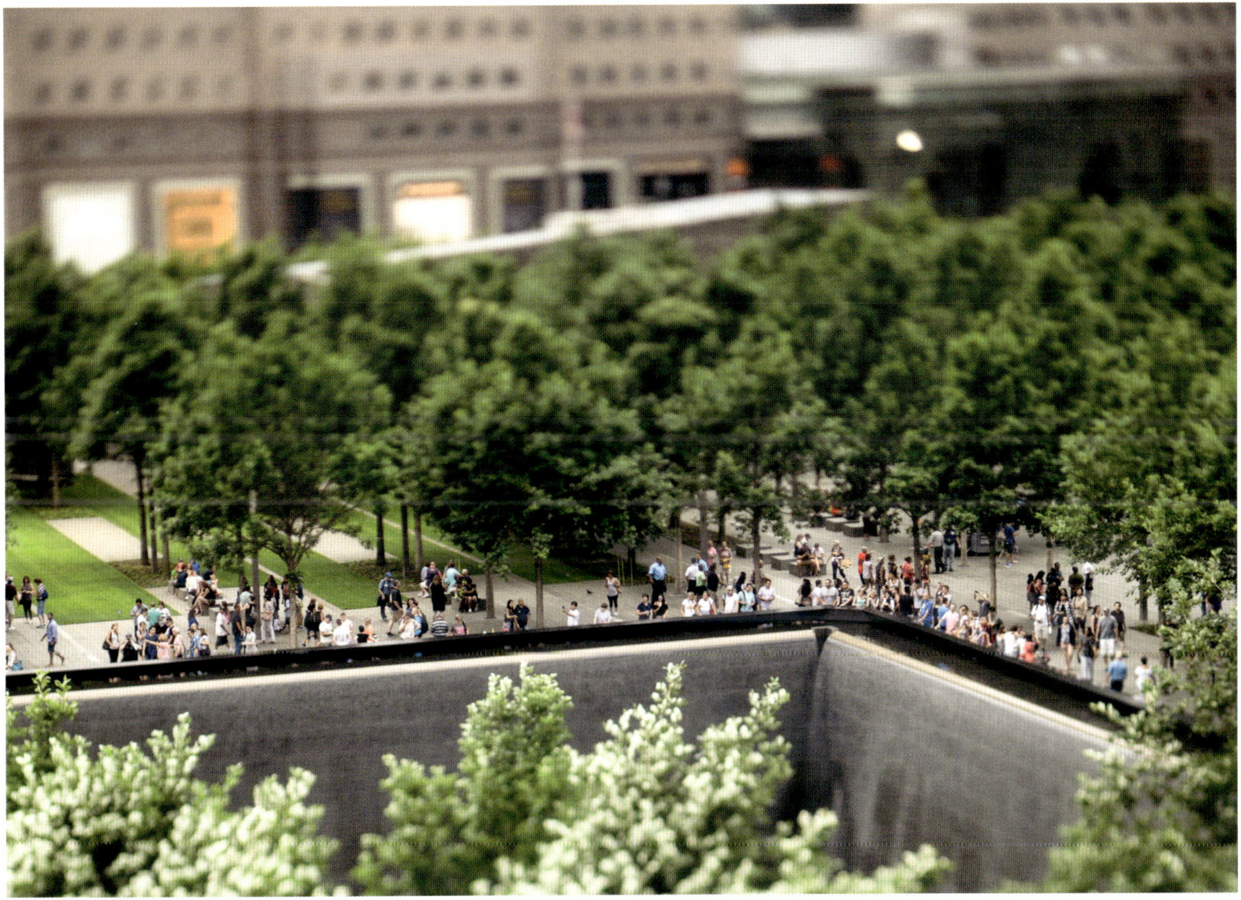

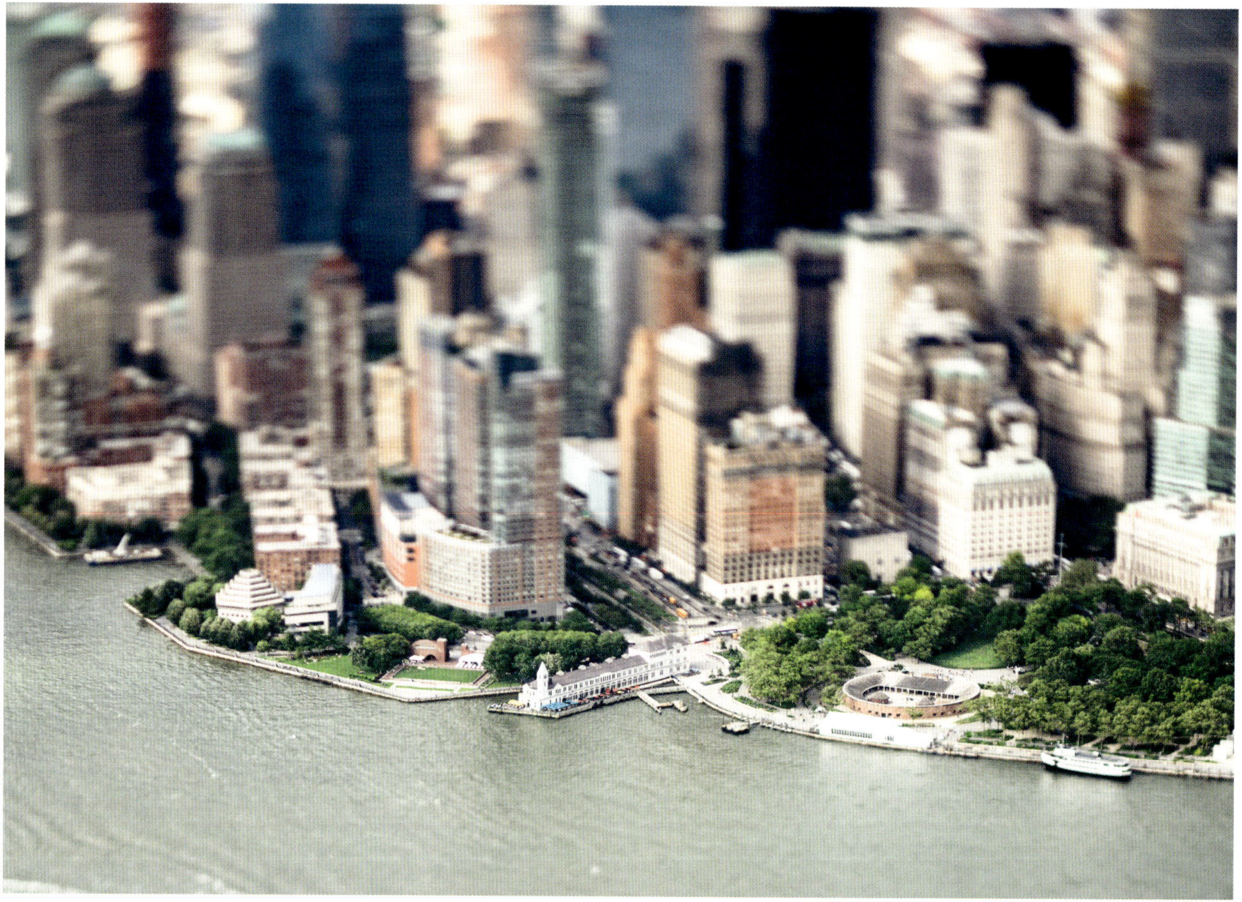

Battery Park

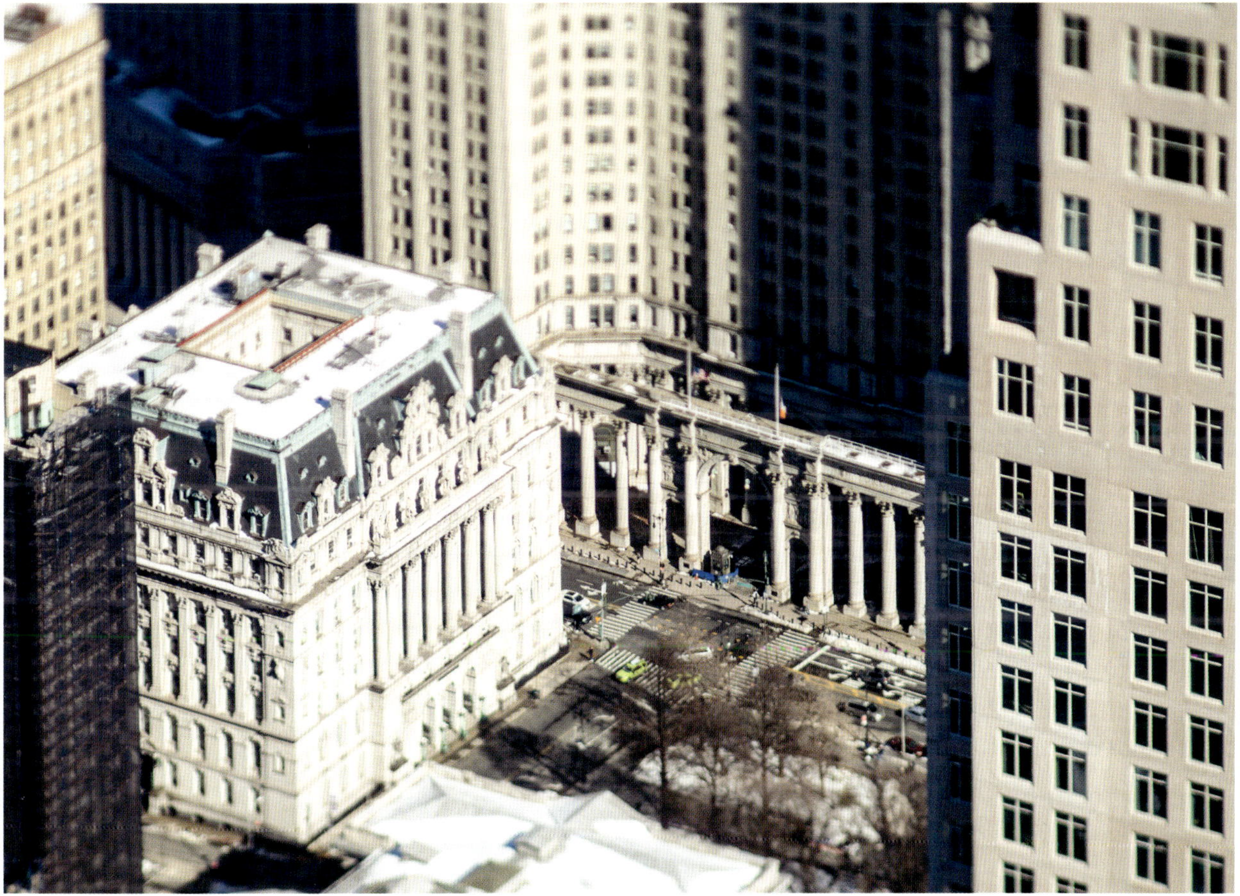

Centre Street

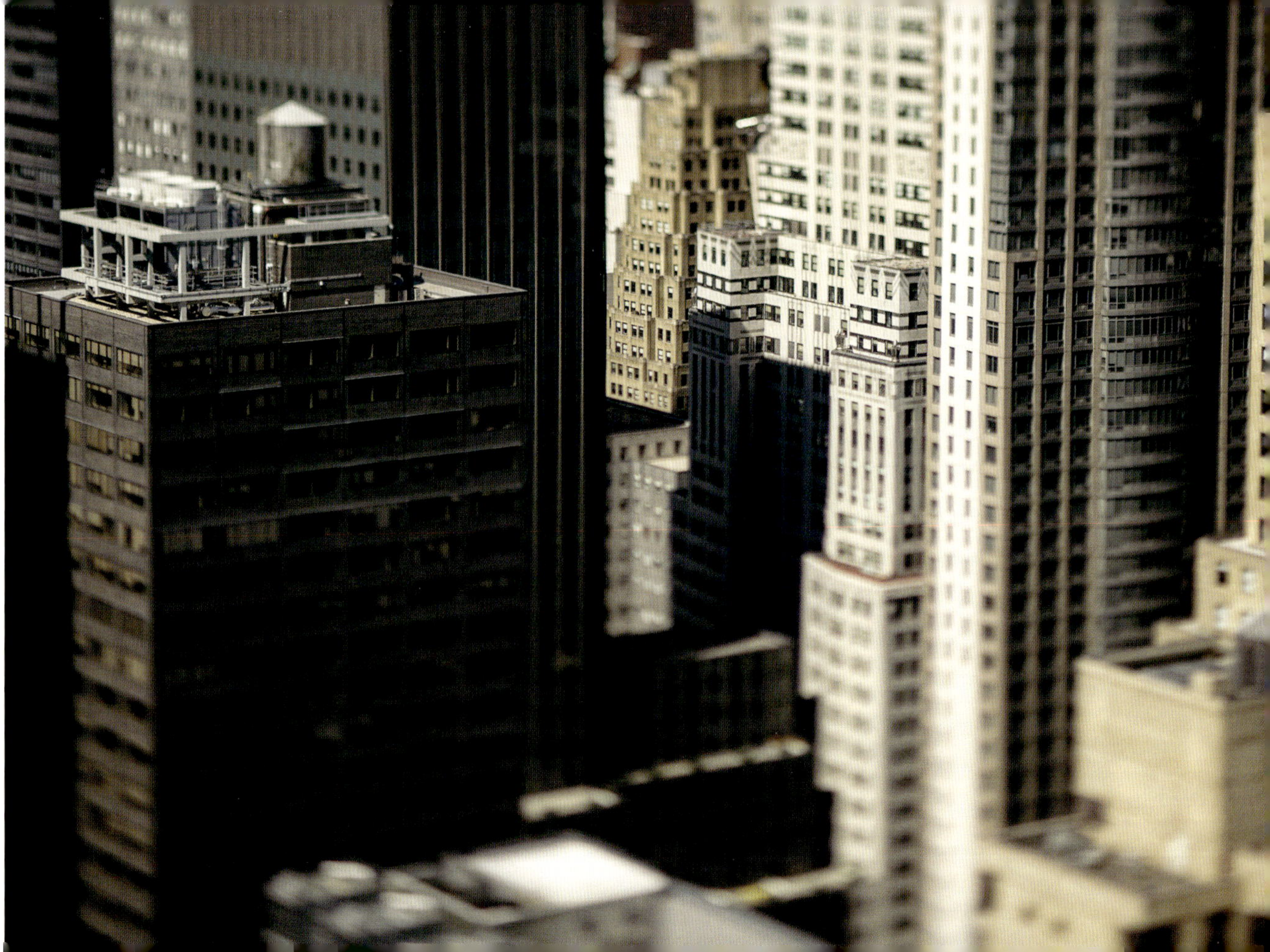

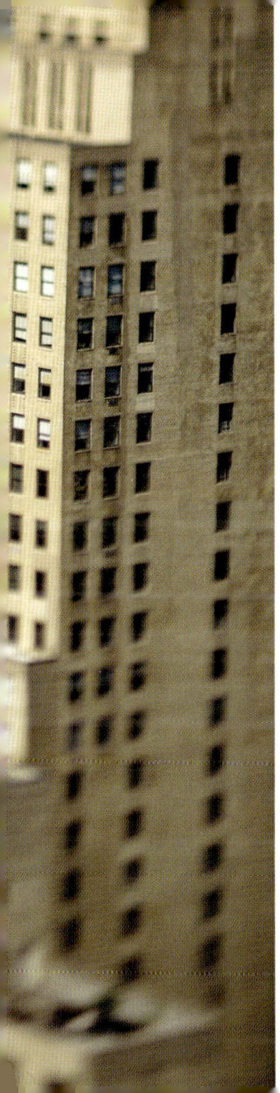

City of prose and fantasy, of capitalist automation, its streets a triumph of cubism, its moral philosophy that of the dollar. New York impressed me tremendously because, more than any other city, it is the fullest expression of our modern age.

Leon Trotsky

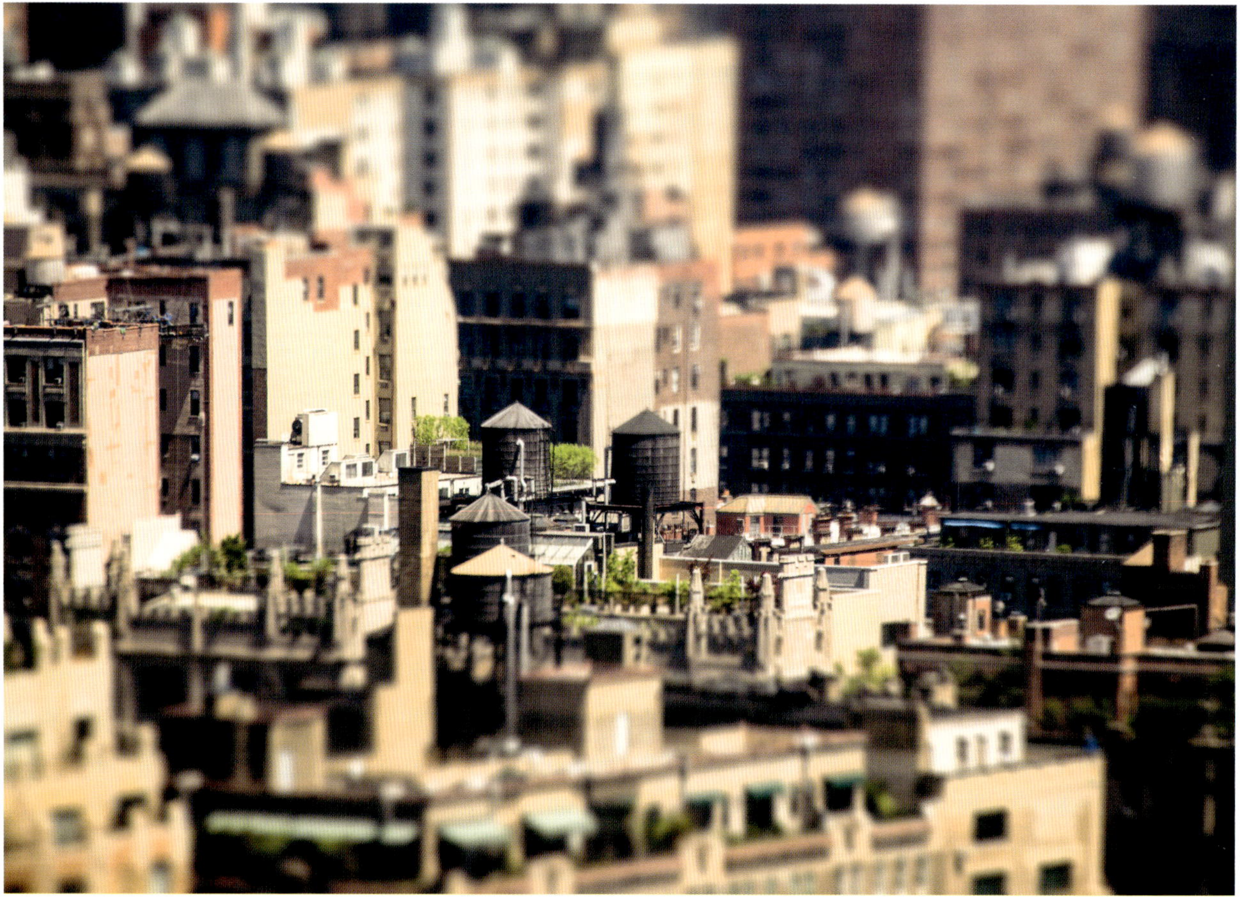

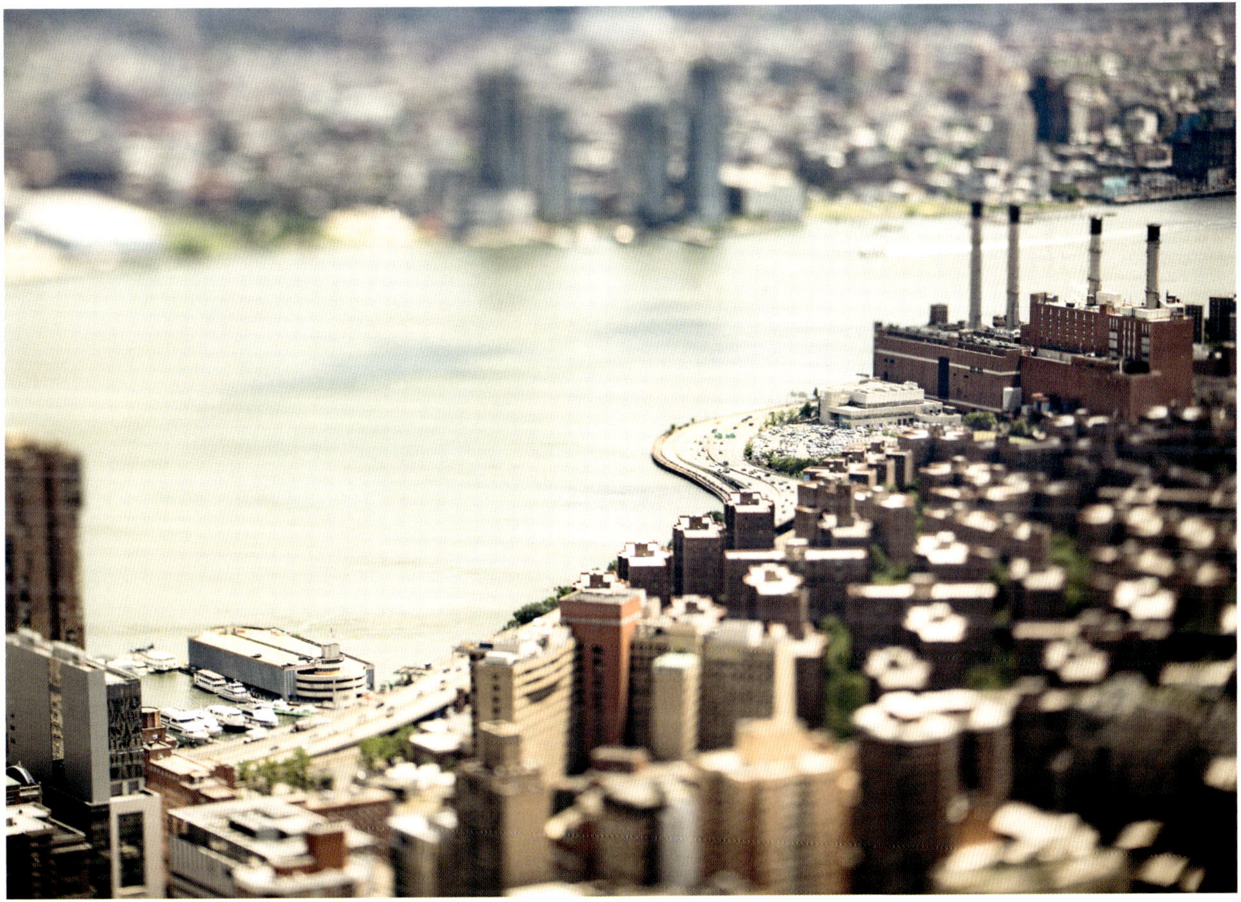

FDR Drive, East River

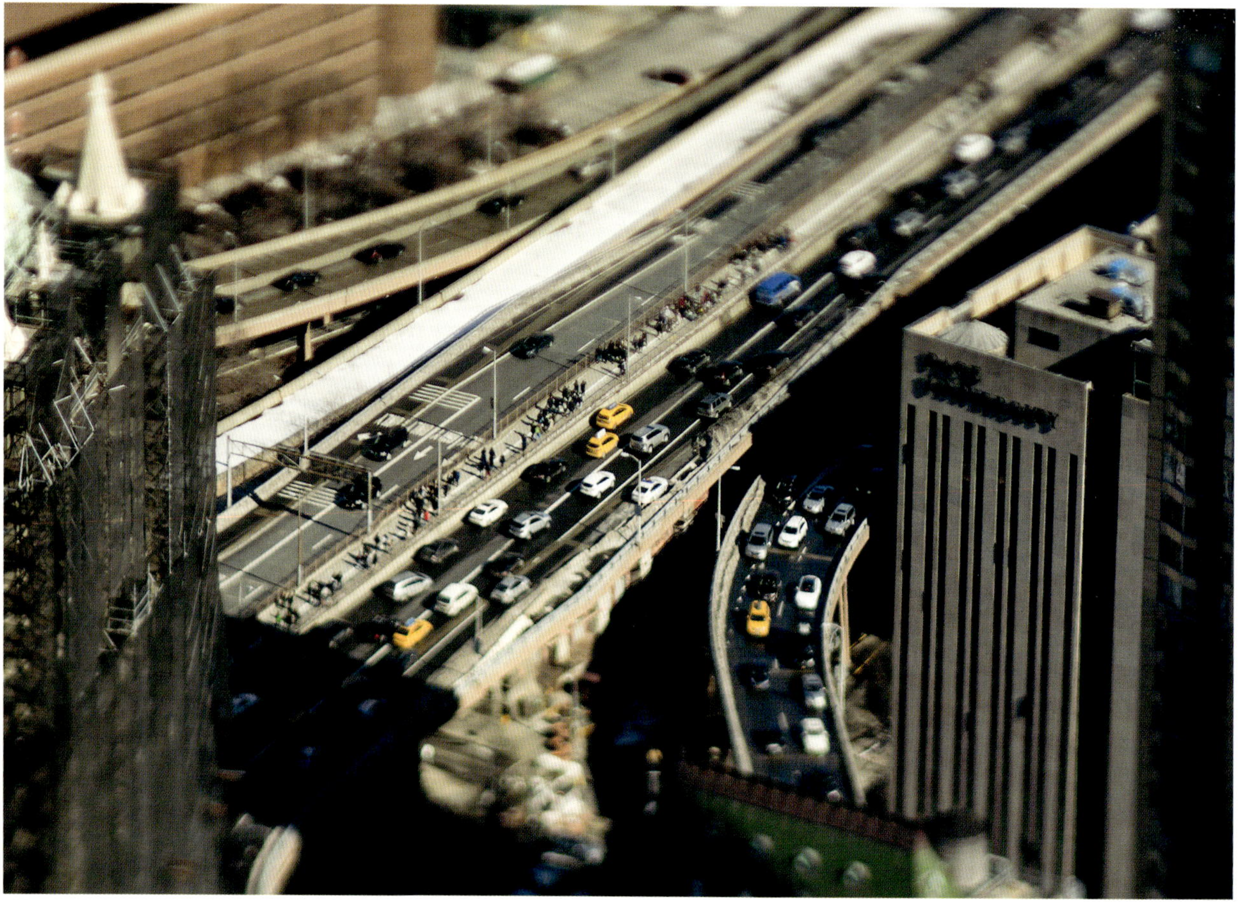

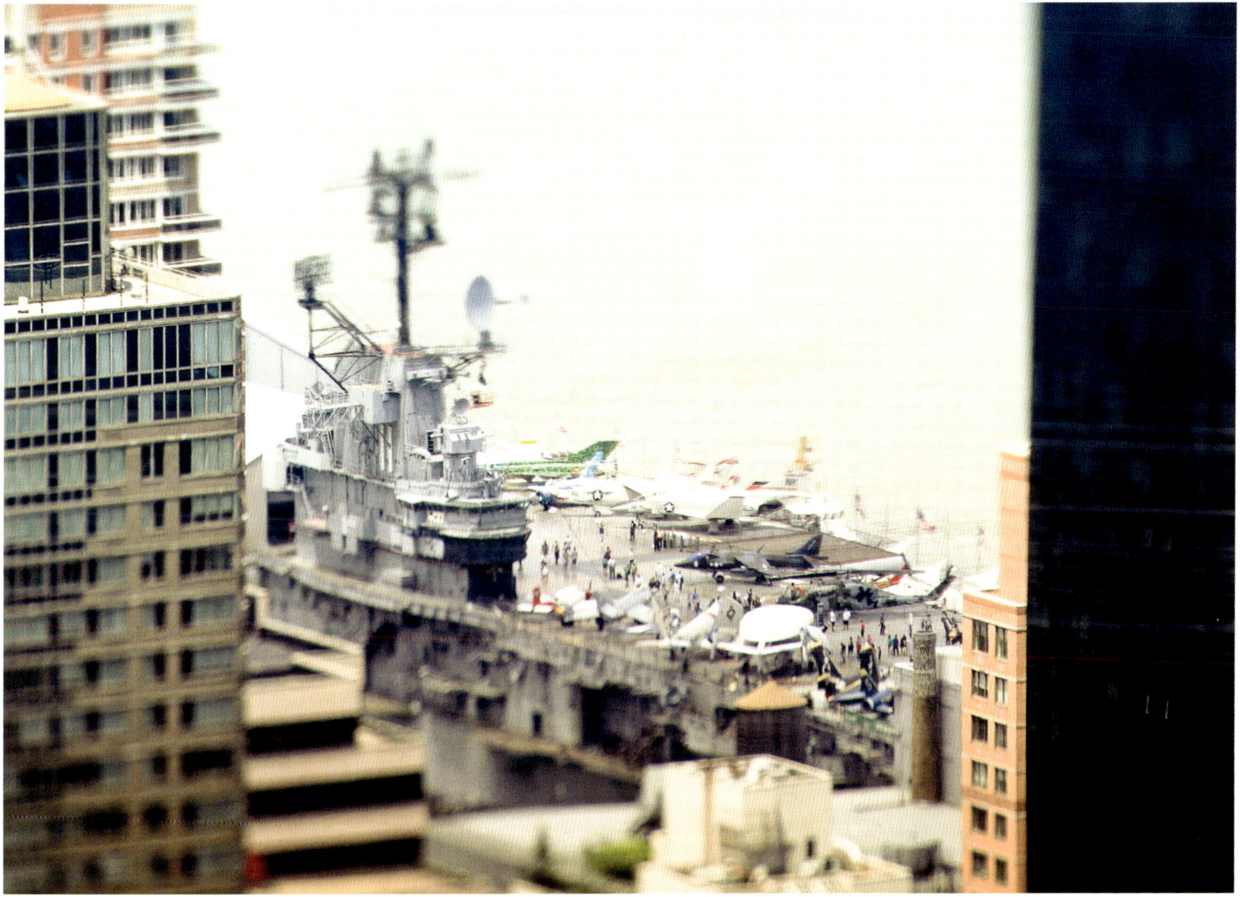

Intrepid Sea, Air & Space Museum

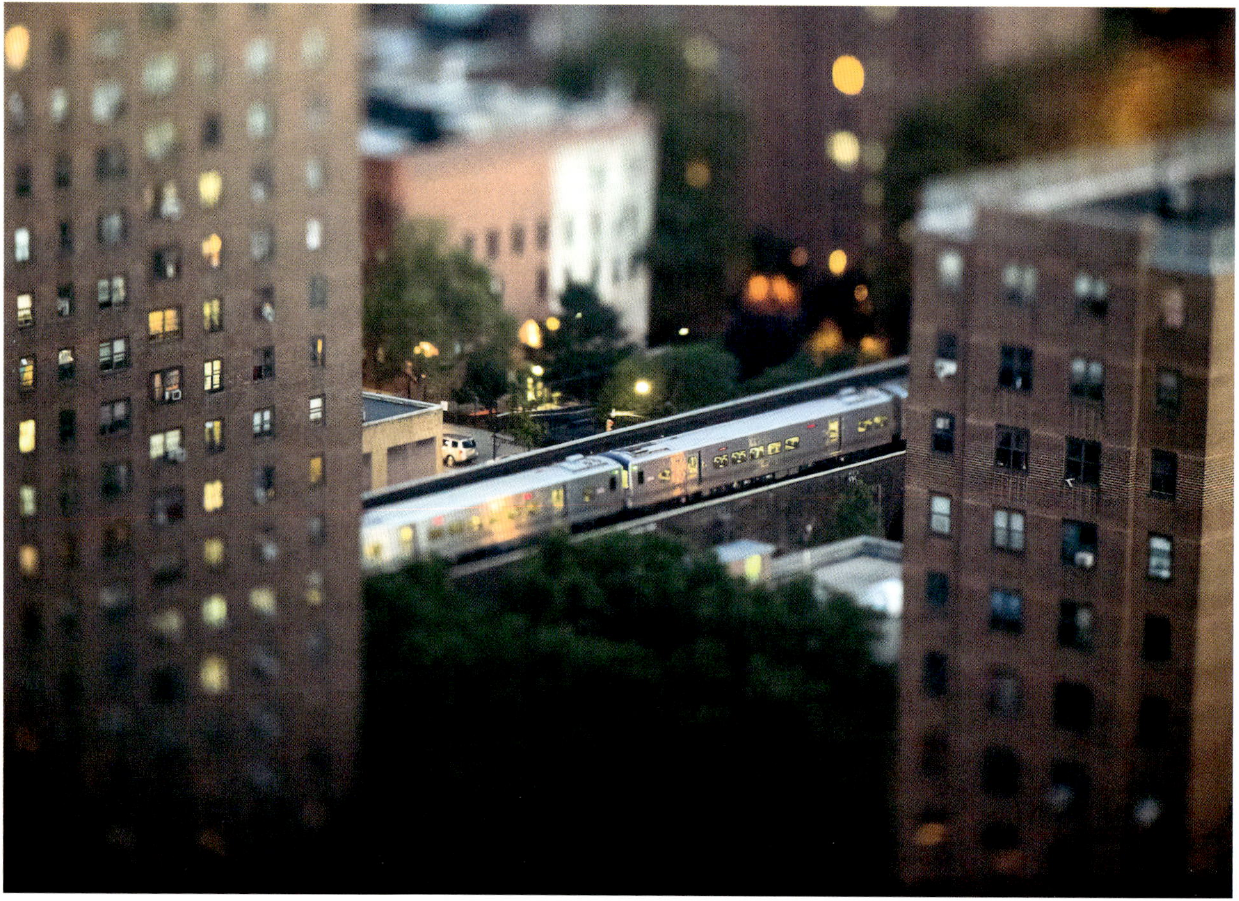

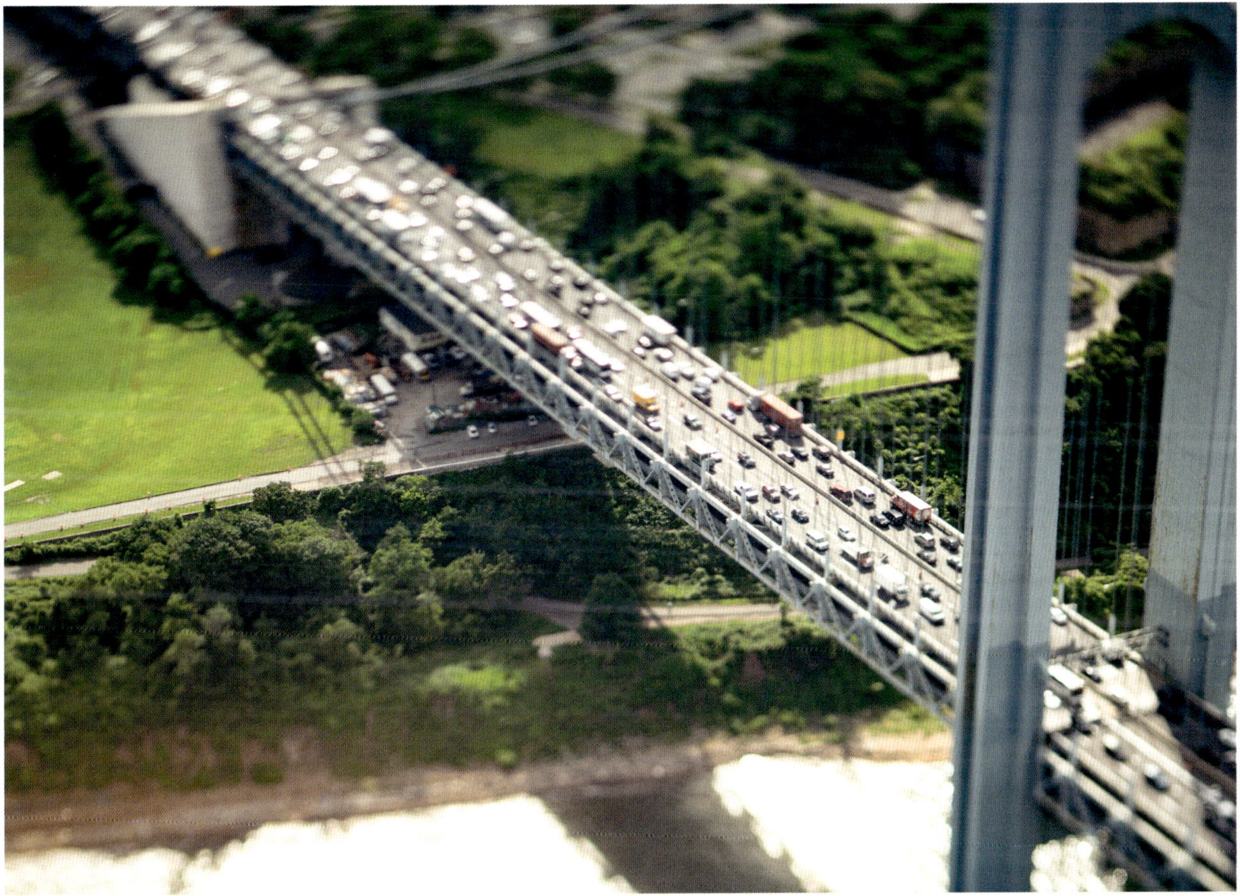

Verrazano-Narrows Bridge

Highline, Chelsea

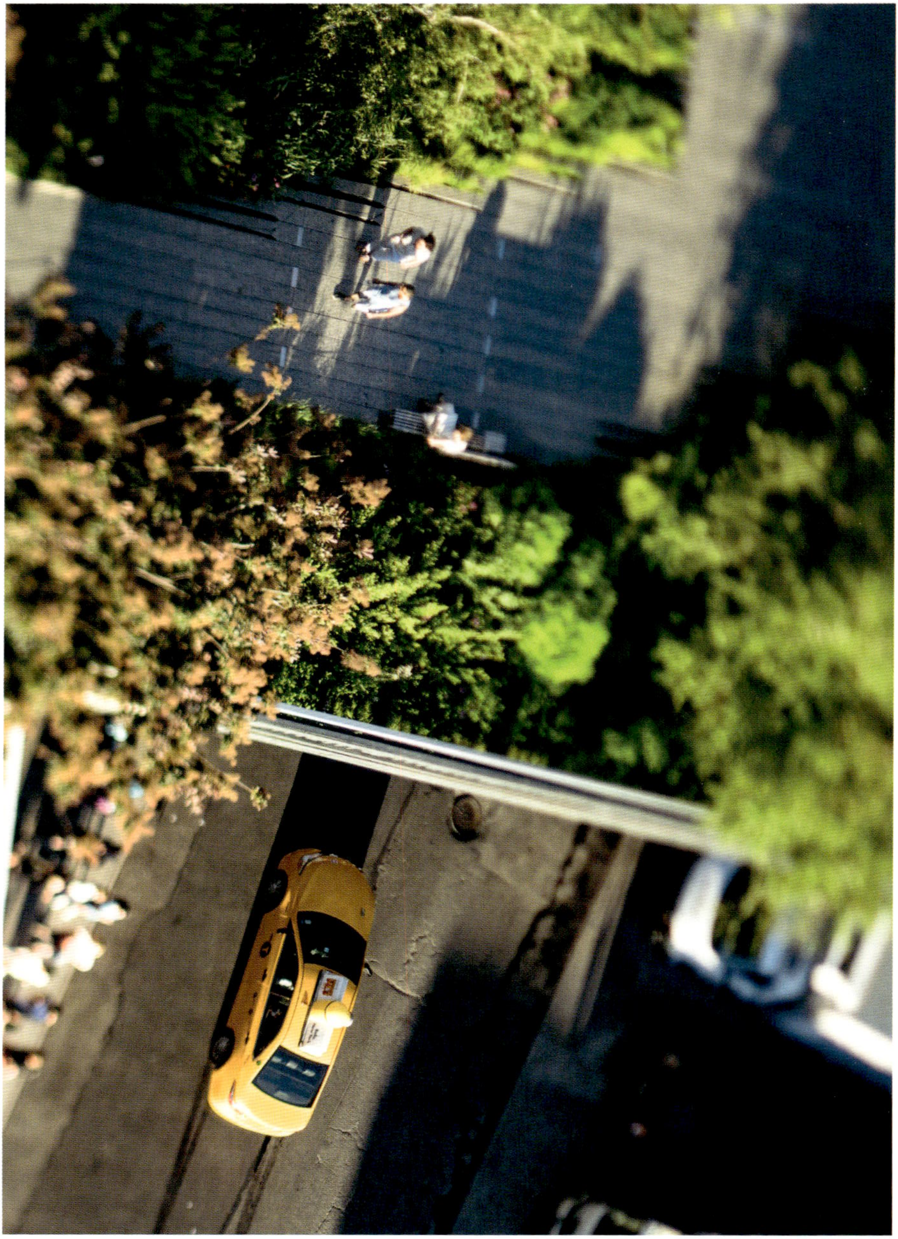

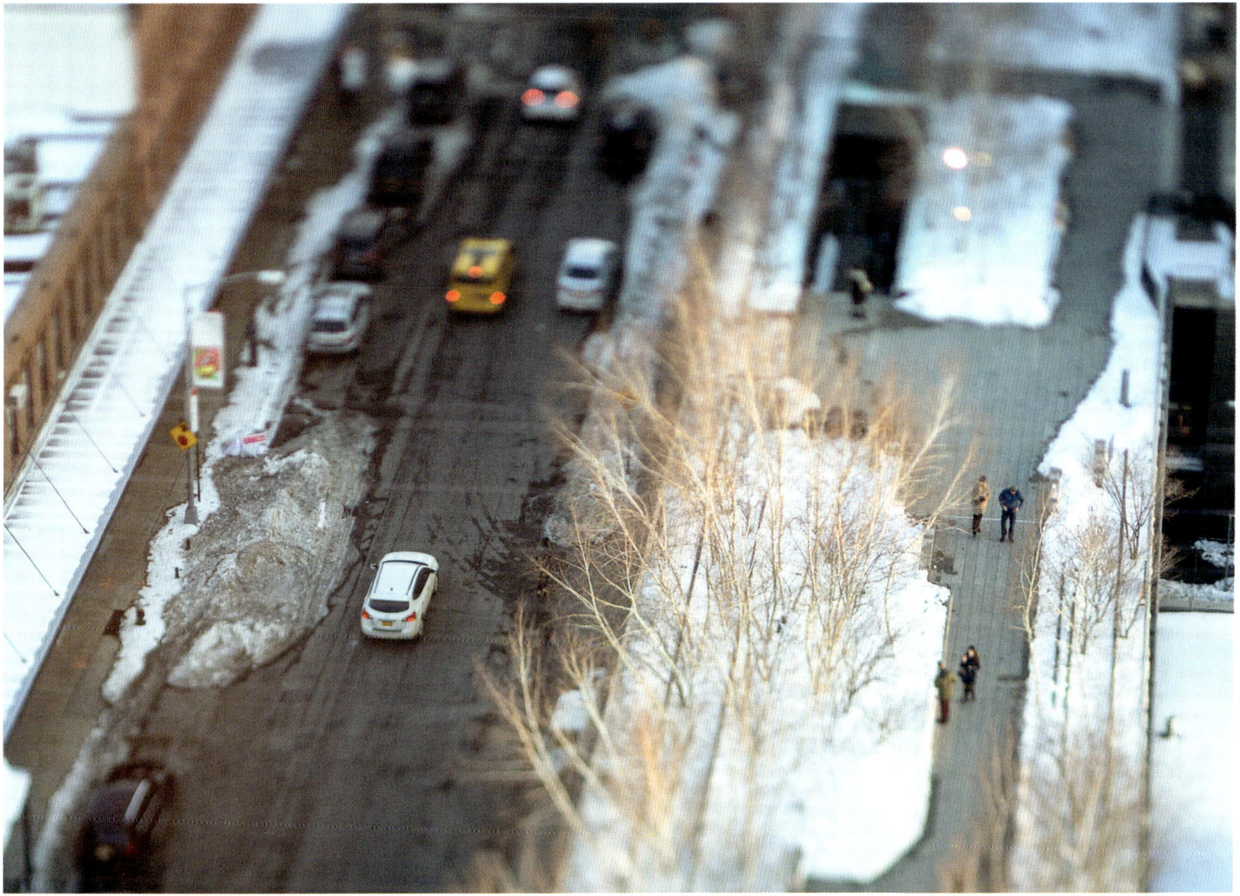

Highline, Chelsea

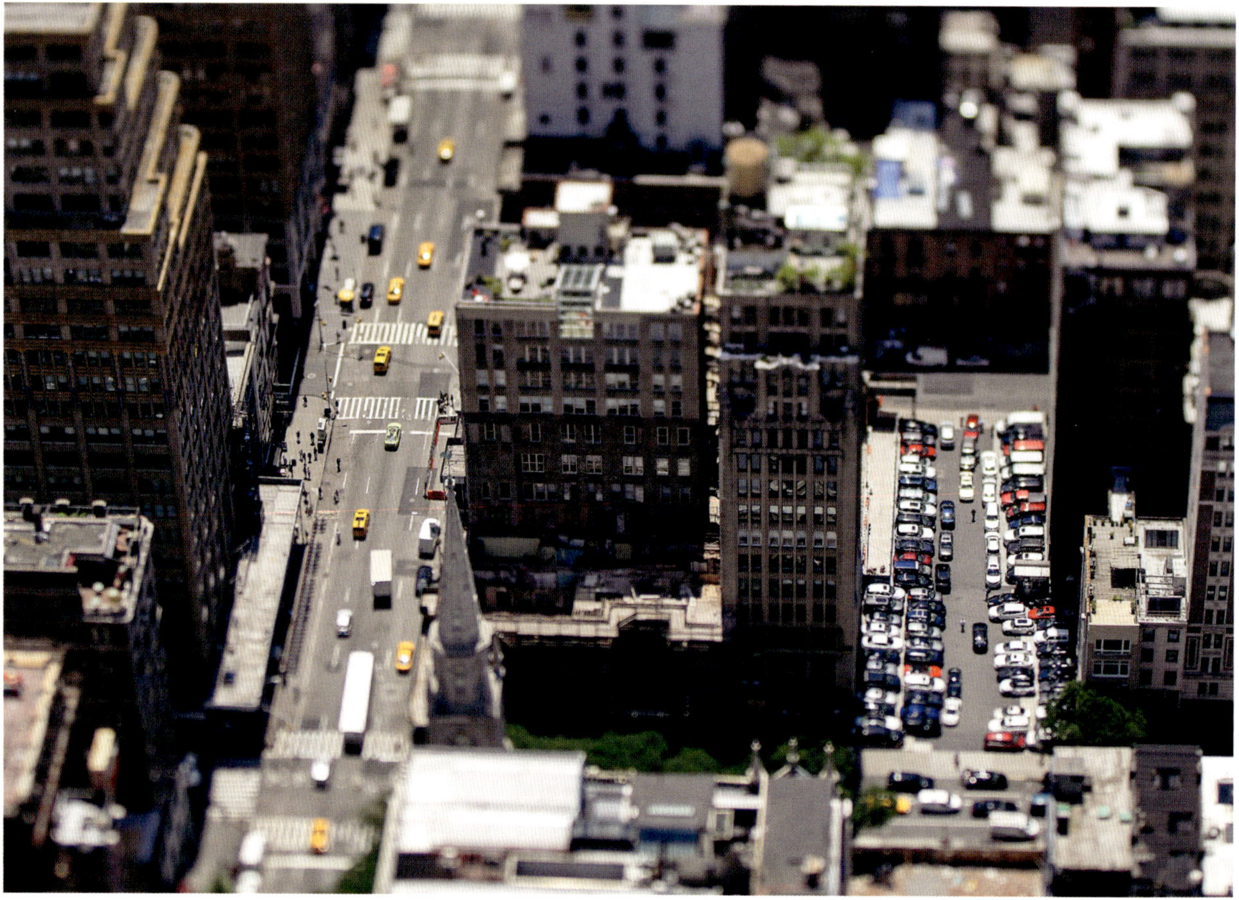

5th Ave

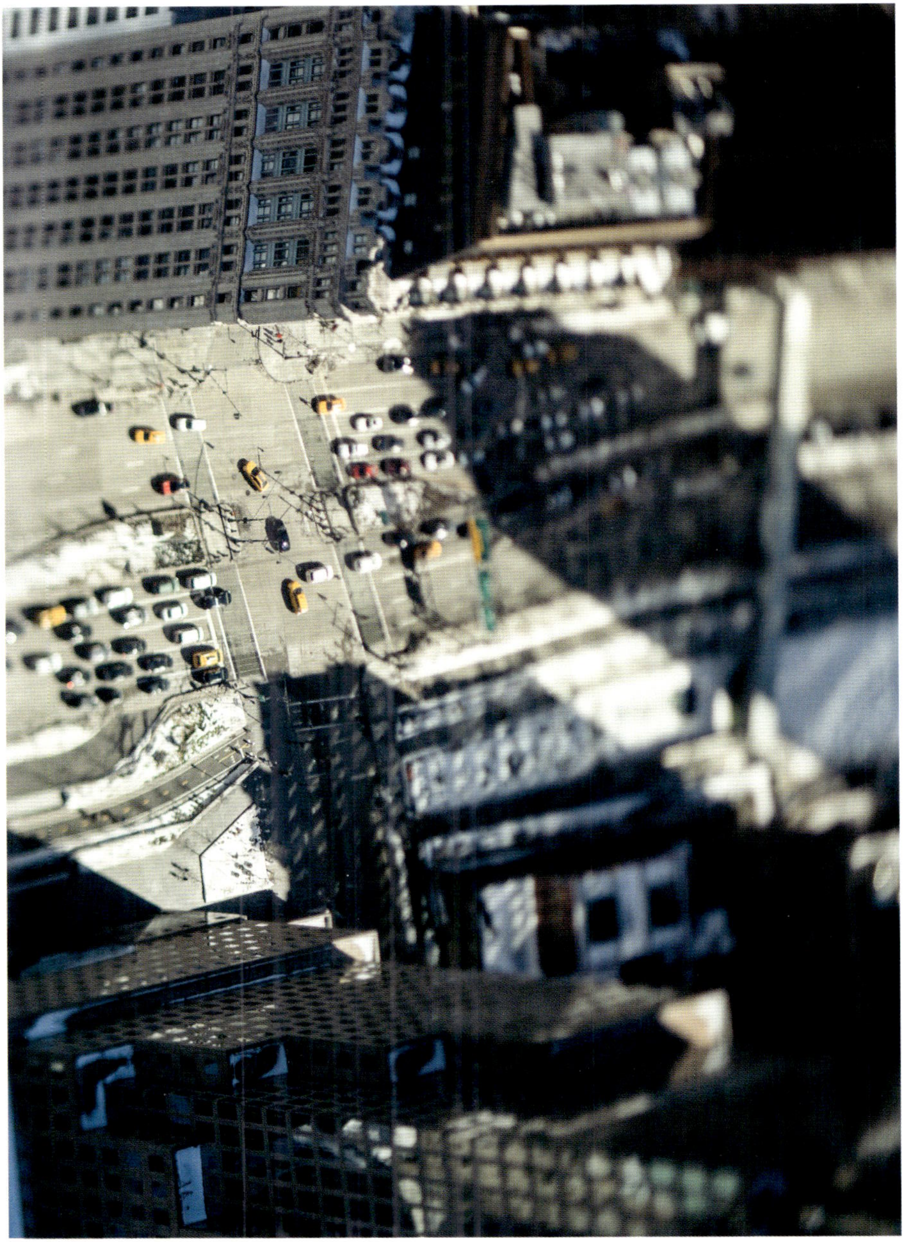

Albany Street

A lot of the time when I write about the person that I love, I feel like I'm writing about New York.

Lana Del Rey

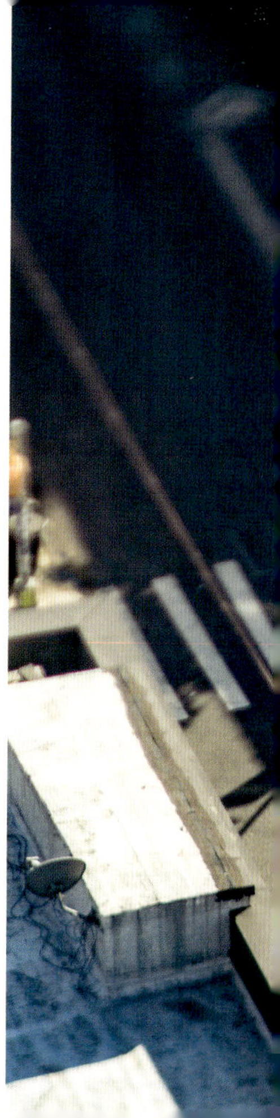

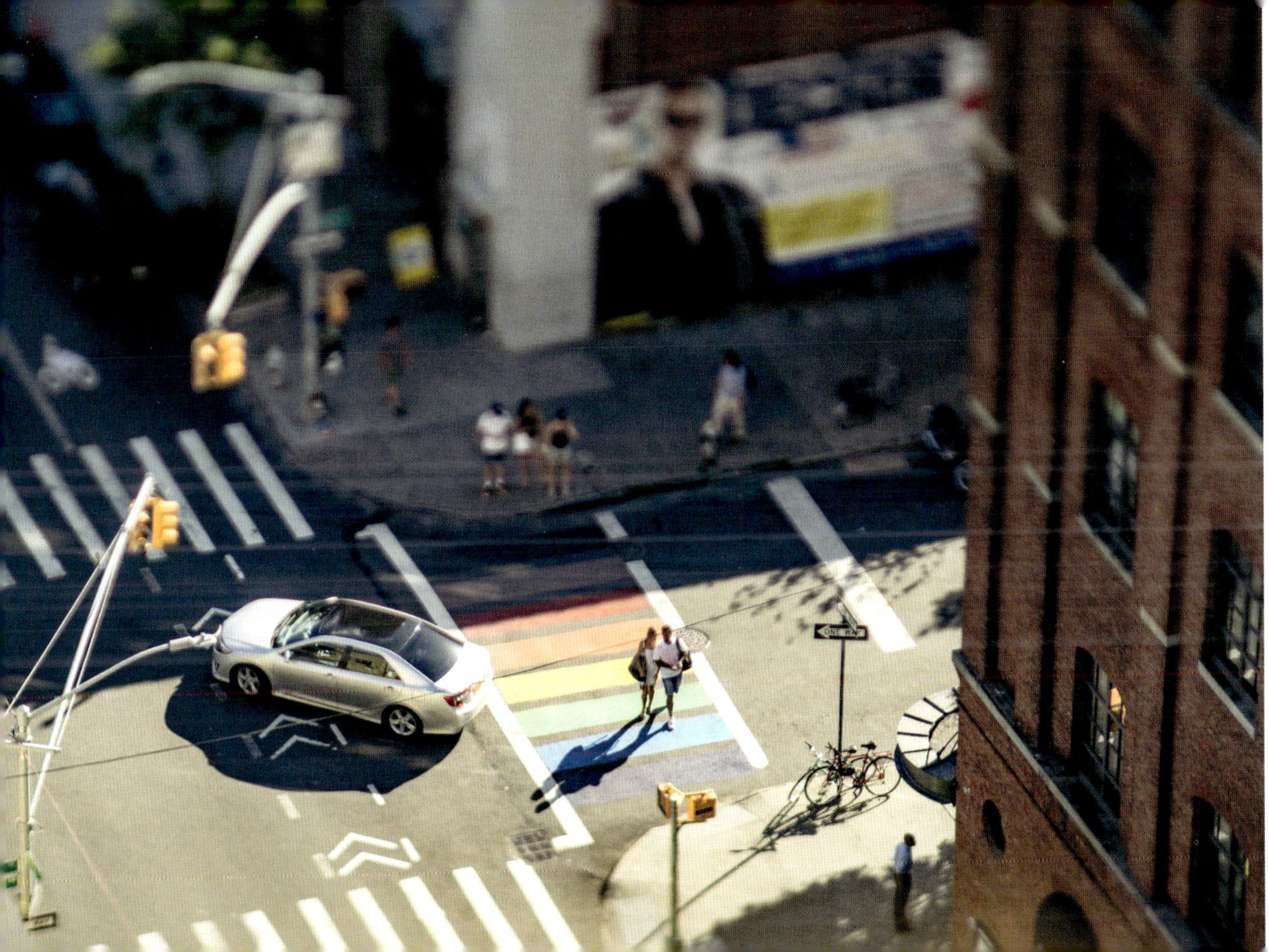

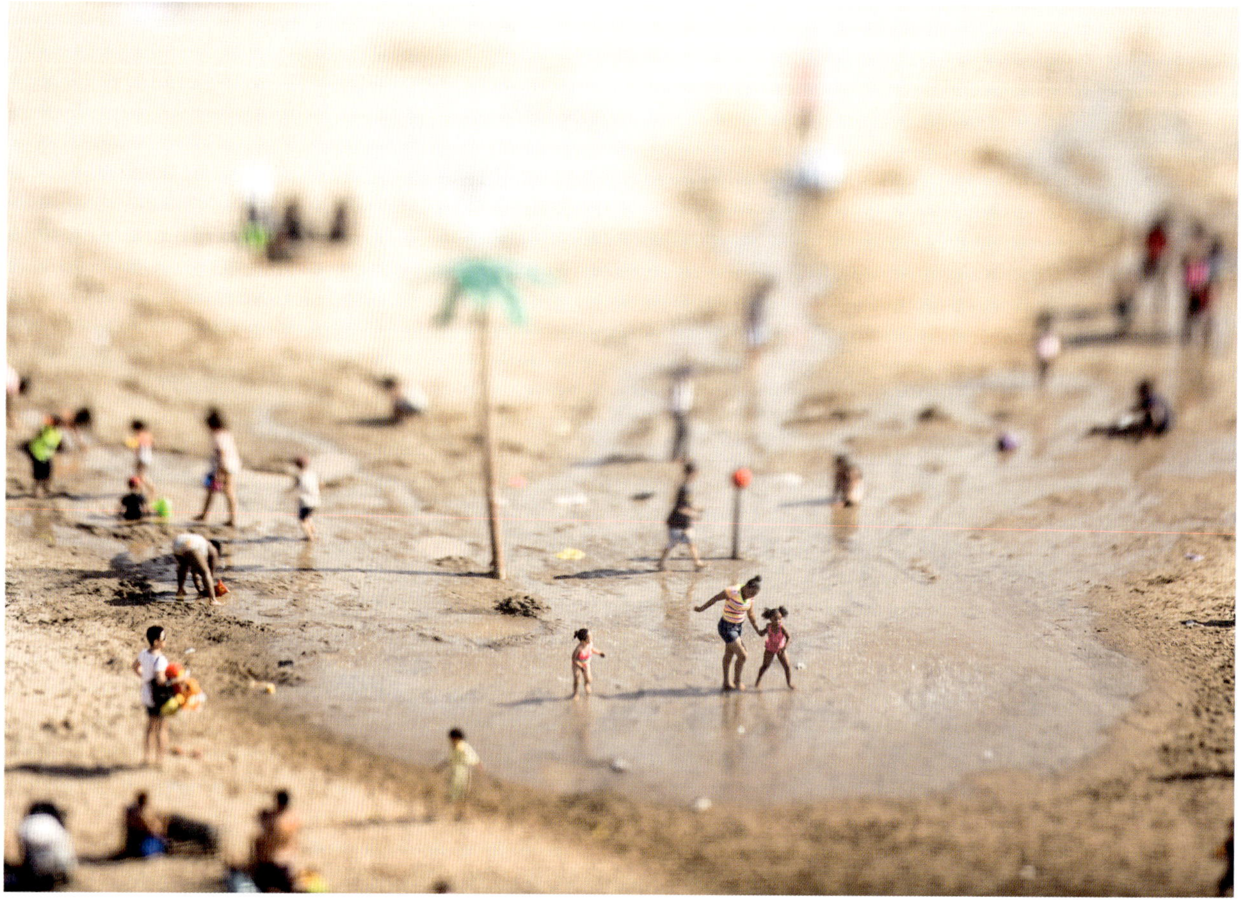

Coney Island Beach

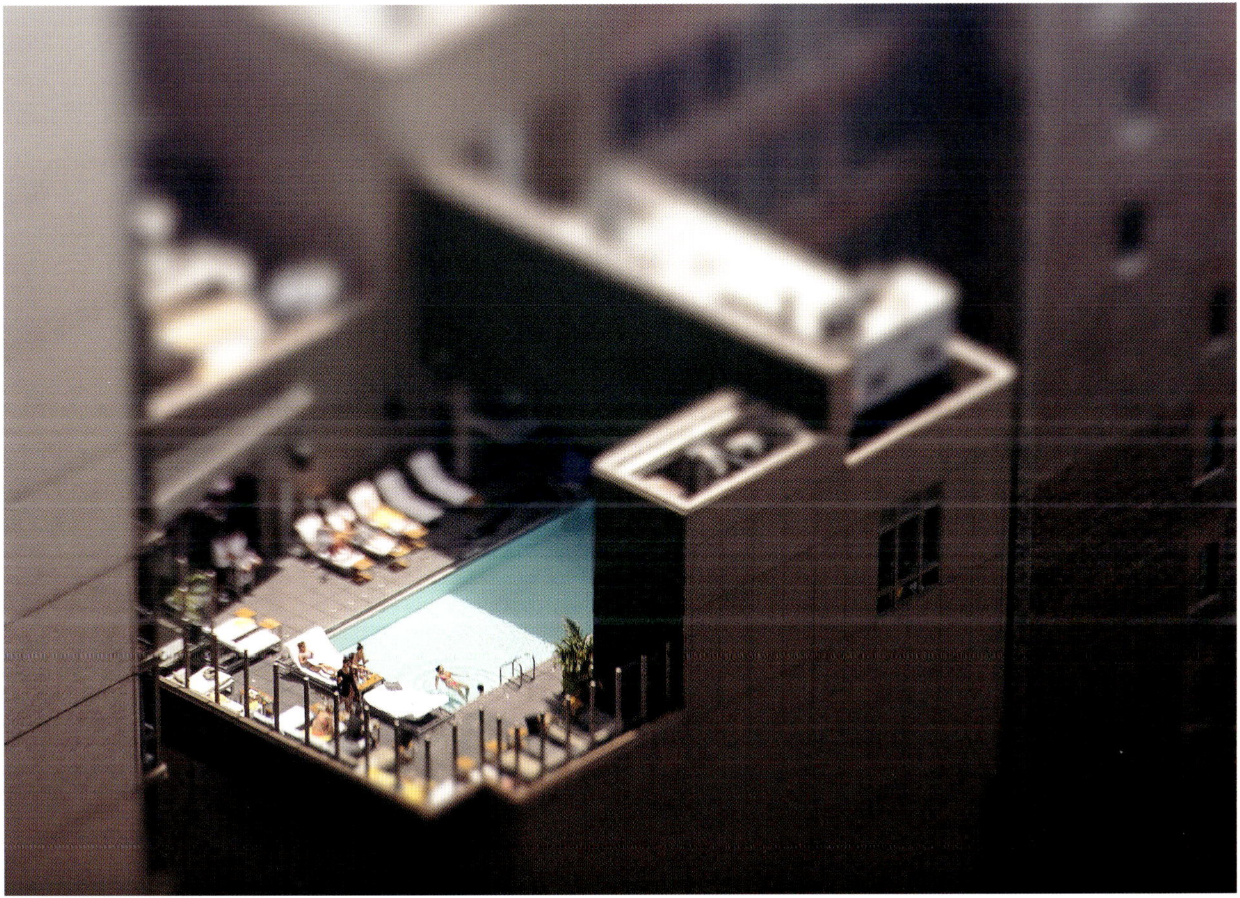

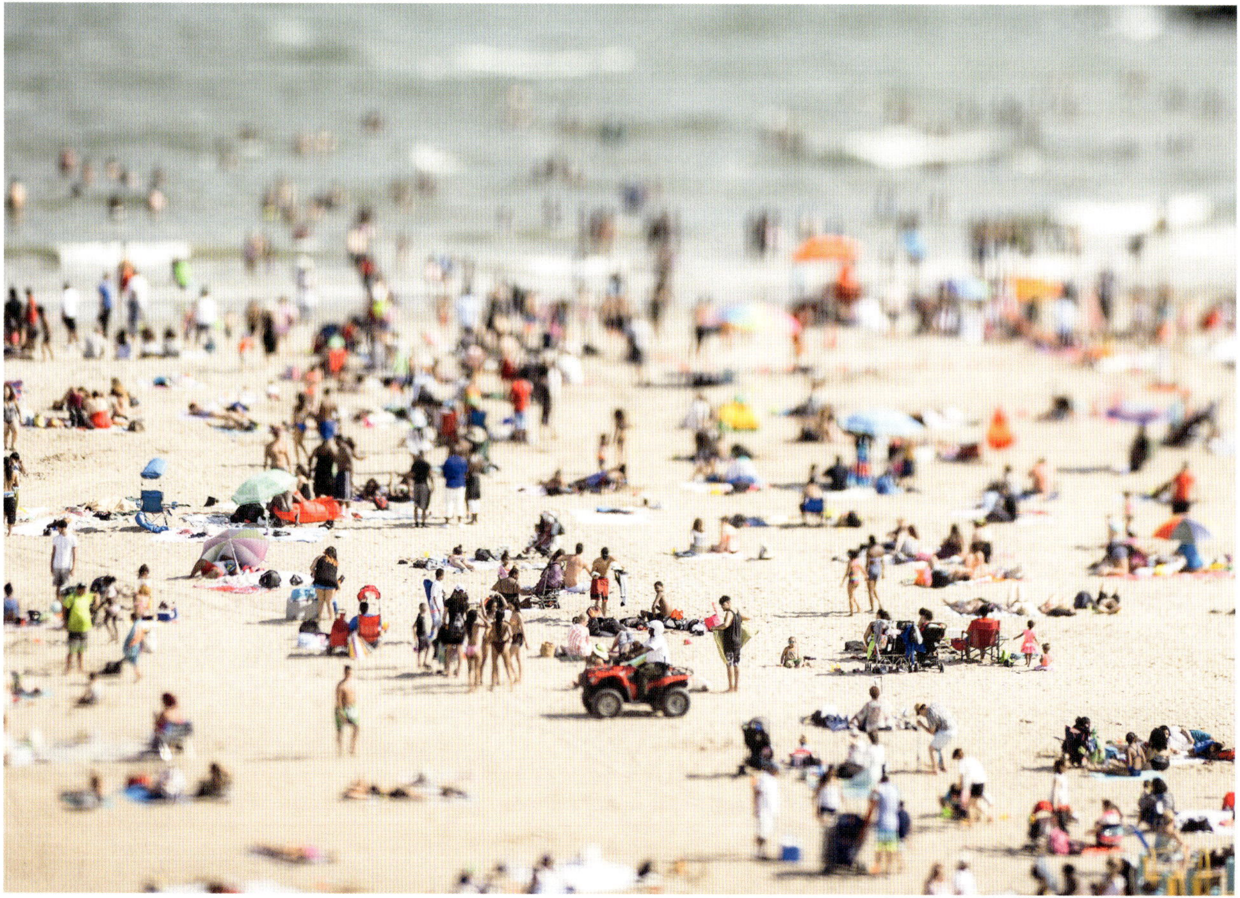

Coney Island Beach

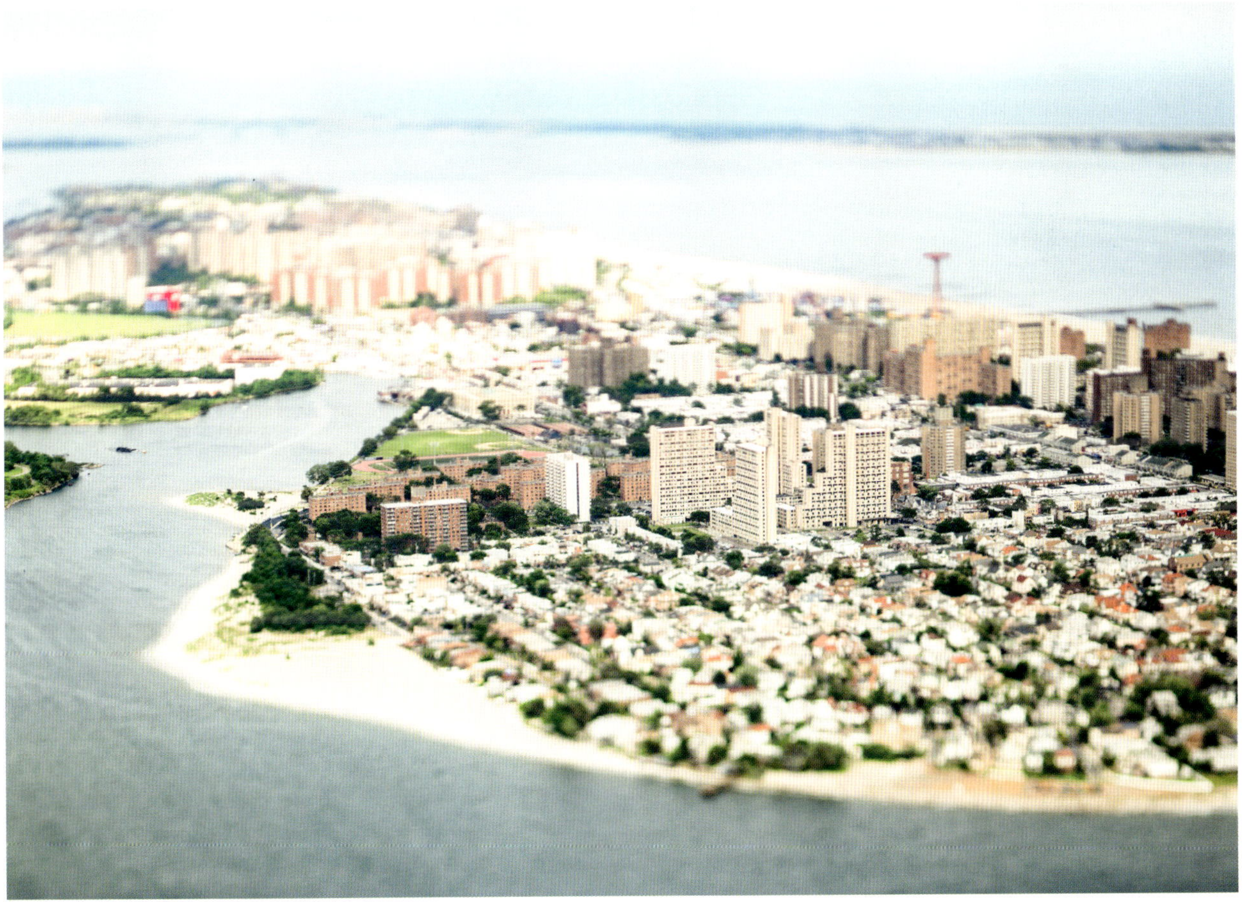

Seagate, Brooklyn

New York is the biggest collection of villages in the world.

Alistair Cooke

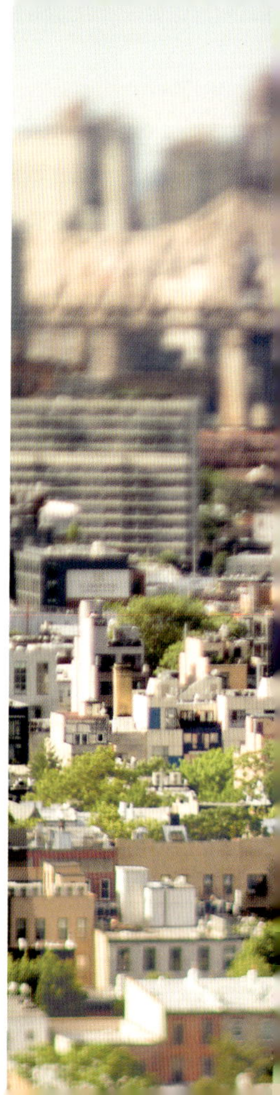

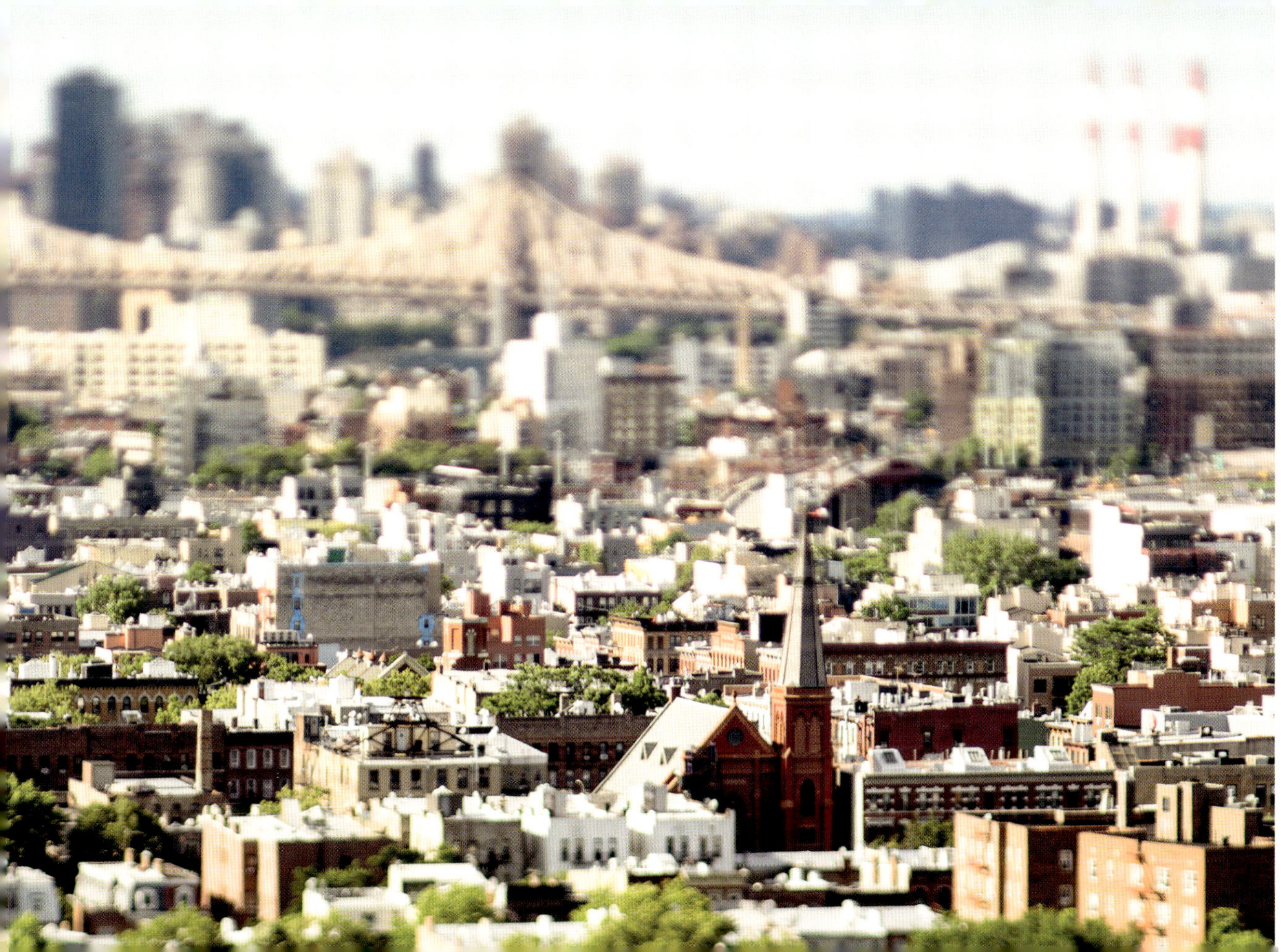

Greenpoint, Brooklyn

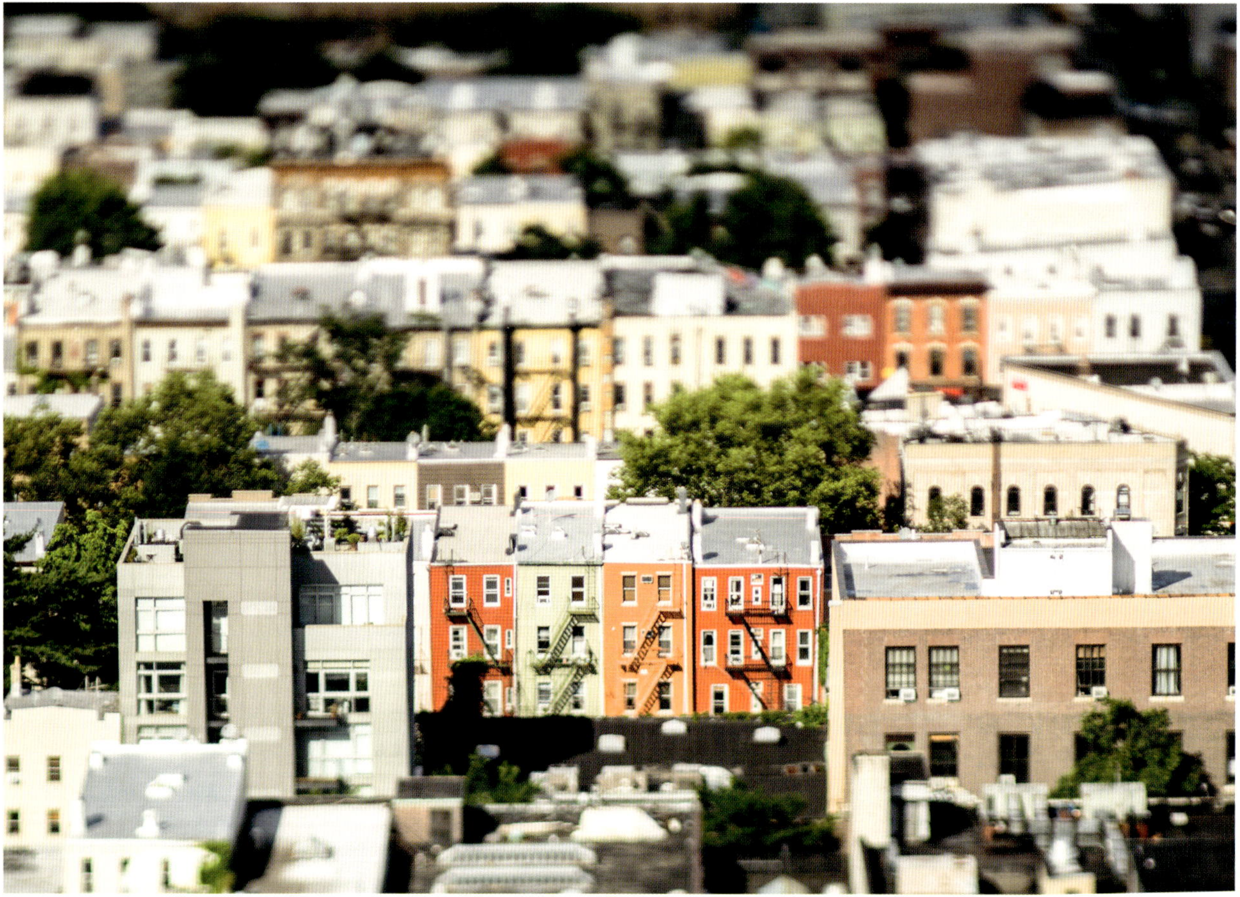

Greenpoint, Brooklyn

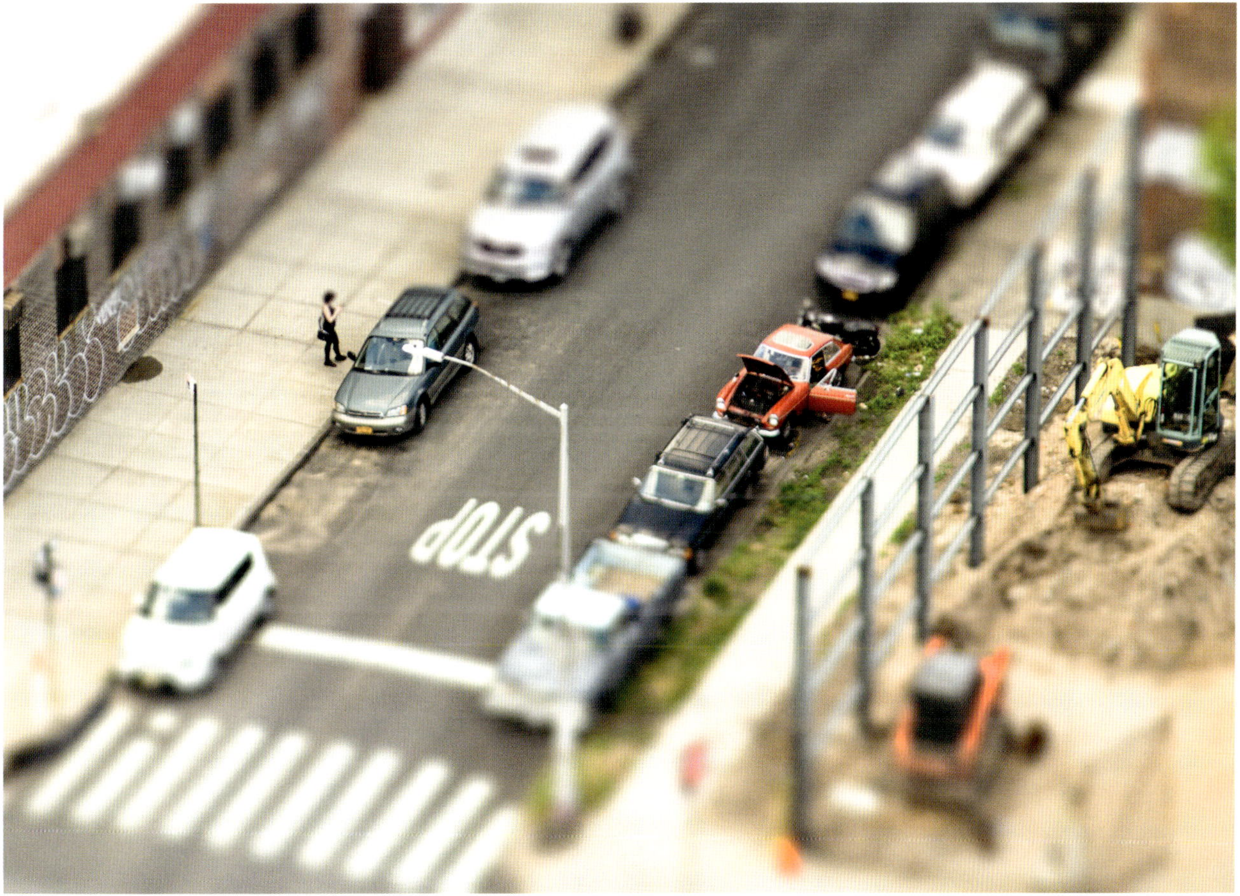

Greenpoint, Brooklyn

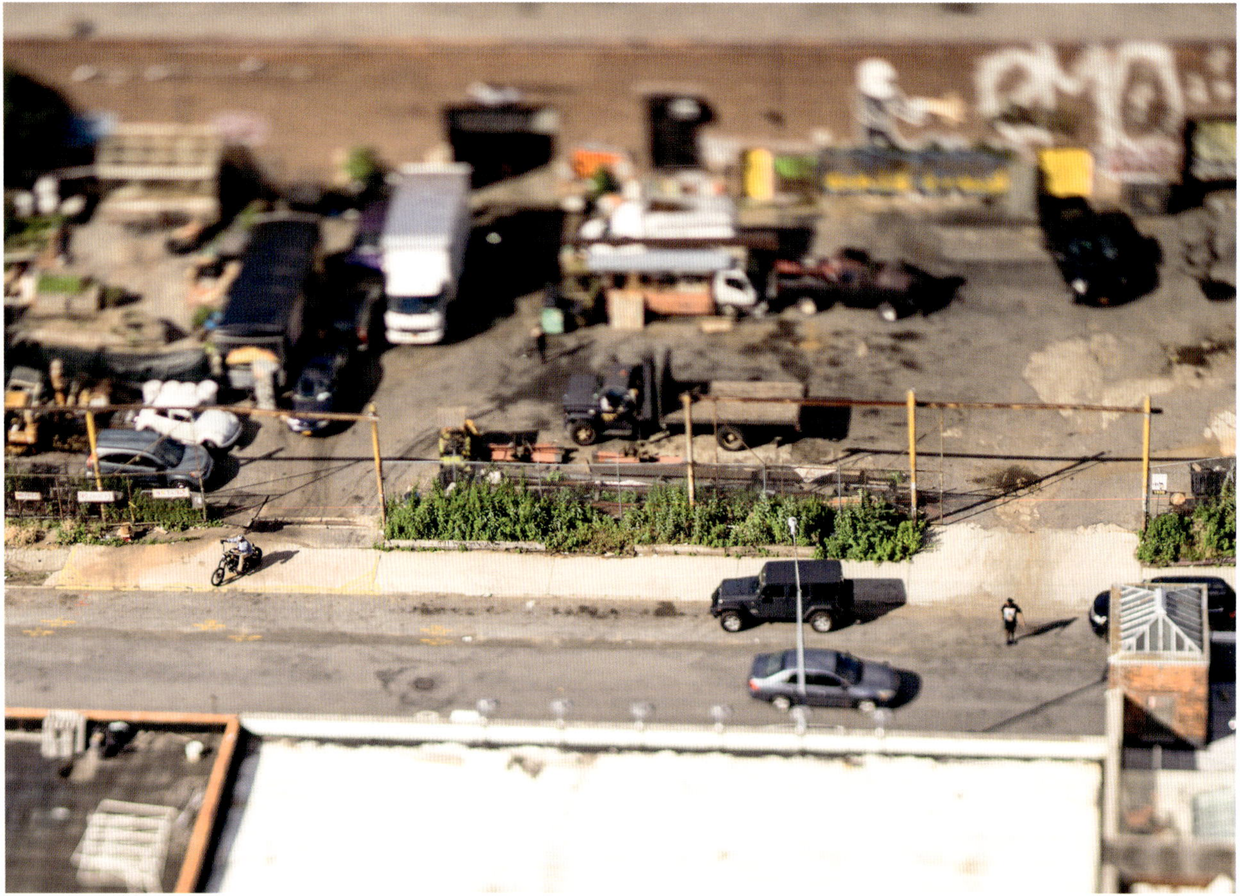

Greenpoint, Brooklyn

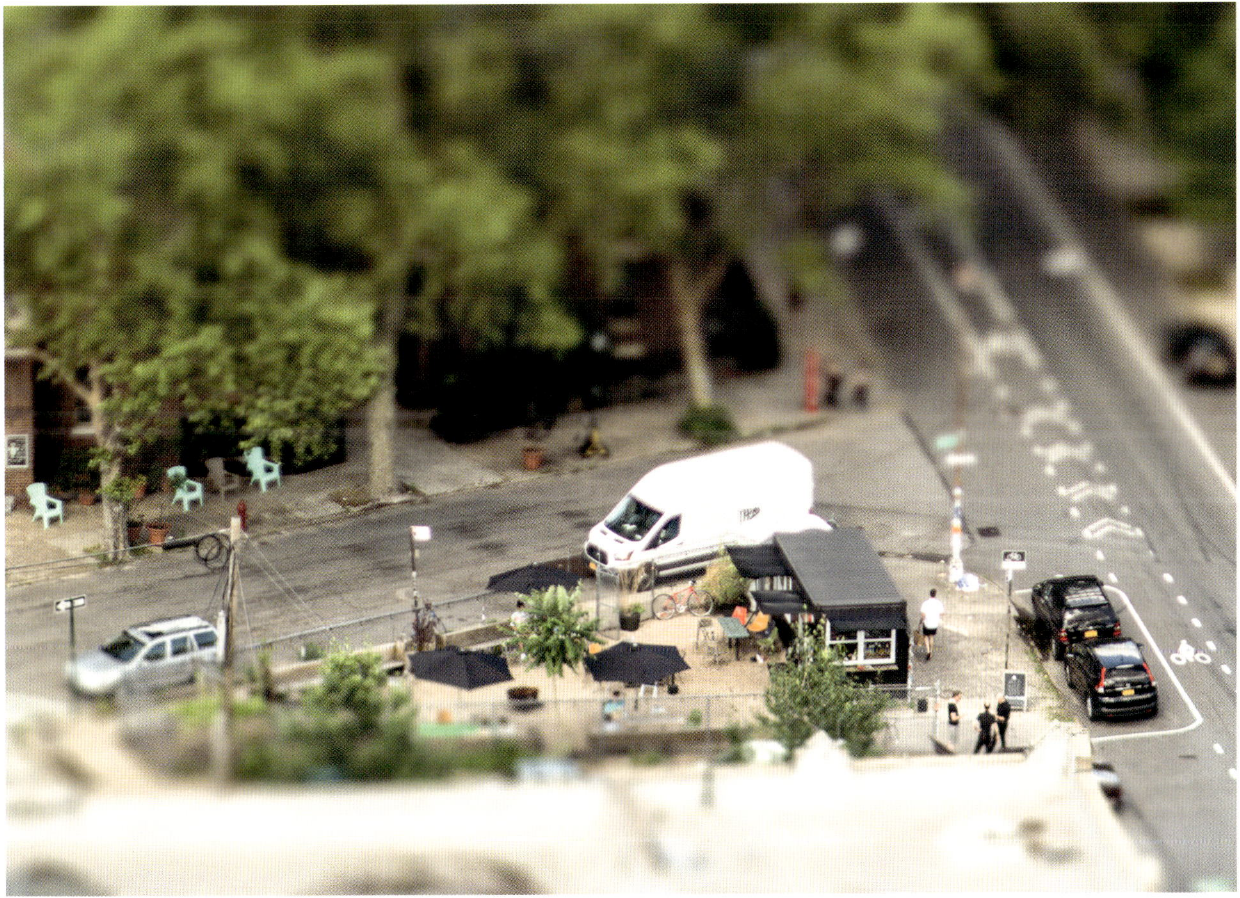

The Lot, Brooklyn

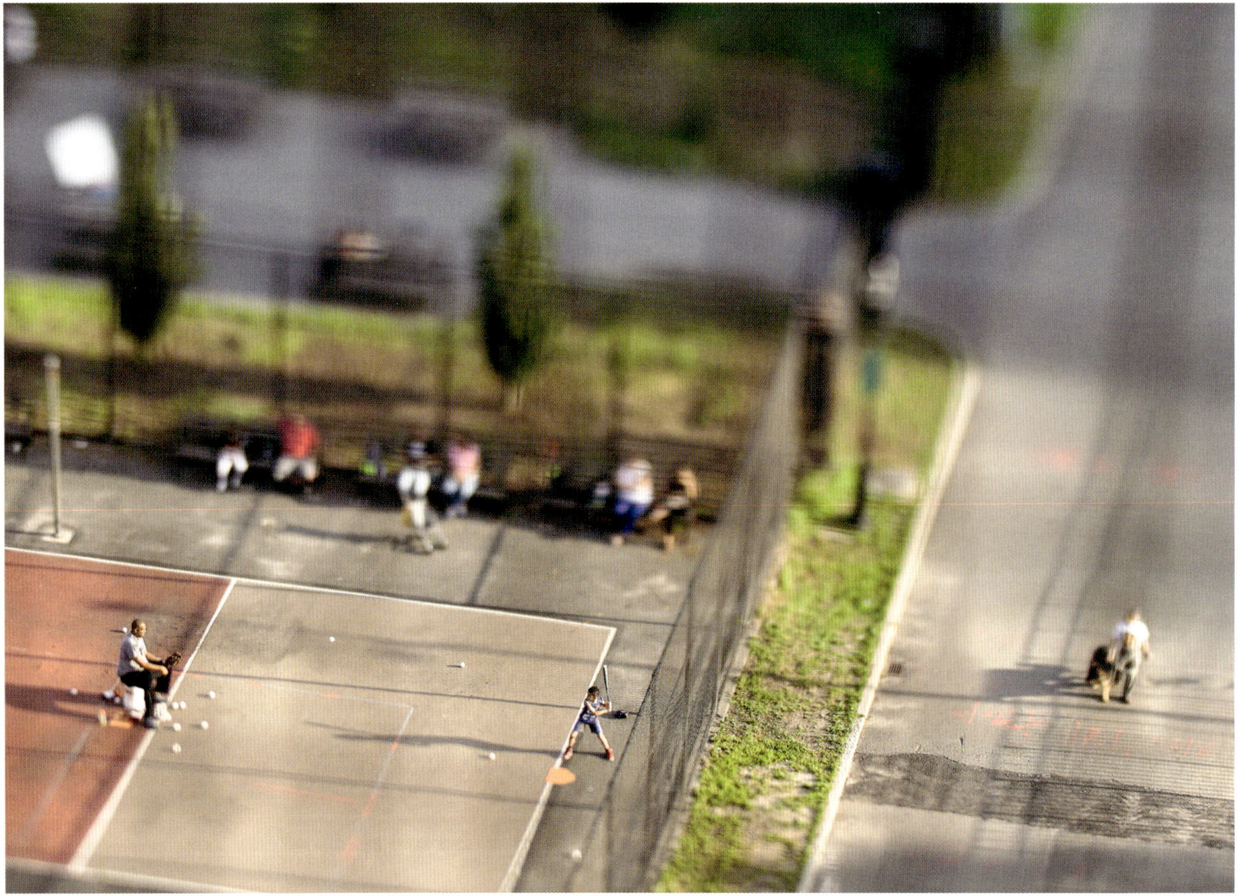

East River Park

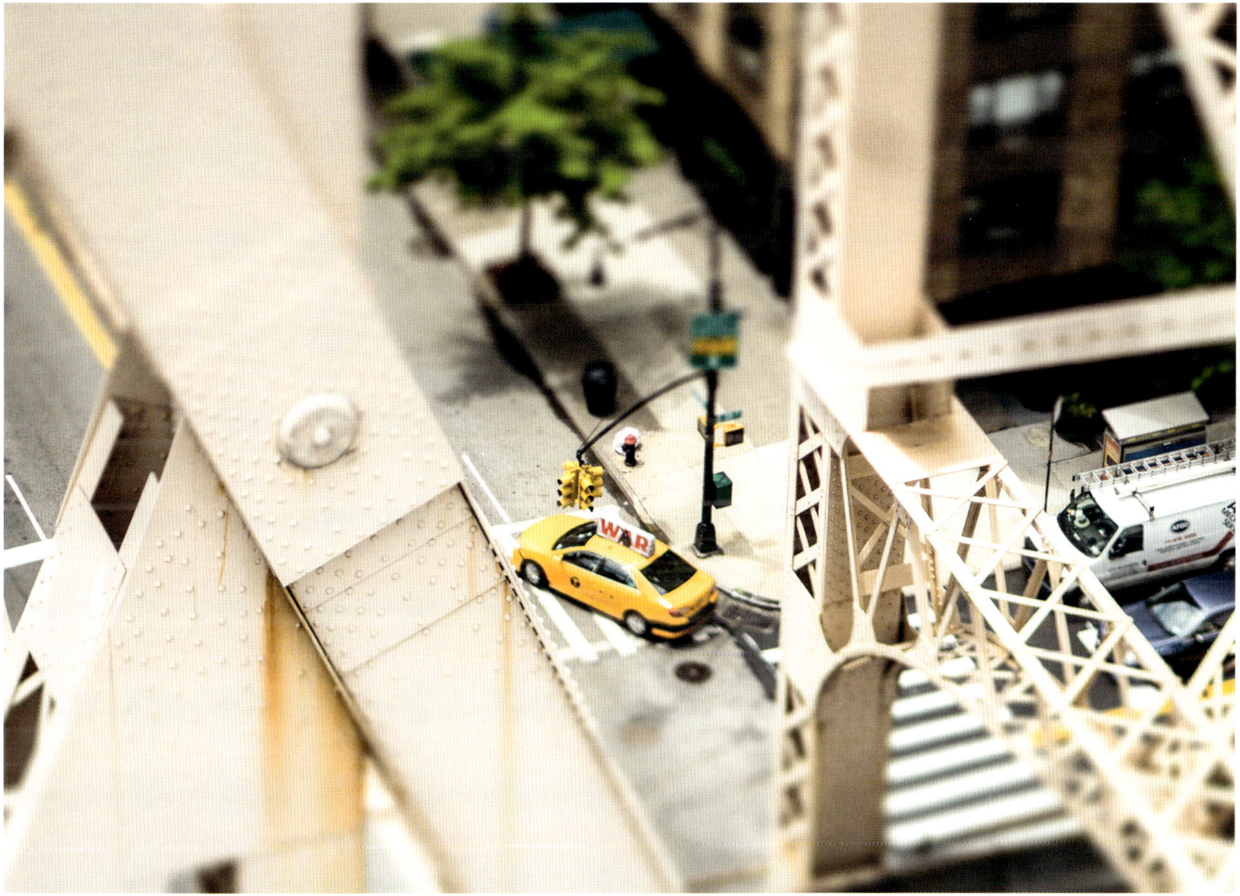

59th Street

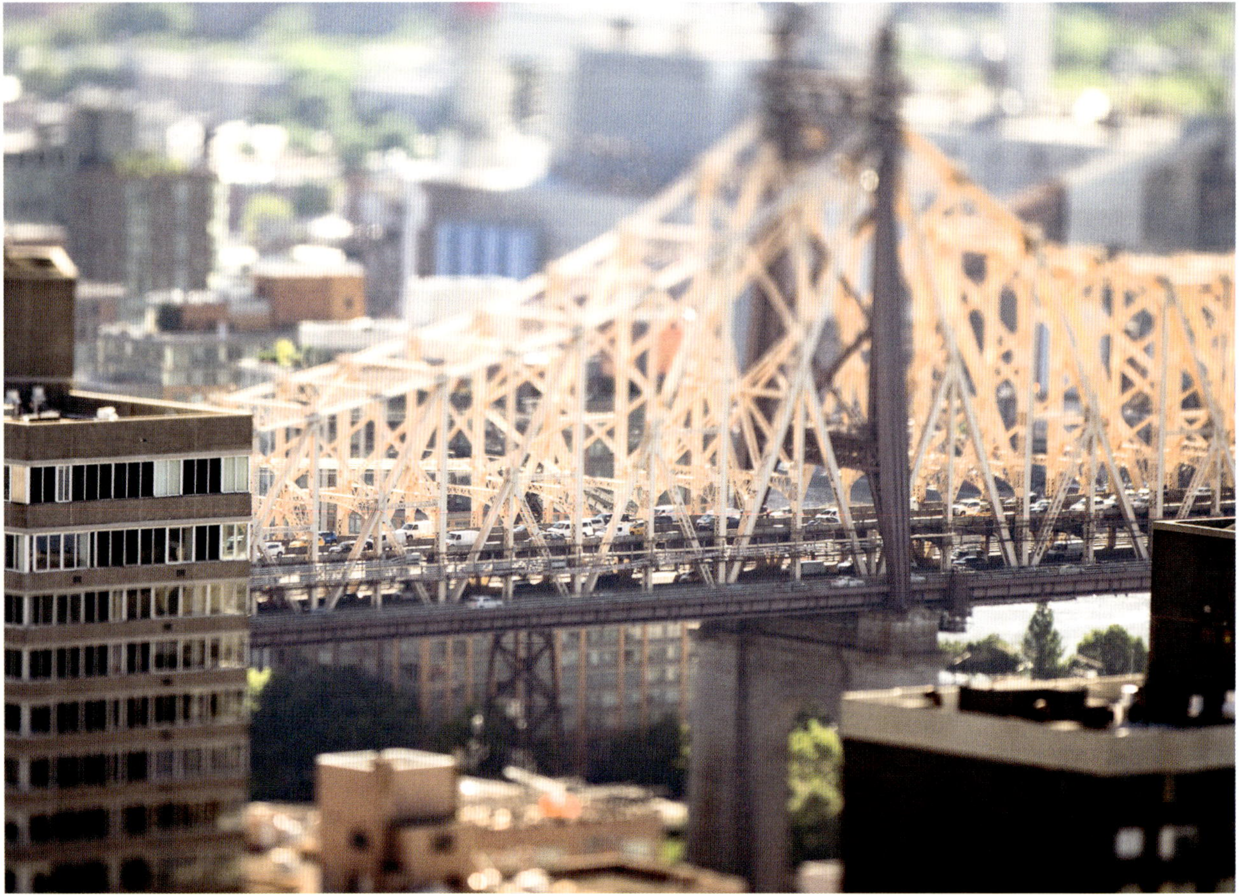

Queensborough Bridge

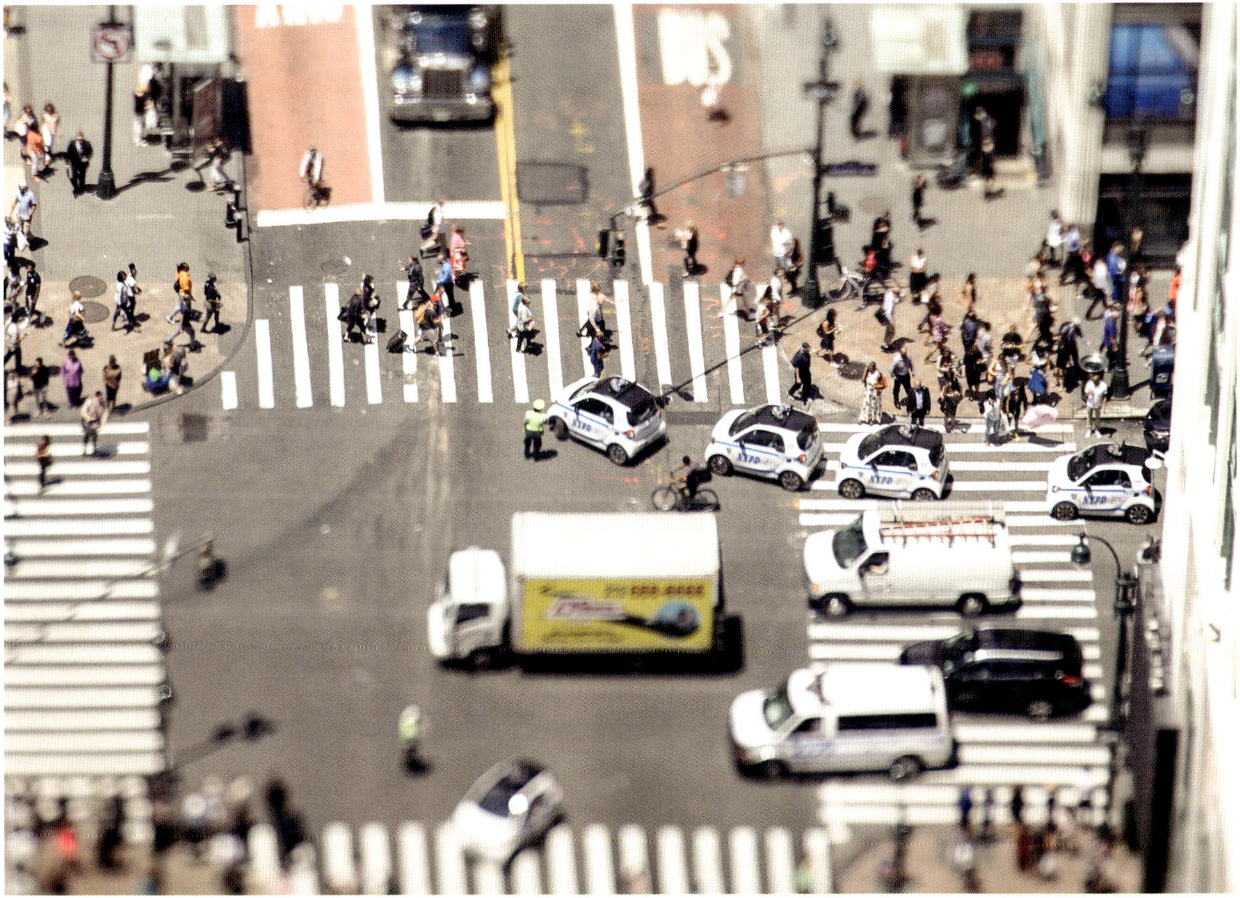

Midtown Manhattan

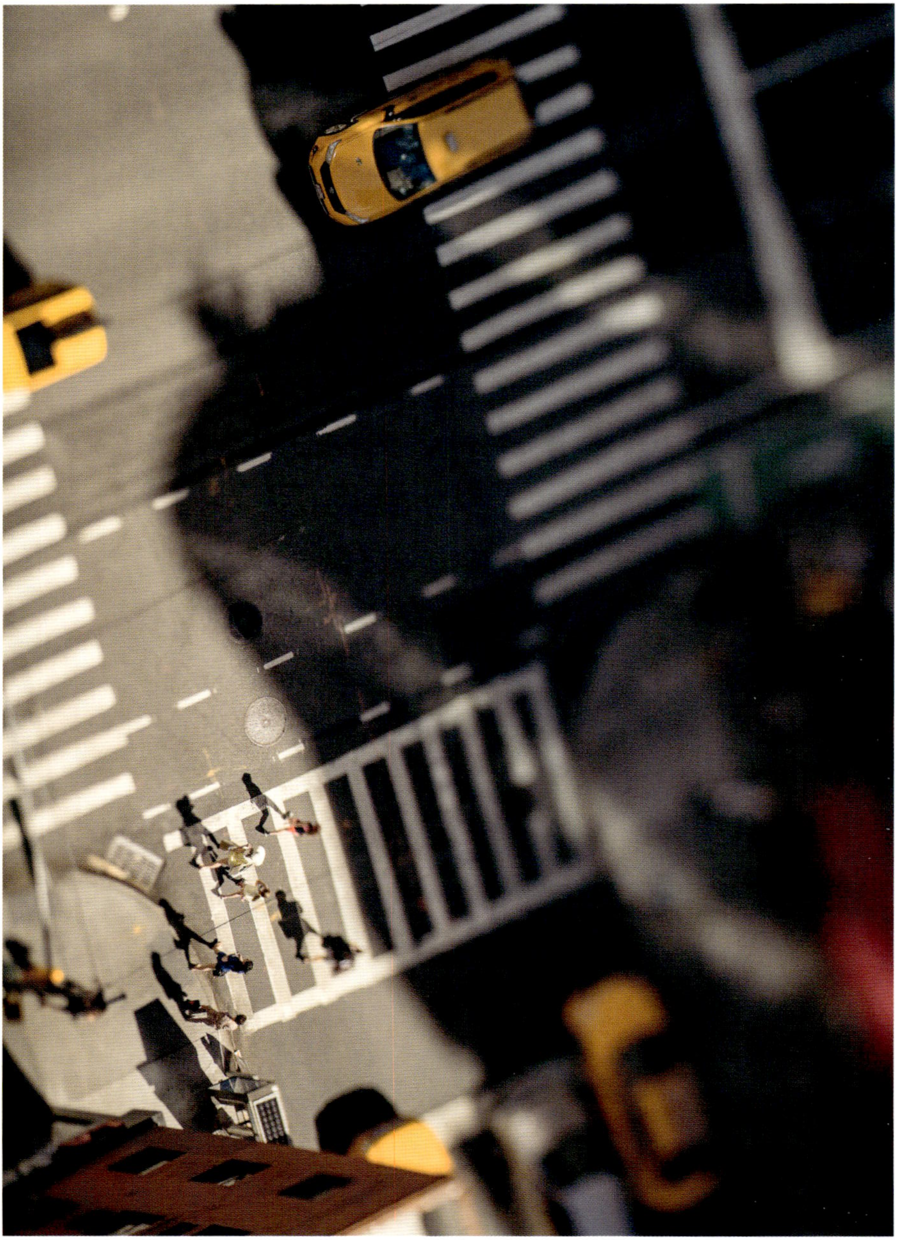

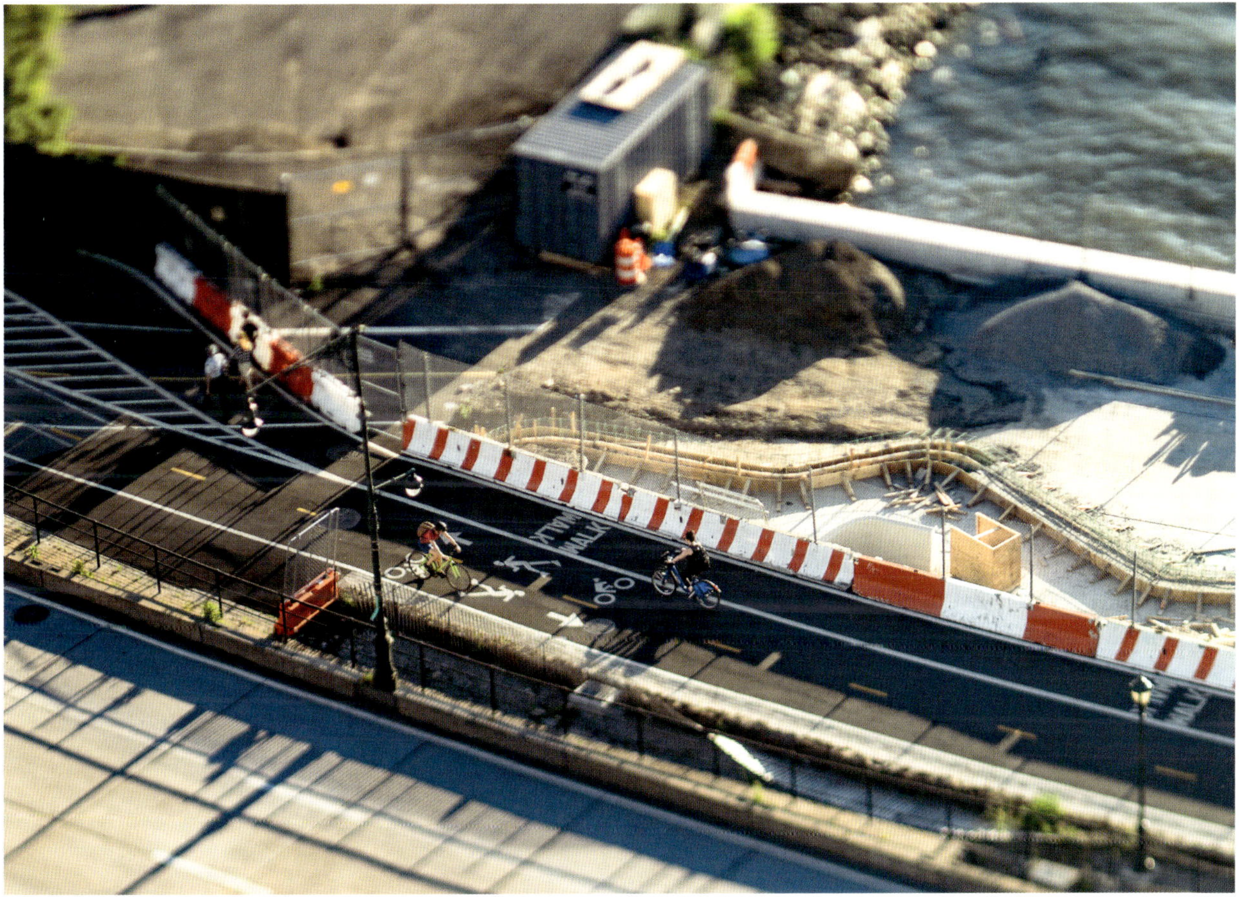

Hudson River Greenway

It was never built for the comfort
and happiness of its citizens,
but to astonish the world.

Susan Ertz

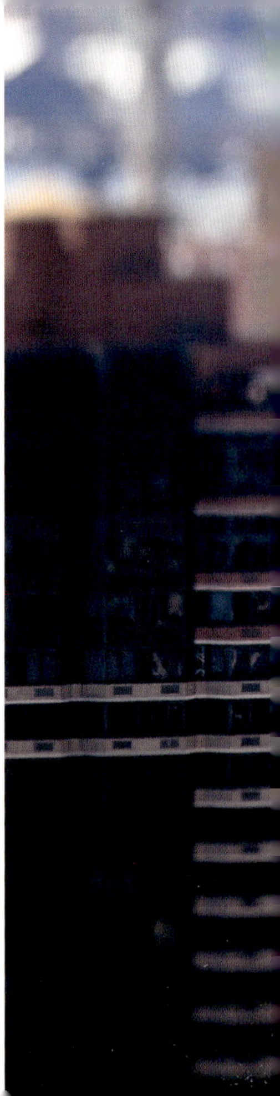

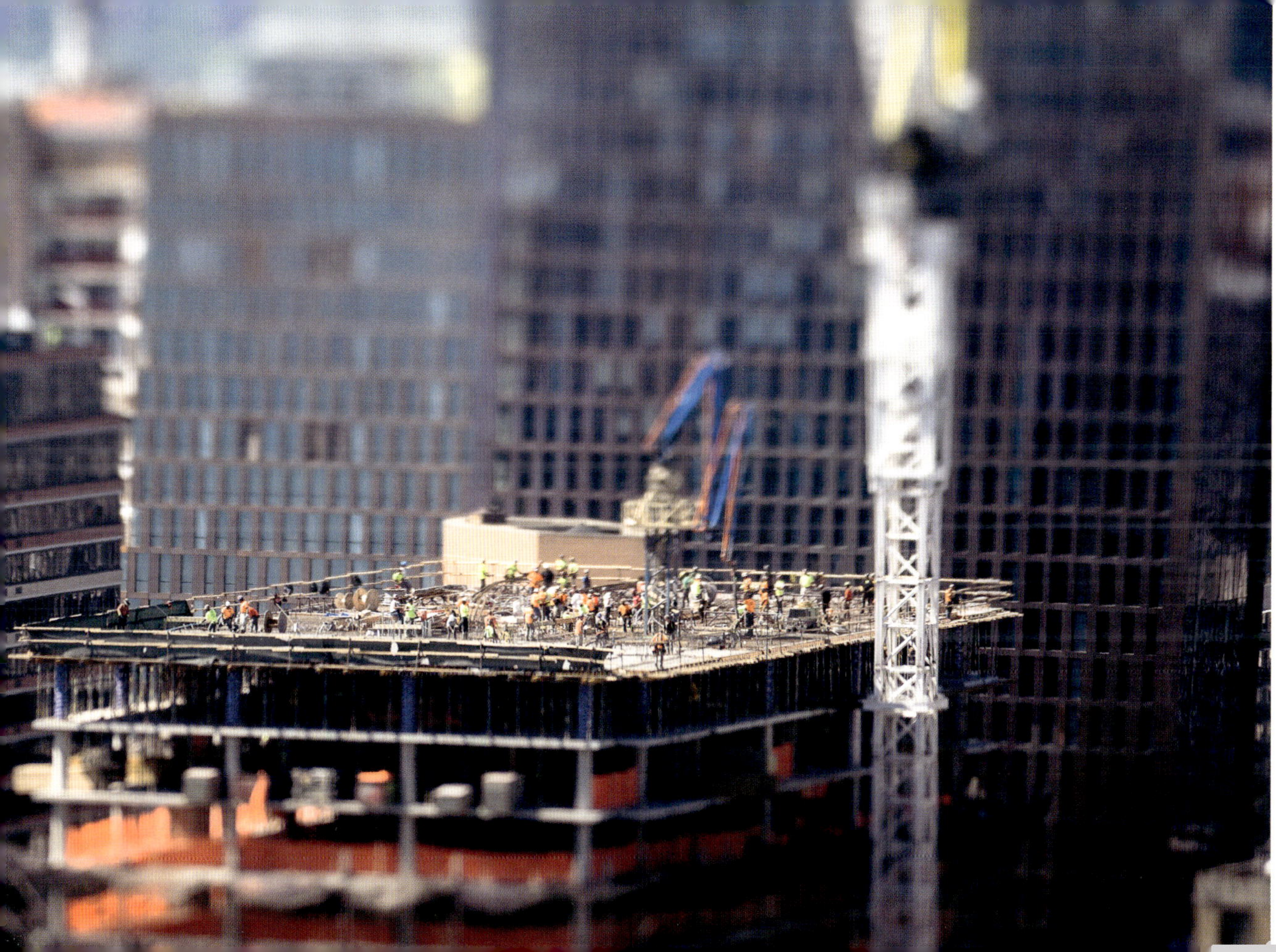

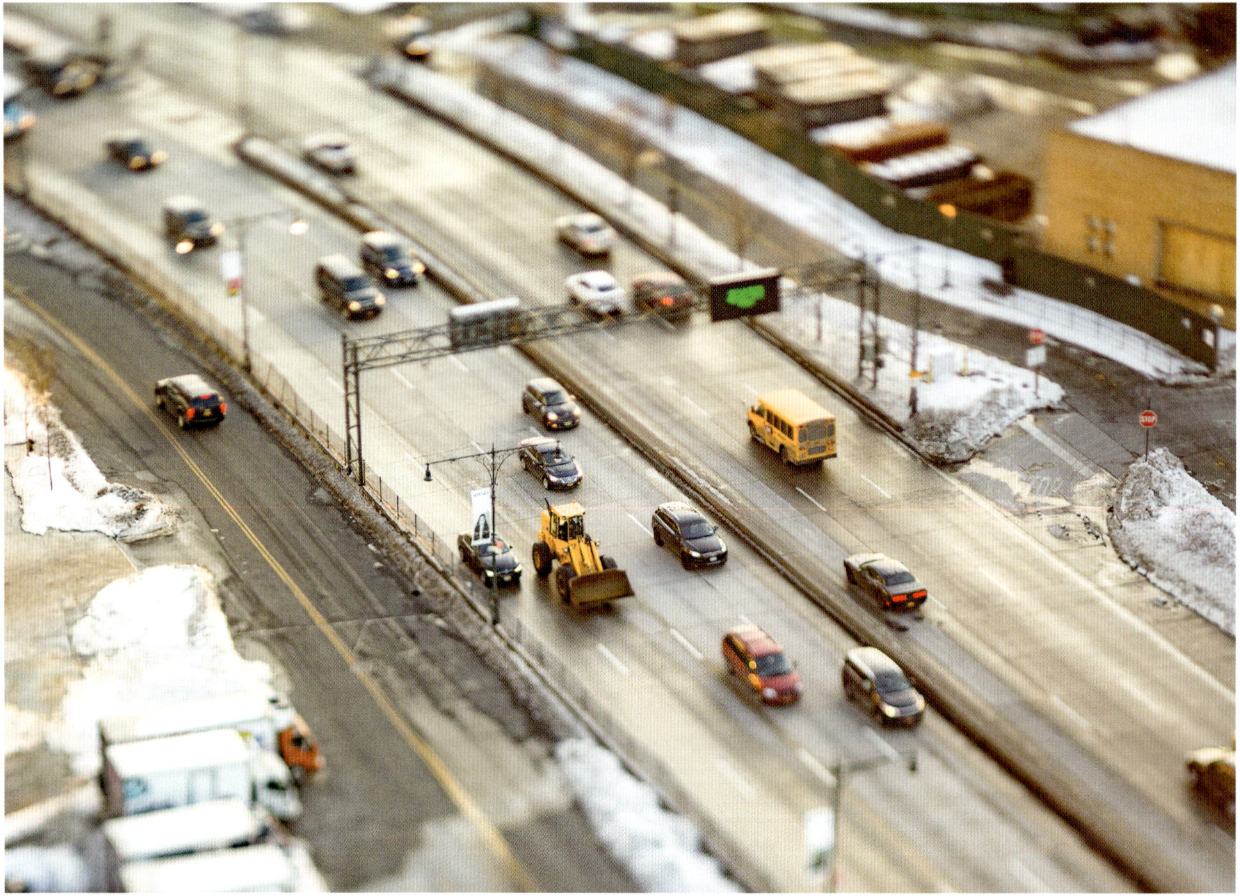

1st Ave

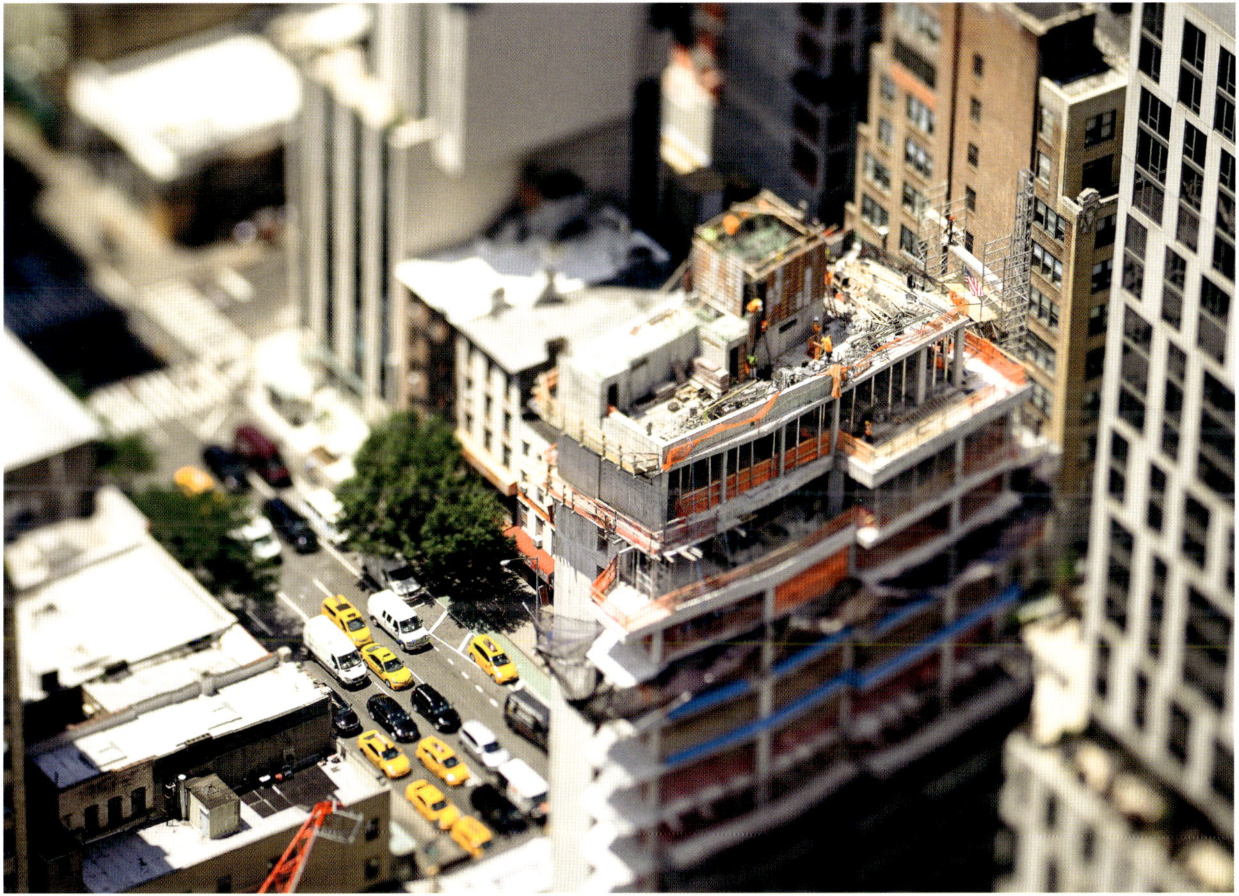

6th Ave

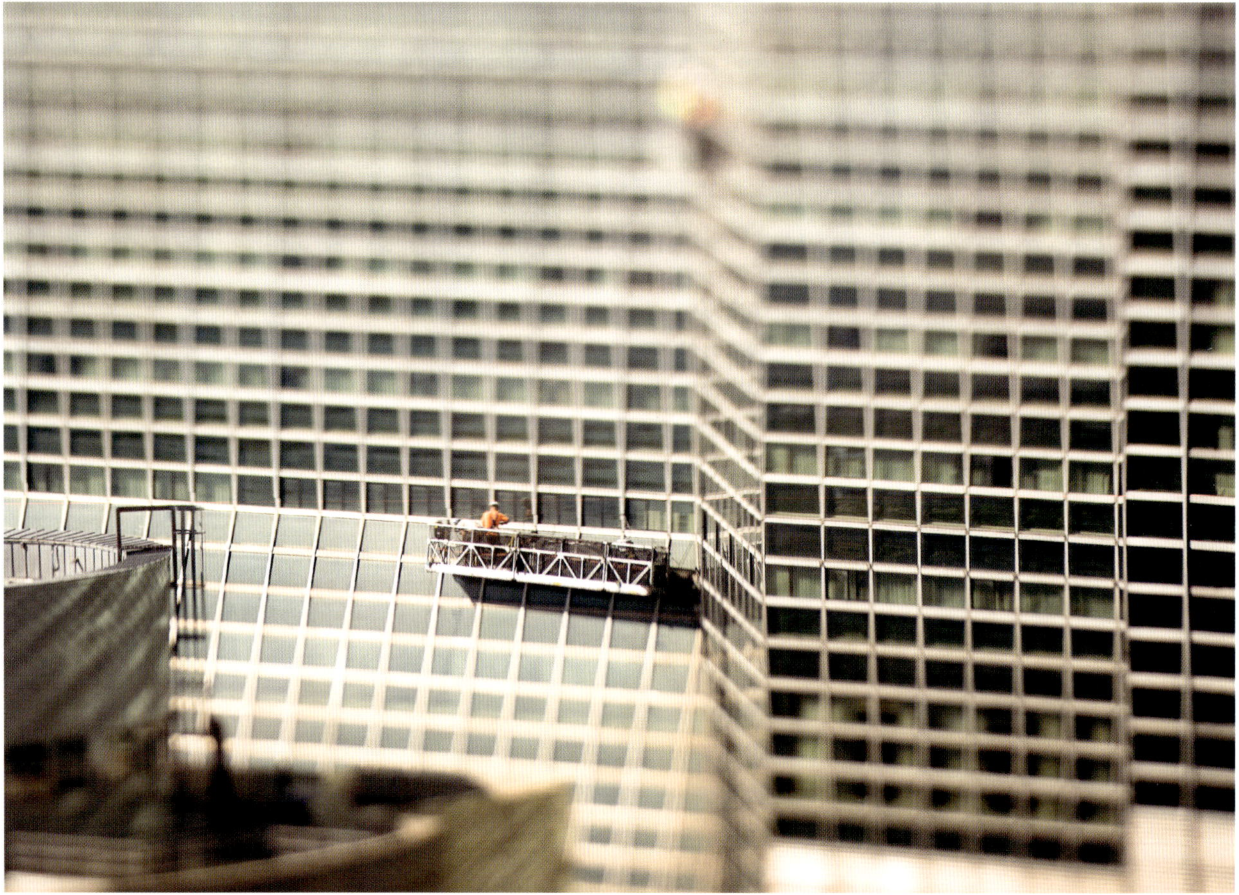

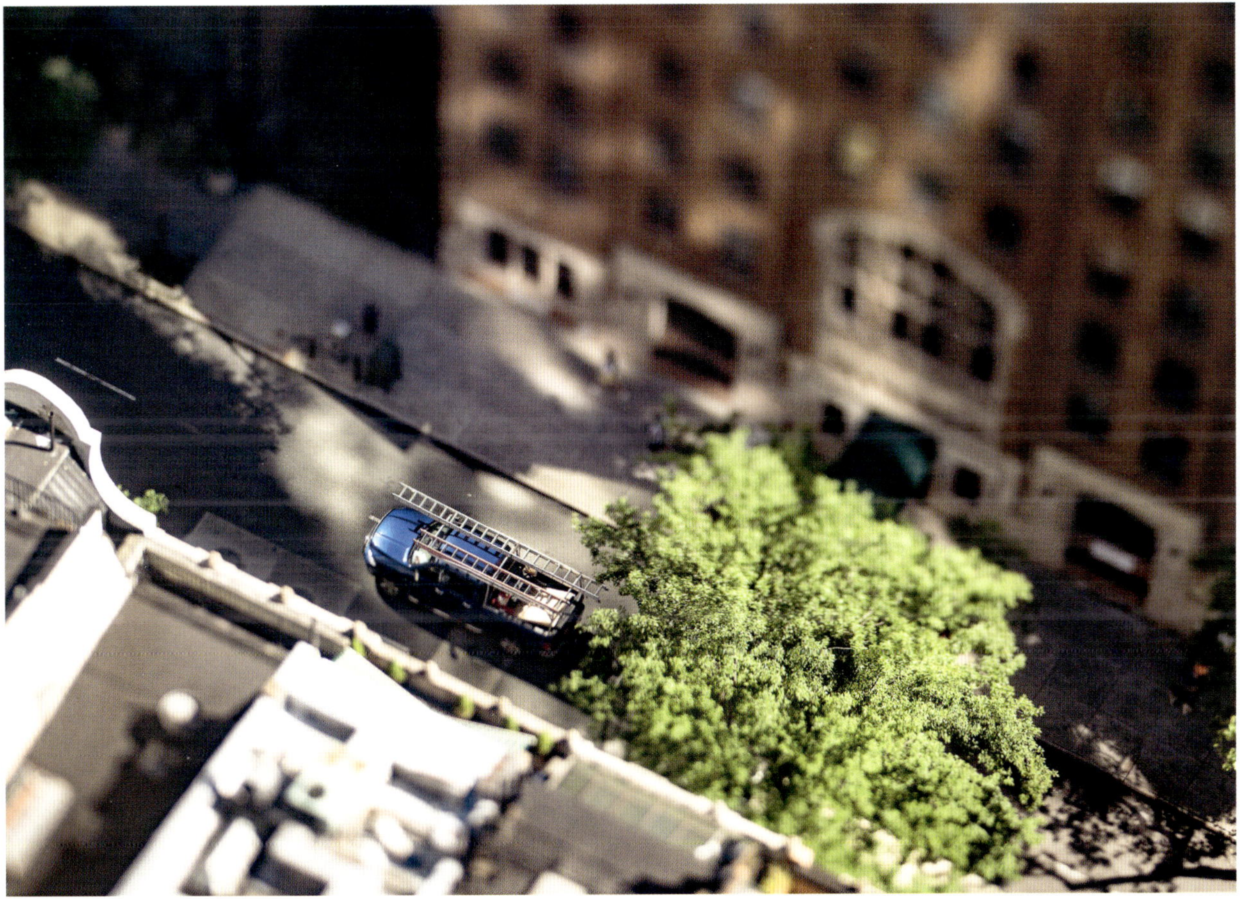

Midtown East

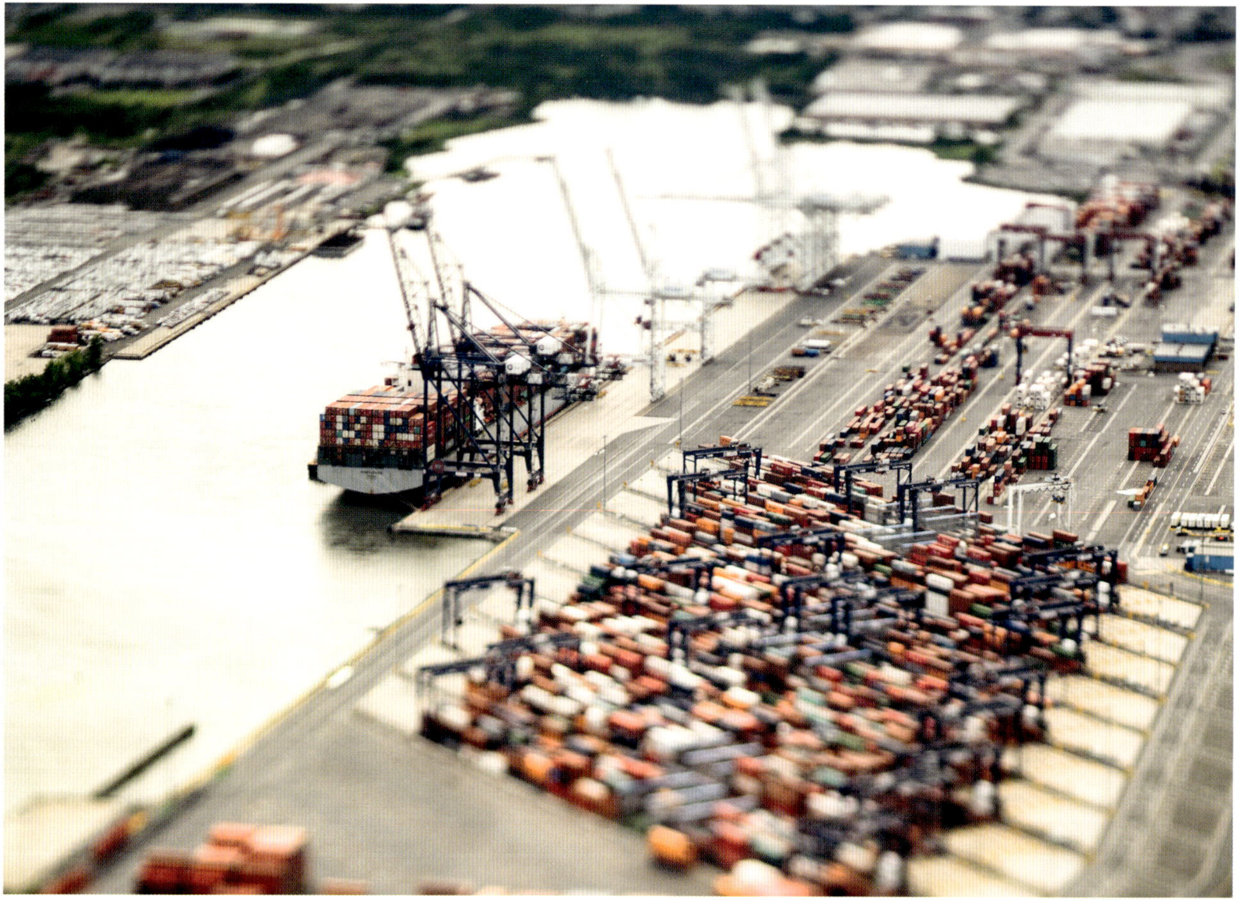

Bayonne, New Jersey

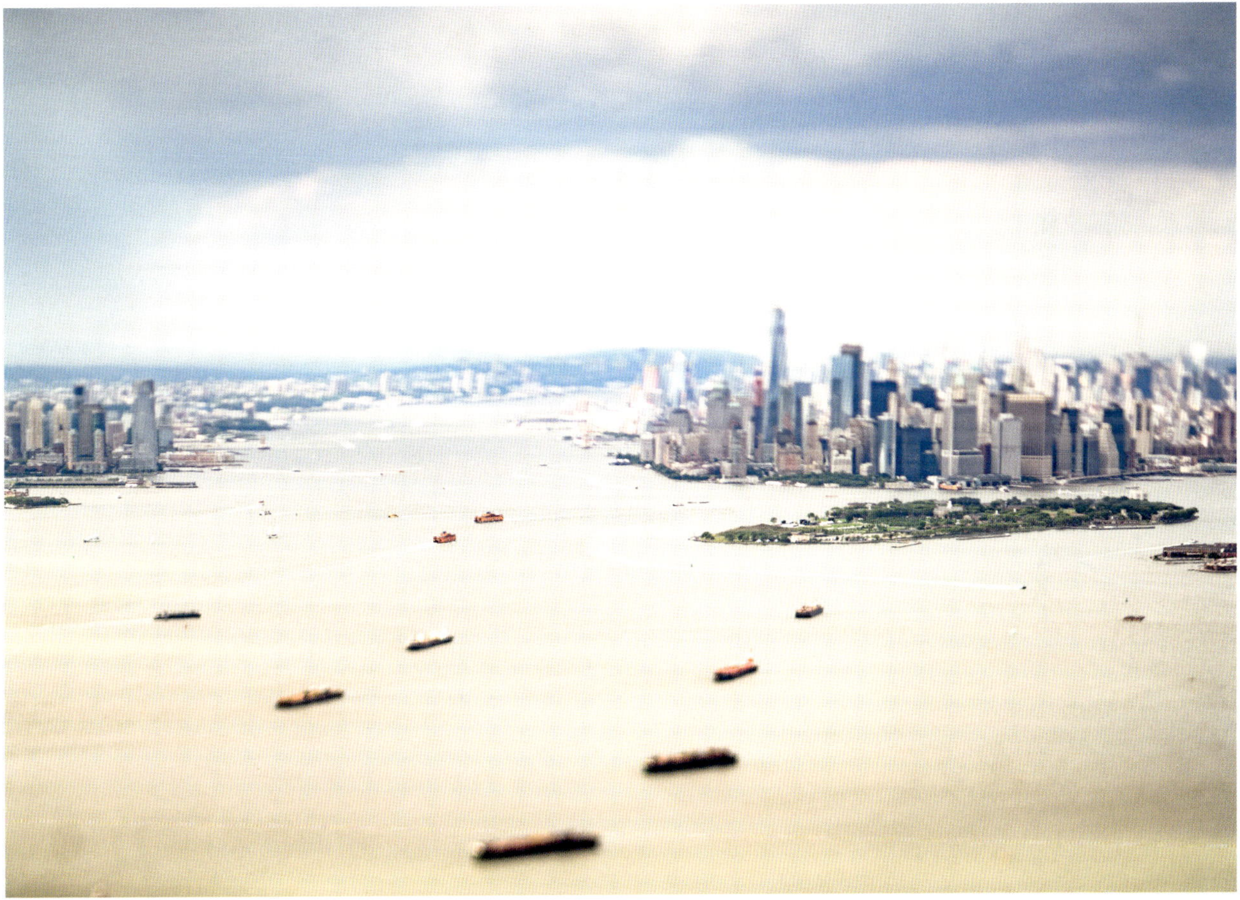

Upper Bay

Paulus Hook, New Jersey

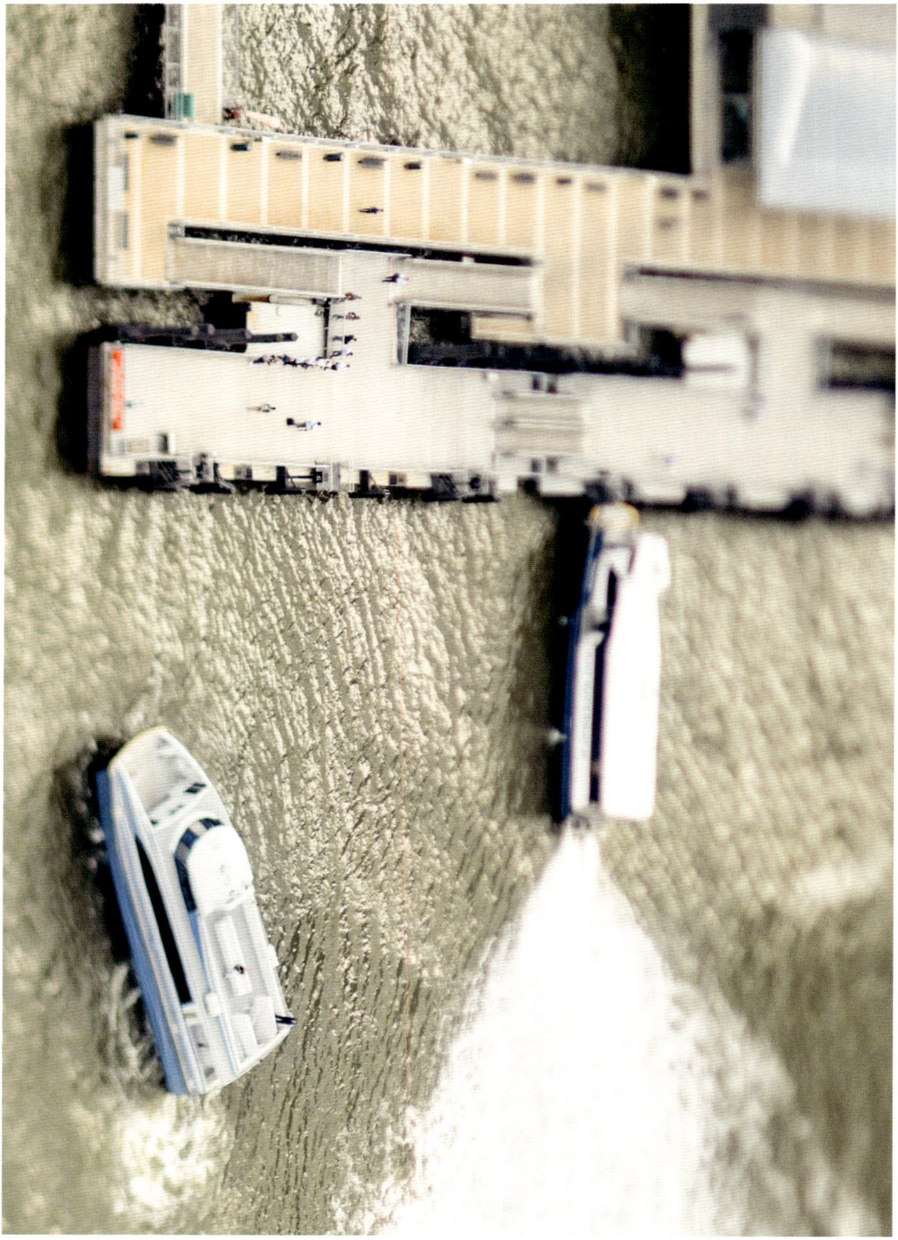

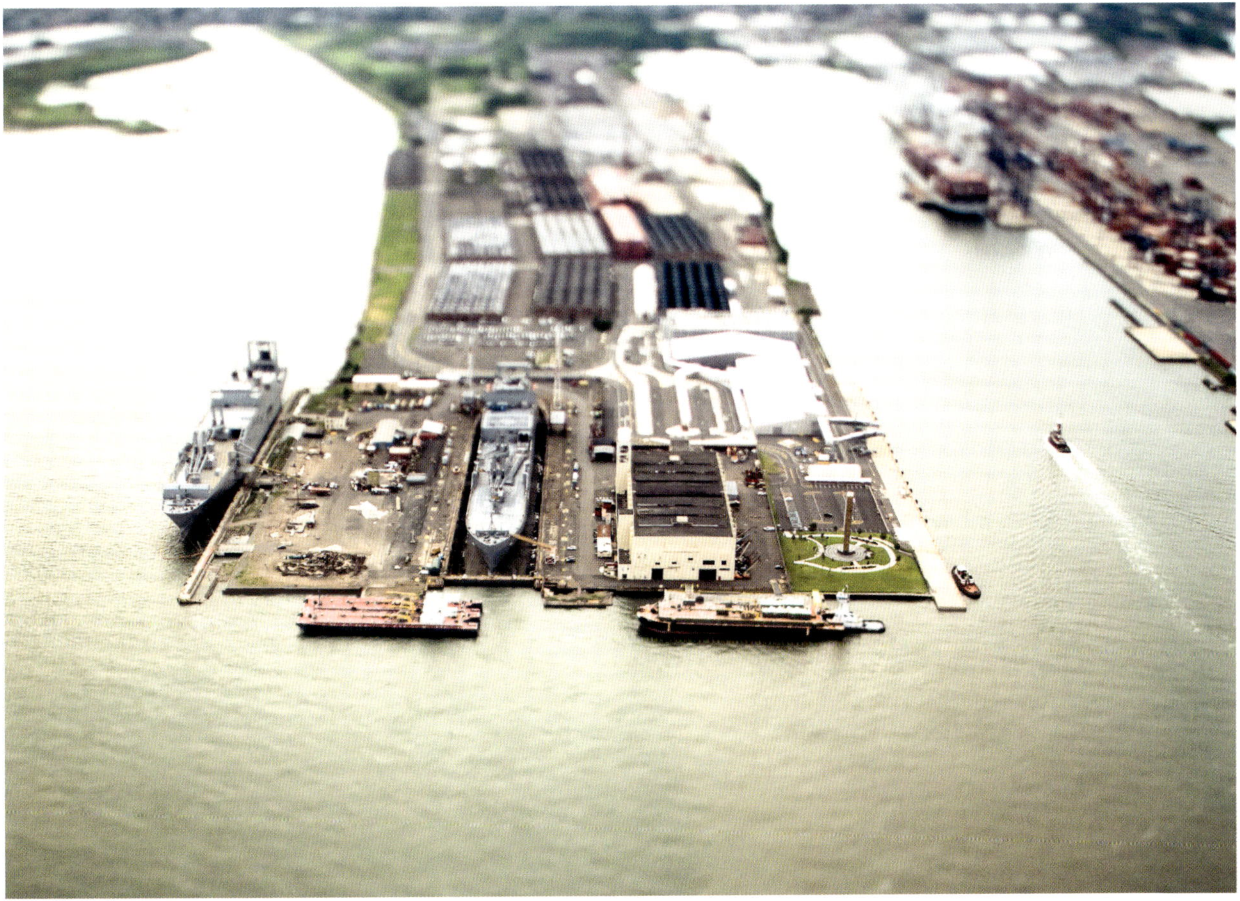

Bayonne, New Jersey

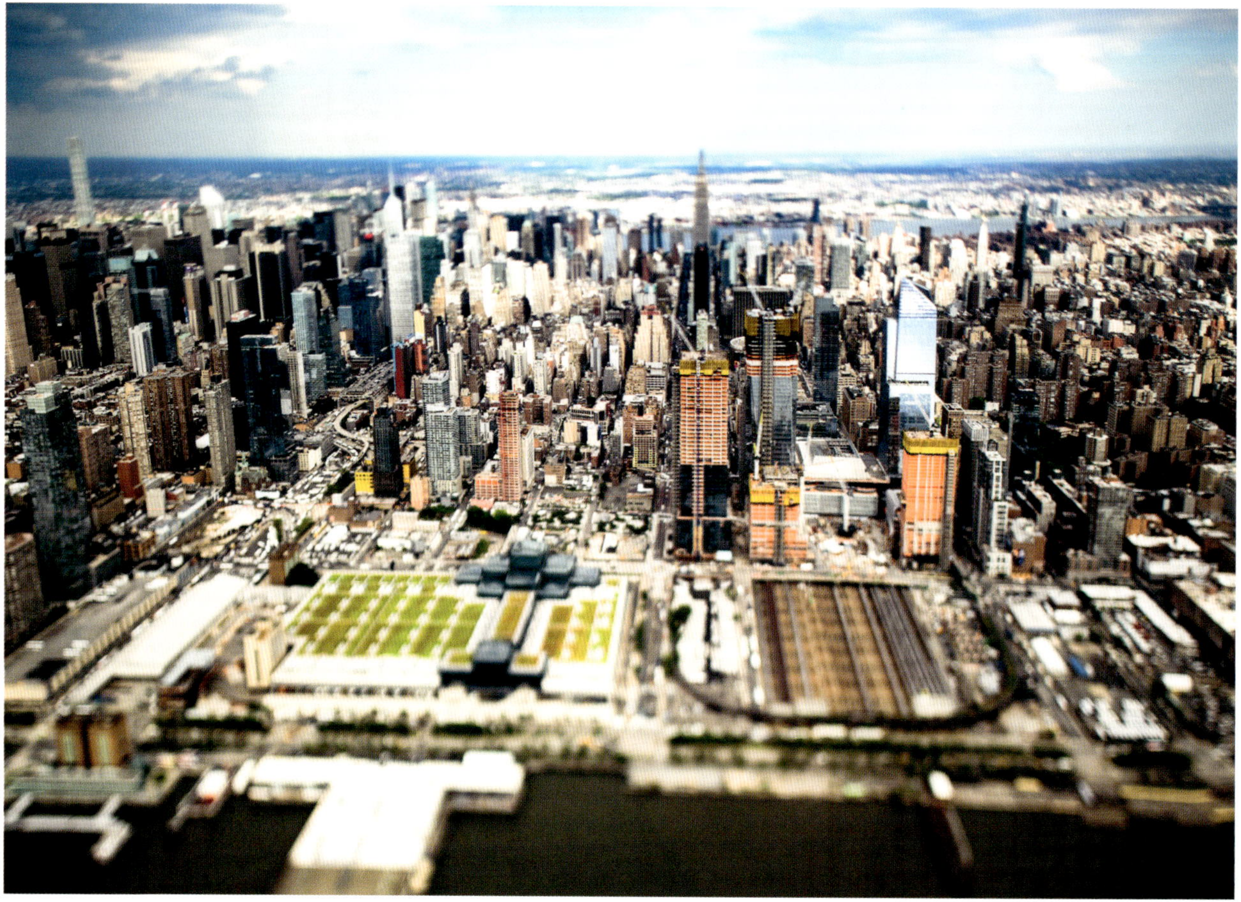

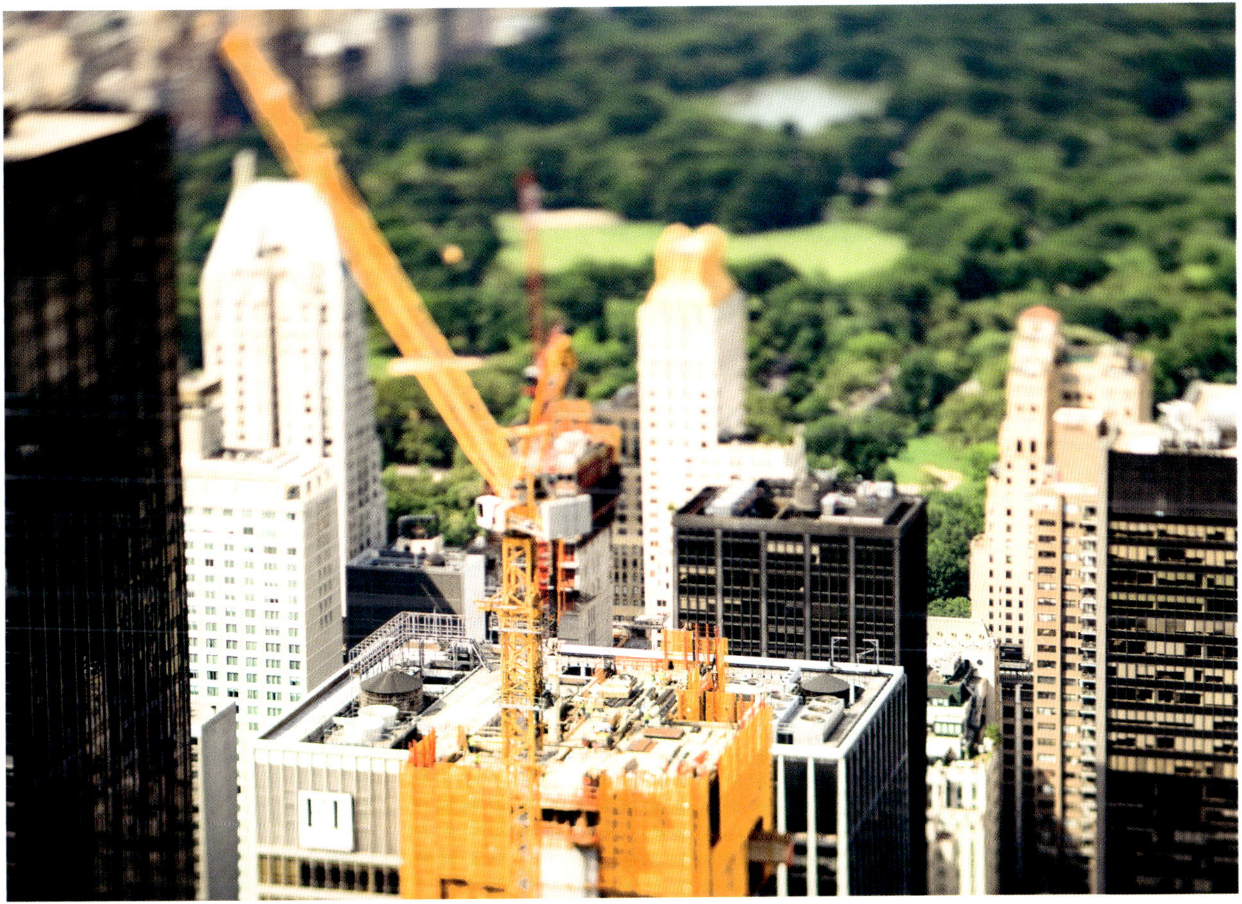

One belongs to New York instantly,
one belongs to it as much in five minutes
as in five years.

Tom Wolfe

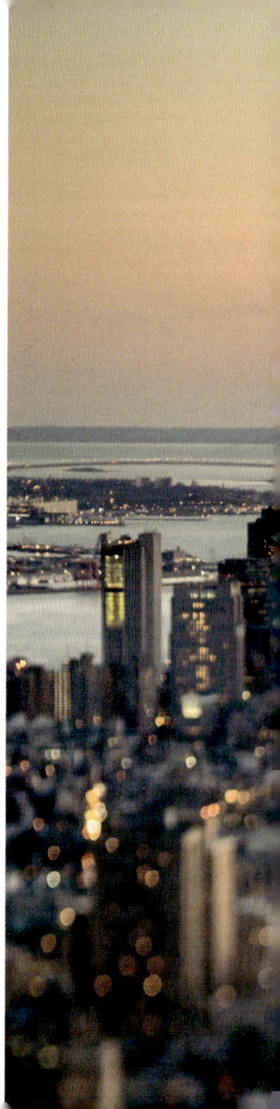

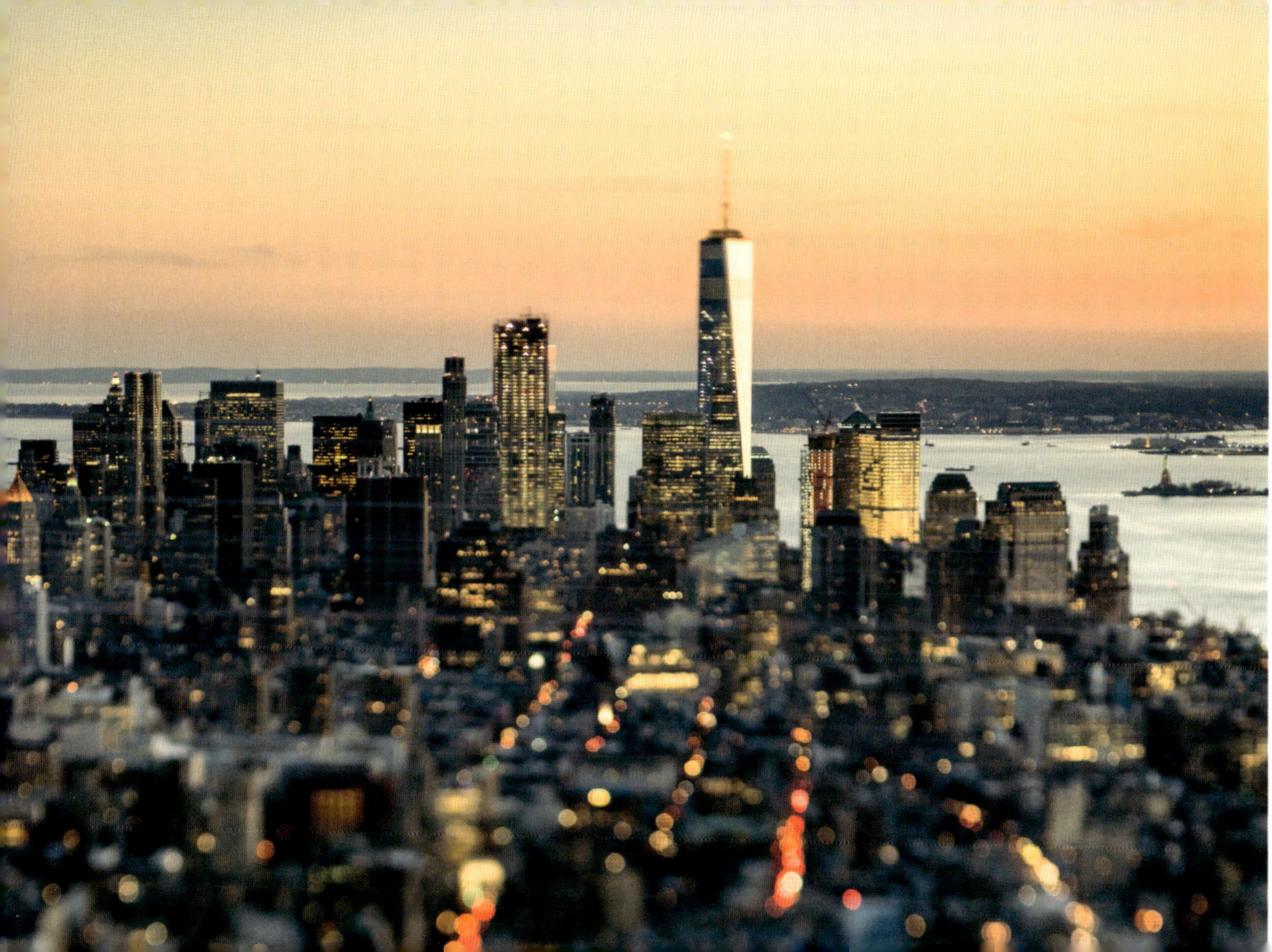

Lower Manhattan Skyline

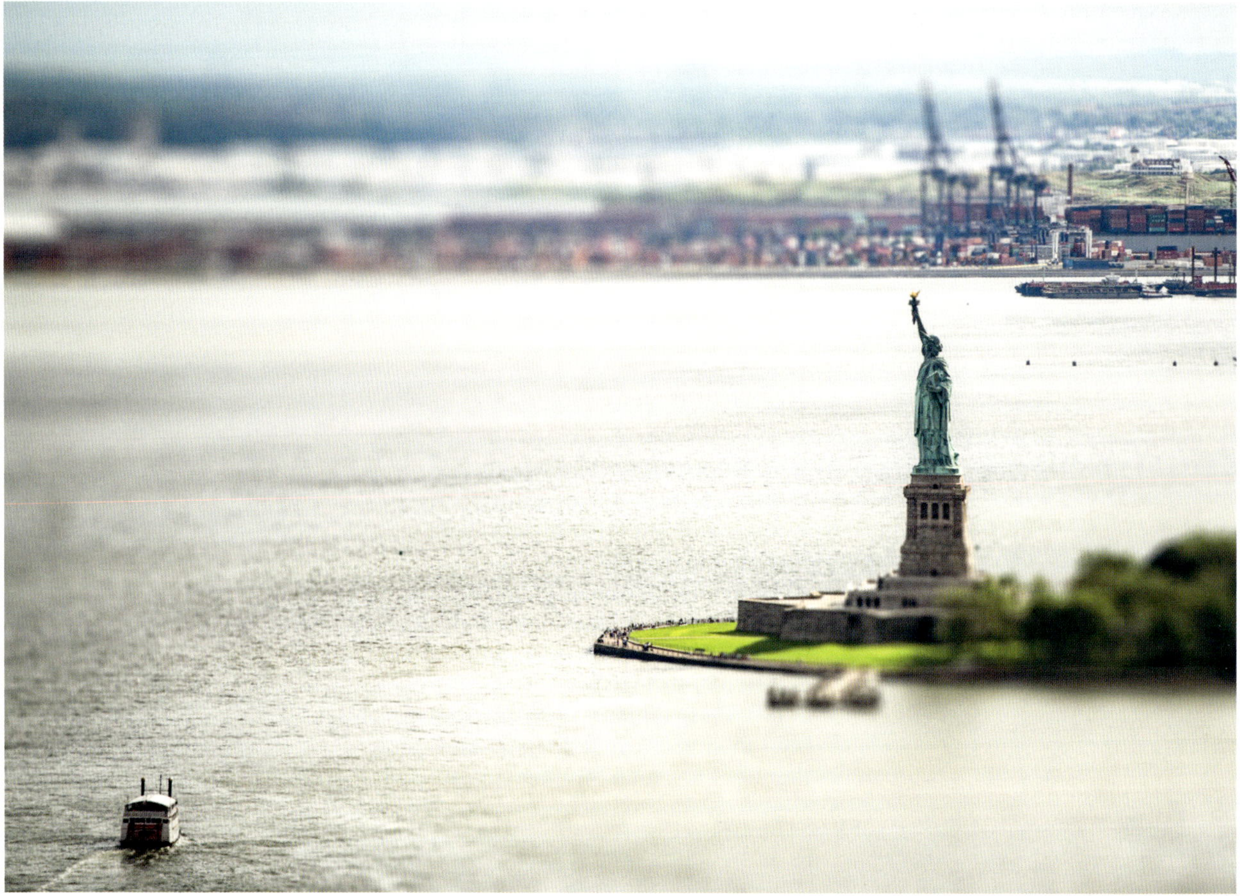

Statue of Liberty

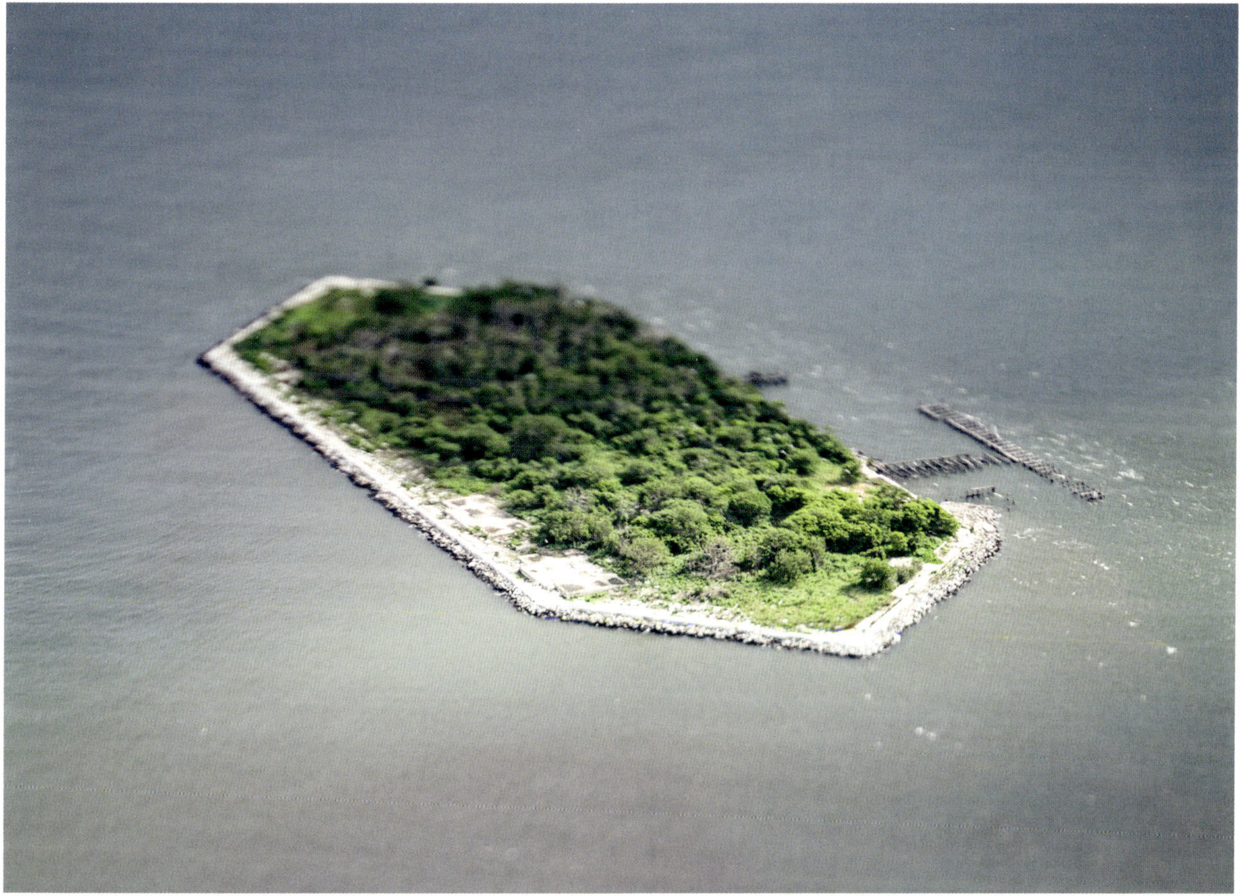

Hoffman Island

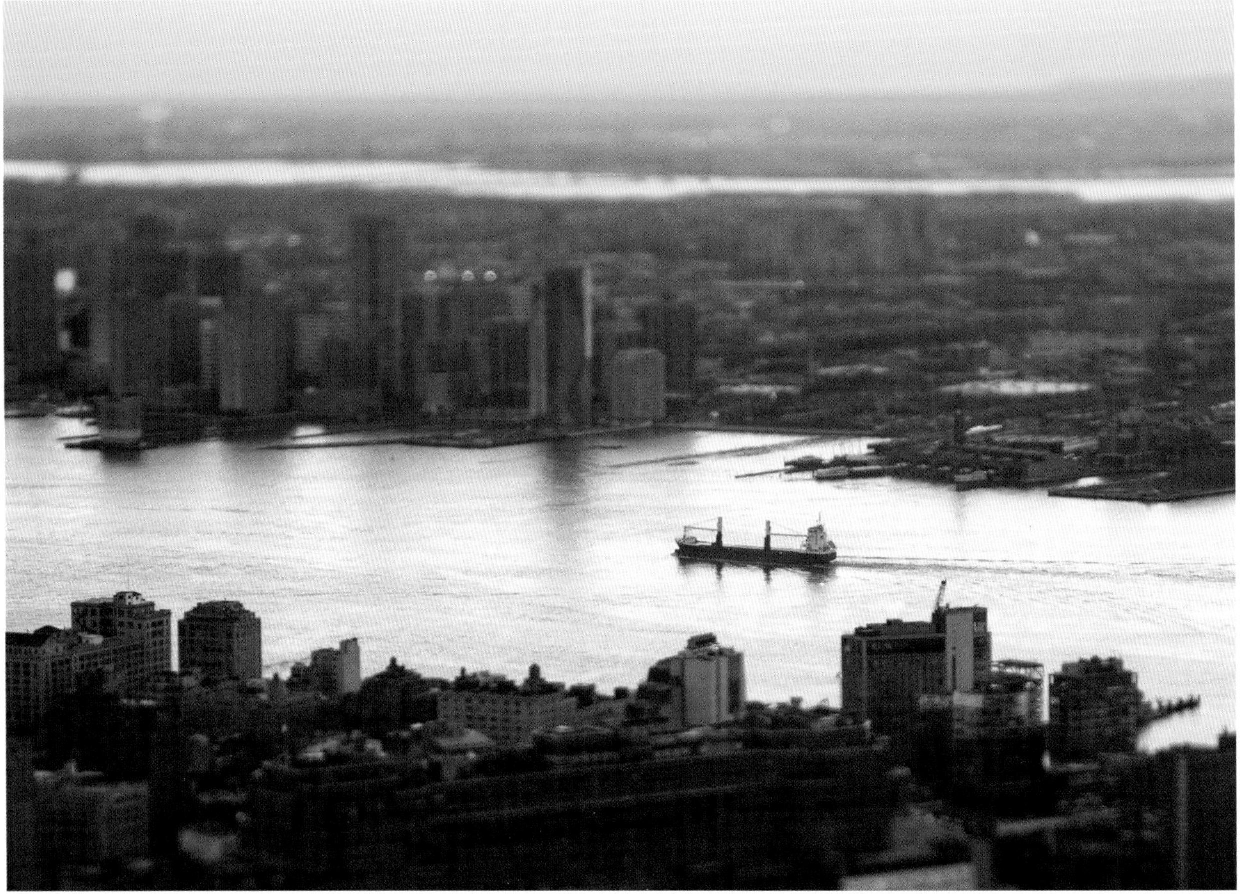

Hudson River

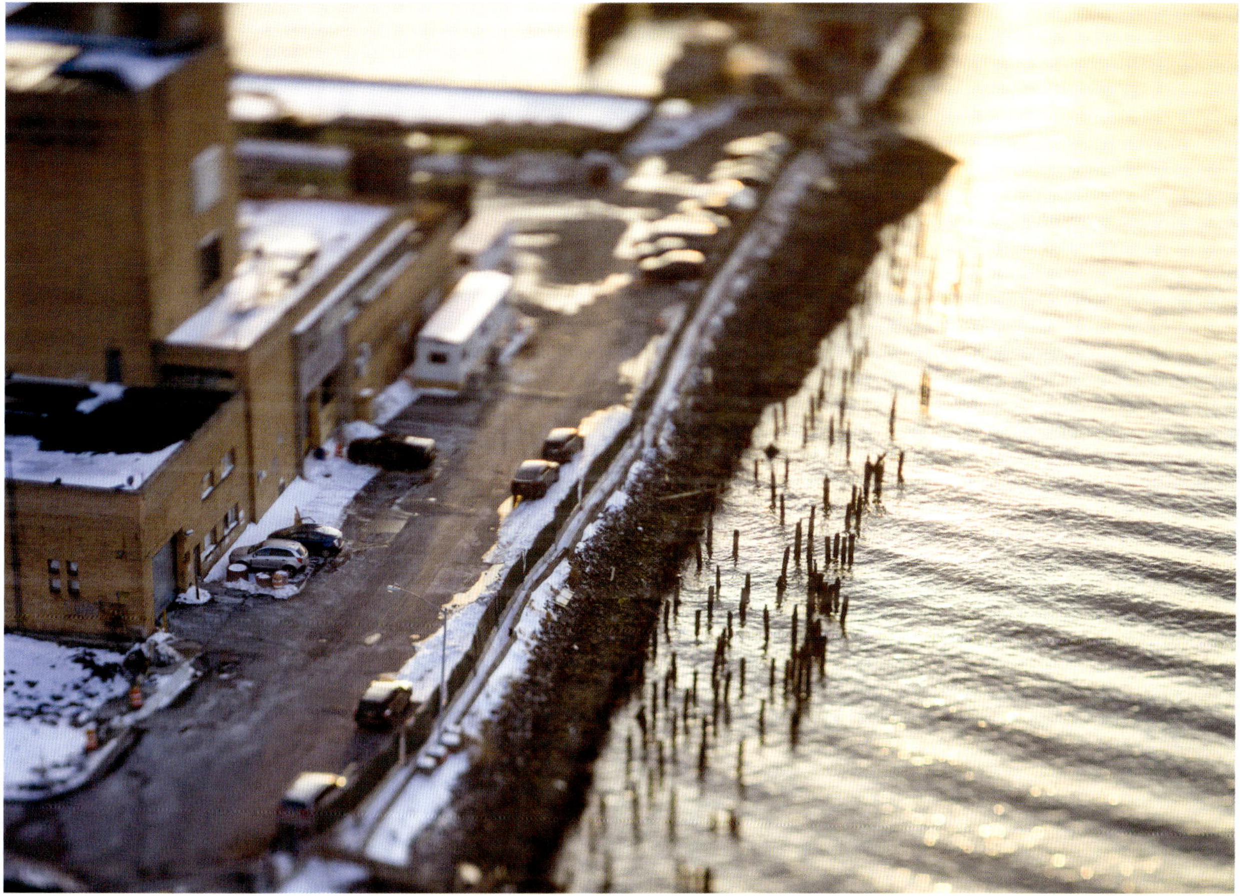

Hudson River

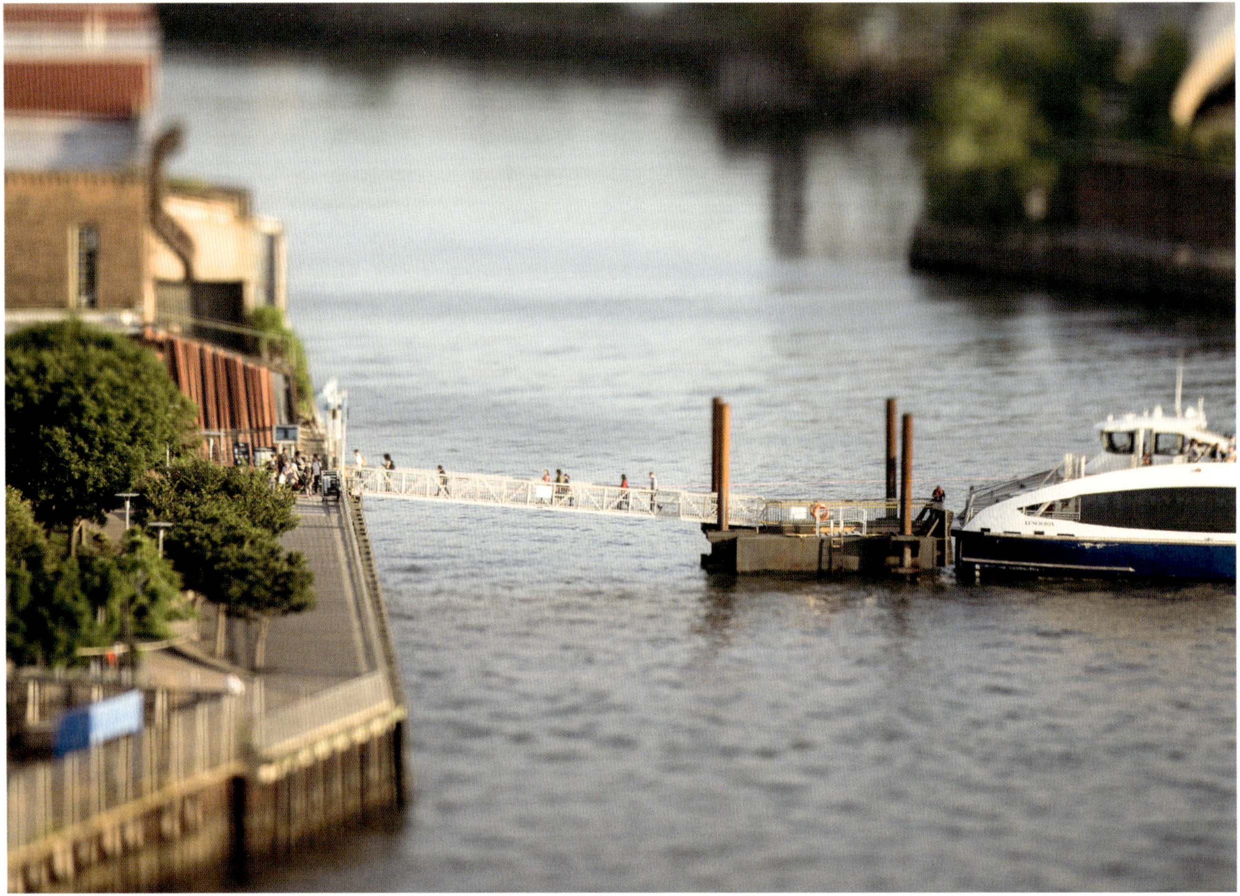

South Willamsburg Ferry

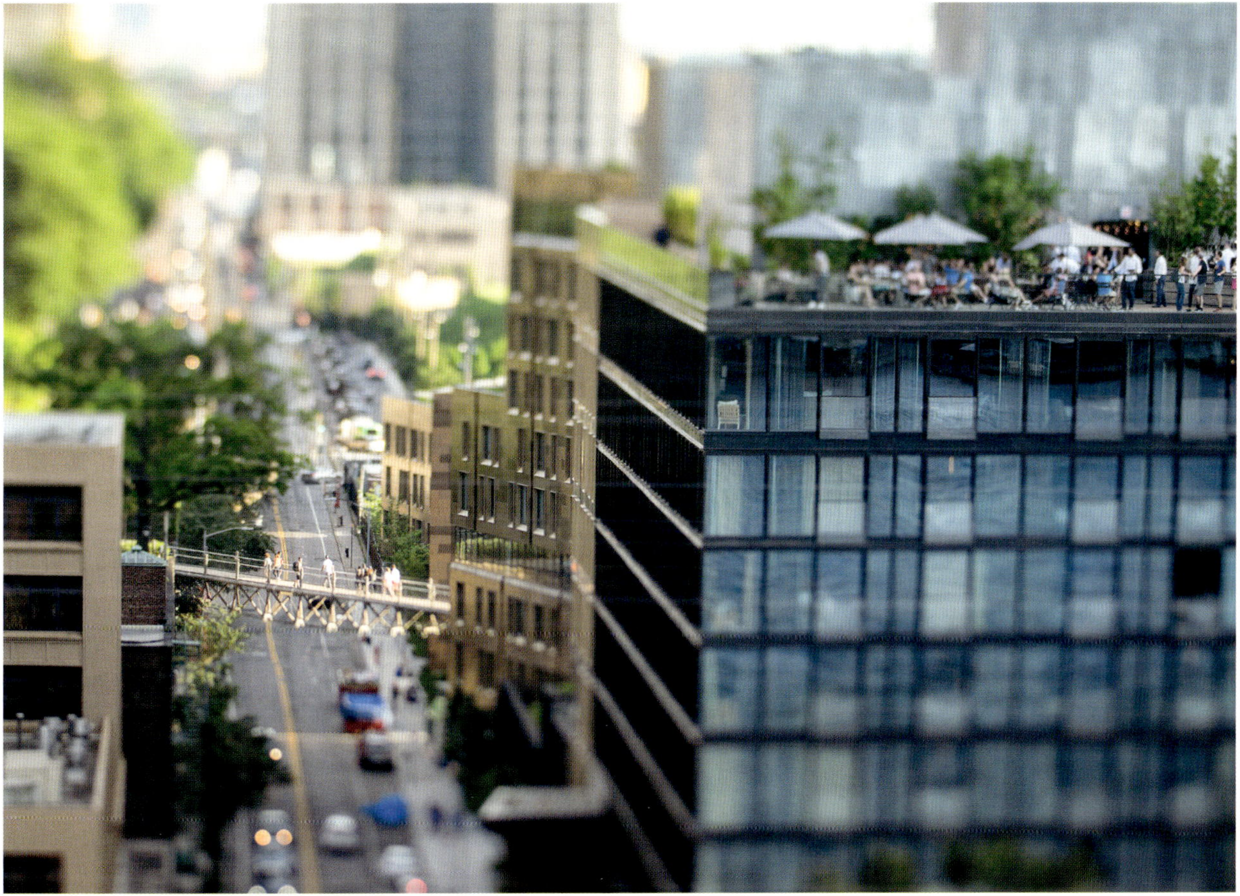

Squibb Park Bridge, Brooklyn

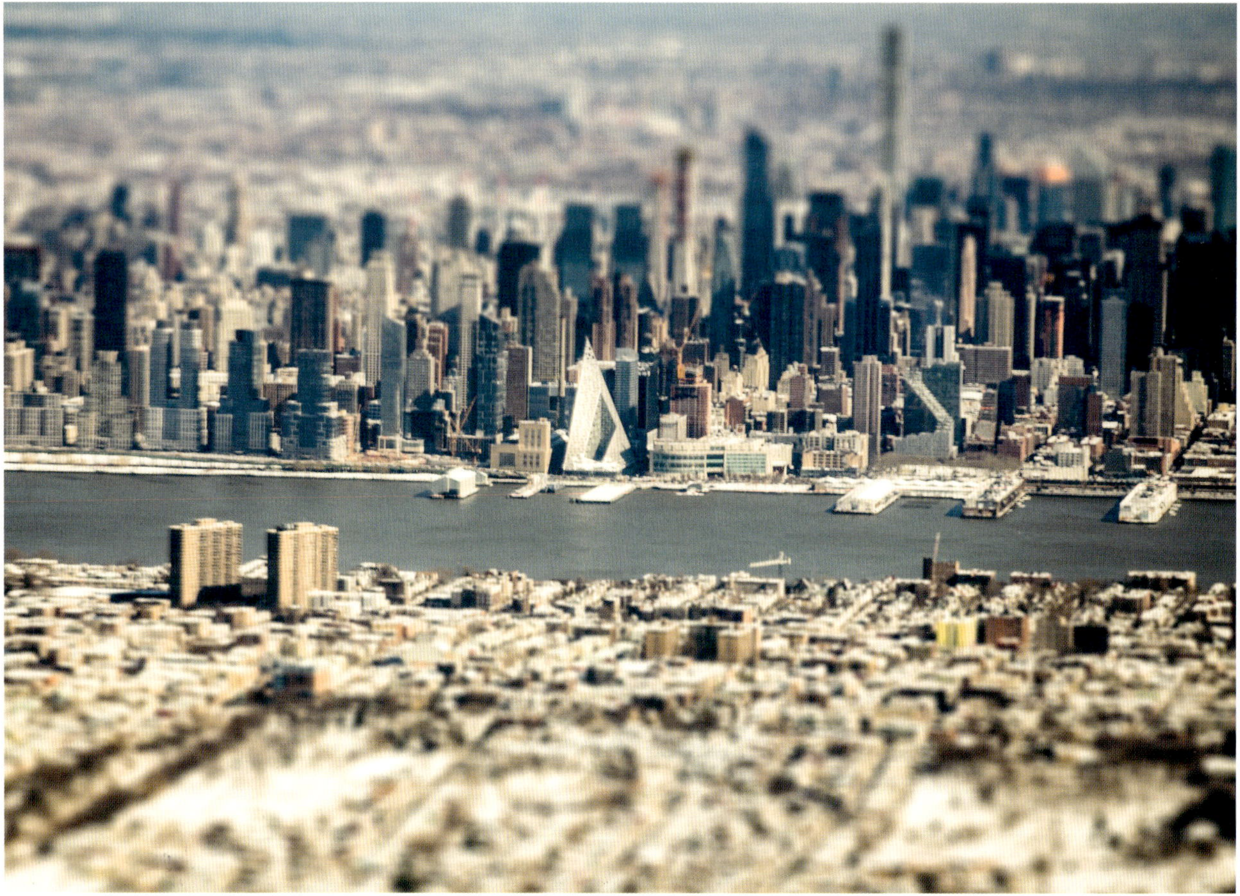

Midtown West, Hudson River

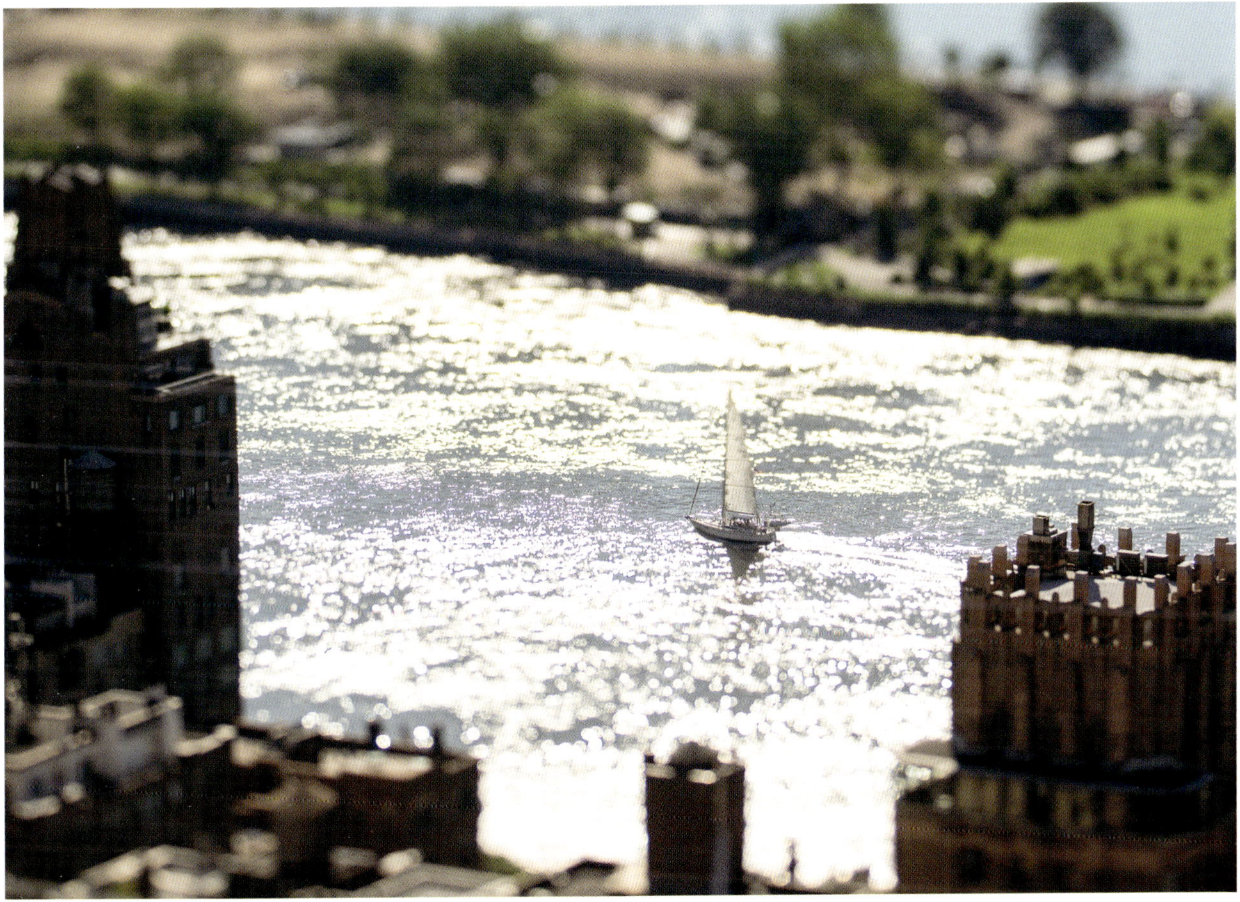

East River

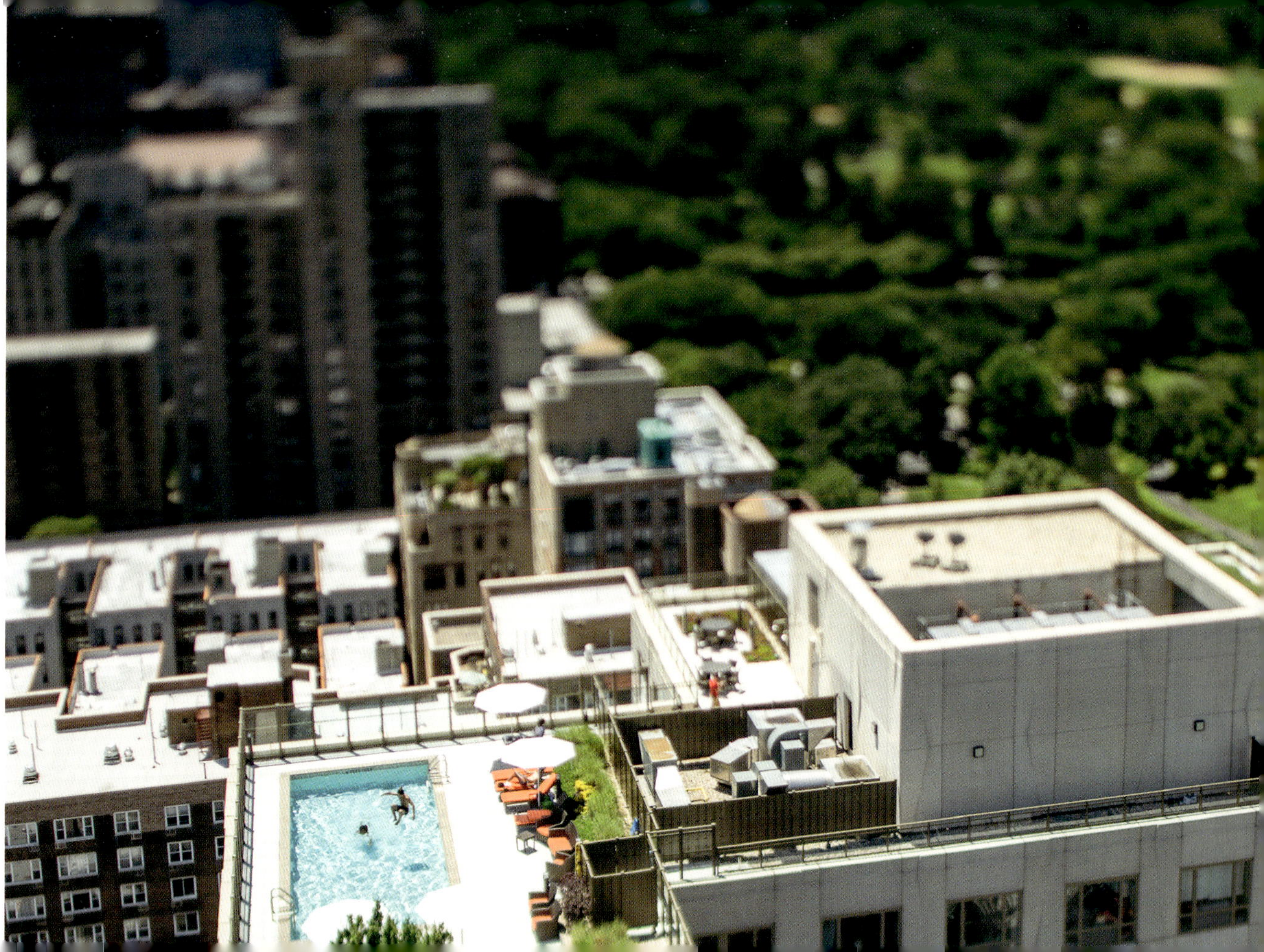

5th Ave, Central Park

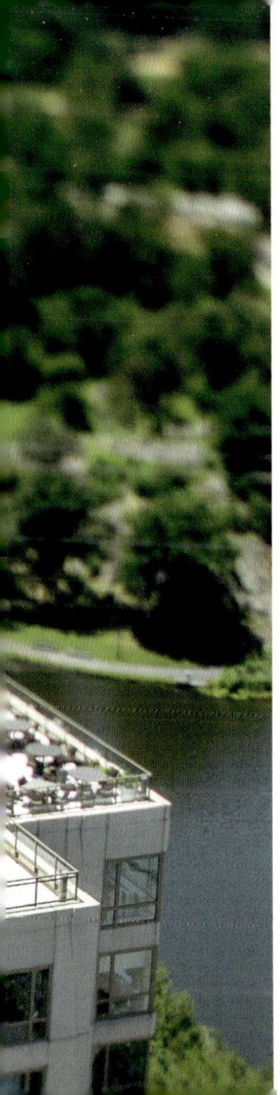

The true New Yorker secretly believes that people living anywhere else have to be, in some sense, kidding.

John Updike

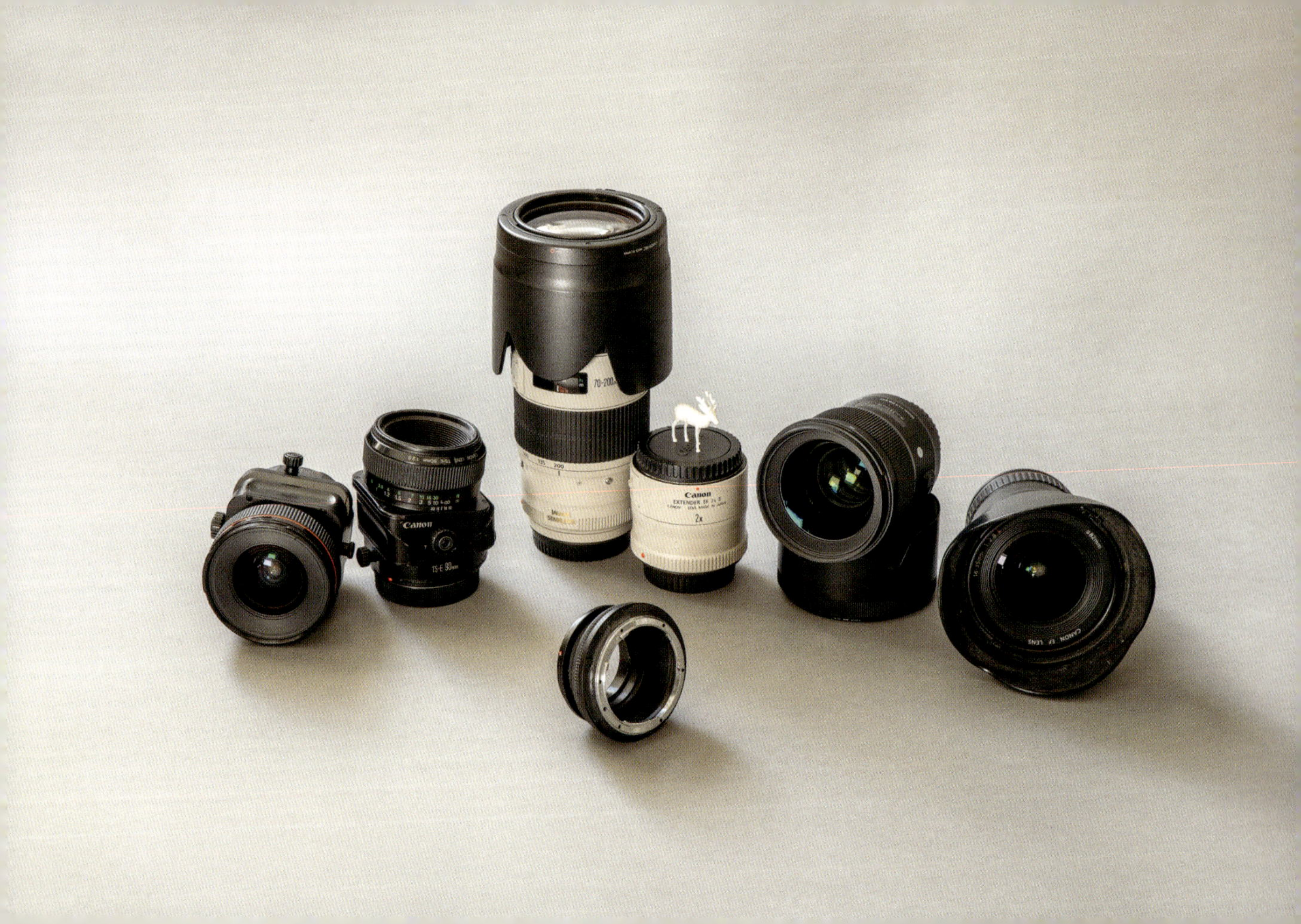
70-200
Canon
TS-E 90mm
Canon
2x
CANON EF LENS

How does Tilt-Shift work?

Unconsciously, our mind interprets Tilt-Shift photos as images of something very small. Whether or not a photo looks miniature is up to the individual who is looking. The sharpness in Tilt-Shift photographs looks very much like macro-photography or photographs of a small object. For example, if you photograph a ladybug, then only a small part of the image is really sharp—both the top and the bottom parts of the image stay blurred or "out of focus". Tilt-Shift mimics this effect and that is possible in two ways. You either use specific Tilt-Shift lenses, or you take the photographs using a regular lens and you process the images digitally afterwards — nowadays, many smartphones also have a Tilt-Shift function.

In this book almost all photos were shot with Tilt-Shift lenses, or regular lenses mounted on a home-made rubber adaptor. By twisting this adaptor you create and control the "out of focus" area in the photographs. I created the adaptor to give me the option of using high quality commercial camera lenses and using them as a Tilt-Shift lens on “mirrorless cameras.” I was able to use any lens angle ranging from wide angle to ultra-telelens for this photography book.

Only two photos were taken with a normal lens and then processed digitally with Tilt-Shift. Most of the images’ color and contrast were optimized for a "miniature feel." The biggest challenge in this book was finding the right resources for photographing from a great height. This bird’s eye view is essential for obtaining the miniature effect. My wholehearted gratitude goes to everyone who assisted me on my way up there to photograph the city.

JASPER LÉONARD

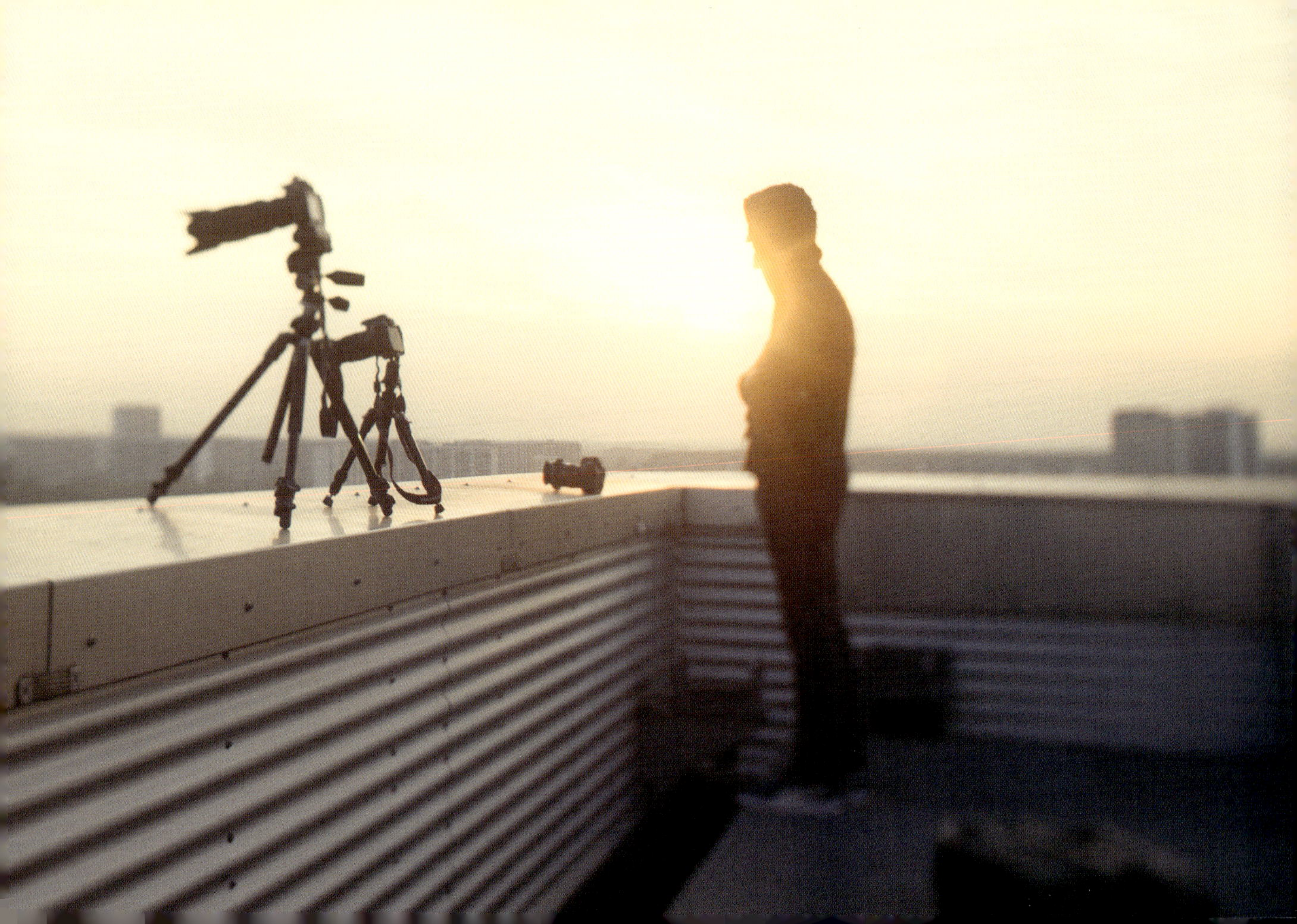

Special thanks to:

Lannoo publishers, Niels Famaey, Patrick van Rosendael, Robert Nagys and the House of Essex, Meredith A. Conti and the MTA Metro-North Railroad, Consul General Cathy Buggenhout, NYU, with special thanks to Nate and Olivia Mehran Roodsaz, Sam Huygelen, Marie Taminau, Pascal Petit, Jelle Maréchal, and all the great observatories and rooftop bars.

For behind the scenes photographs and videos check #newyorkresized on Facebook or Instagram.

This book is
MARKED

MARKED is an initiative by Lannoo Publishers.
www.marked-books.com

Sign up for our MARKED newsletter with news about new and forthcoming publications on art, interior design, food & travel, photography and fashion, as well as exclusive offers and events.

Photography: Jasper Léonard
Texts: Jasper Léonard
Copy-editing: Kate Mayne
Book design & typesetting: Jelle Maréchal

If you have any questions or comments about the material in this book, please do not hesitate to contact our editorial team: markedteam@lannoo.com

D/2017/45/176 – NUR 652
ISBN: 9789401443395
www.lannoo.com

#AREYOUMARKED